DISCARDED
P9-AAY-749

PROFESSIONAL DEVELOPMENT AND INSTITUTIONAL NEEDS

Professional Development and Institutional Needs

Edited by

GILLIAN TROREY and CEDRIC CULLINGFORD
University of Huddersfield, UK

Ashgate

Published by
Ashgate Publishing Limited
Gower House
Croft Road
Aldershot
Hampshire GU11 3HR
England

Ashgate Publishing Company
131 Main Street
Burlington, VT 05401-5600 USA

Ashgate website: http://www.ashgate.com

British Library Cataloguing in Publication Data
Professional development and institutional needs. -
(Monitoring change in education)
1.Teachers - In-service training 2.Teachers - Training of
I.Trorey, Gillian II.Cullingford, Cedric
370.7'11

Library of Congress Control Number: 2001099937

ISBN 0 7546 1277 5

Printed and bound in Great Britain by Antony Rowe Ltd, Chippenham, Wiltshire

Contents

List of Figures and Tables

Notes on Contributors

Steve Belbin is Head of Dallas Road Primary School, Preston, Lancashire.

Dr John Blewitt is Lecturer in the Centre for Continuing Education at the University of Bradford and consultant for the Learning and Skills Development Agency *Good Practice in Sustainable Development Education* project.

Dr Rachel Brooks is Lecturer in the Department of Education at the University of Southampton.

Dr Julia Corkindale is Senior Lecturer and staff development co-ordinator at Kingston Further Education College.

Cedric Cullingford is Professor of Education at the University of Huddersfield.

Christopher Day is Professor of Education at the University of Nottingham.

Steve Dinham is Professor in Education Leadership at the University of New England, Armidale, New South Wales.

Dr Christopher Greenfield is Head of the International School at Sherborne College, Dorset.

Ros Ollin is Principal Lecturer in Post-Compulsory Education and Training in the School of Education and Professional Development, and member of the Staff Development Group of the University of Huddersfield.

Richard Pring is Professor and Head of the Department of Educational Studies at the University of Oxford.

Dr Adrian Raynor is a former head teacher now working as an NPQH trainer and freelance consultant.

Dr Catherine Scott is a Lecturer in Statistics in the School of Psychology at the University of Western Sydney, Australia.

Helen Swift is Principal Lecturer and Head of Continuing Professional Development in the School of Education and Professional Development, University of Huddersfield.

Dr Gillian Trorey is Head of Staff Development in the School of Education and Professional Development, and member of the Staff Development Group of the University of Huddersfield.

Preface

In all sectors of education, professional development has traditionally been a personal matter; autonomous professionals taking responsibility for their own development as a matter of personal choice. In attempting to meet the demands of external accountability and organisational effectiveness, the personal and professional development of individuals has become marginalised in recent times, further increasing the difficulties of reconciling the needs of the individual and the institution. The new managerial pragmatism assumes that the only investment in the individual that is worthwhile is one that has an immediate and accountable effect on the functioning of the institution. This has resulted in a plethora of instrumental 'staff development' activities that allow little time for systematic reflection and deeper understanding.

Yet, in a time of unprecedented change and complexity in education, the subject of individual development is of great importance; self knowledge, emotional resilience and flexibility are personal attributes that can only contribute to organisational development – the development of a 'learning organisation'.

This book is a study of what is taking place in professional development in education. Through the accounts of researchers and practitioners, it seeks empirical evidence to explore the impact of policy on the professional development of individuals, and the effect of professional development on teaching and school effectiveness. The importance of effective leadership is a recurring theme.

All sectors of education are covered, but the driving principle is not so much to survey all that is taking place but to point up, through case studies, those real incidents, clearly analysed, that can enhance understanding of the issues and lead to the exploration of possible solutions.

Acknowledgements

The editors would like to thank Julie Gledhill and Susan Smith for their help in the preparation of the camera-ready copy.

1 Introduction: Meeting the Needs of the Individual and the Institution

GILLIAN TROREY

> Though initially organizations are creatures of people, they tend over time to become separated from people, functioning independently in pursuit of their own goals and purposes. This has to be bridged somehow.
>
> (Sergiovanni, 1997, p.232)

Professional development has assumed great importance in all sectors of education over the last few years. Facing both external and internal pressures, schools, colleges and higher education institutions have been forced to undergo rapid change. The focus on higher standards and improving quality and the demands of increasing accountability mean that teachers and lecturers have an unprecedented need for ongoing professional development.

Each sector now has standards or 'competencies' for the assessment of performance; performance managed pay is becoming a reality. We have the Teacher Training Agency and the General Teaching Council, the Further Education National Training Organisation and the Institute of Learning and Teaching in Higher Education, as well as more business orientated organisations such as Investors in People.

This situation results in many tensions. National priorities for teacher development, often with funding attached, may mean that the specific development needs of a school, department or faculty, or individuals within them, remain unaddressed. As schools and colleges and higher education departments or faculties have become responsible for their own resources, so staff development is increasingly managed at that level. Head teachers and departmental heads now have responsibility for balancing these external demands against those of their individual school or department, and the needs of their individual staff. One of the themes of this book is the recognition of these competing demands and the debate about ways of resolving them.

The demands for increased quality and public reporting and inspection have resulted, over the last decade, in a more business orientated or 'managerialist' culture. Placing emphasis on strategic development plans and corporate goals has resulted in a lack of recognition of the importance of individual development, a lack of recognition that the teacher or lecturer must be at the centre of any improvement drive. As long ago as 1988, Hewton pointed out that the introduction of school-focused staff development policies would either be seen as 'a positive step towards greater professional autonomy' or 'as a management strategy to increase control and accountability' (Hewton, 1988, quoted in Midwood, 1997, p.186). The evidence arising from the research presented in this book suggests that staff in all sectors perceive the latter to be the case; there are concerns about the erosion of professional autonomy. Yet, unless teachers are involved in the processes of policy development and decision making, they are unlikely to be fully engaged in policy implementation (Bennett et al., 1992). If the policies relate to organisational effectiveness, then:

> ...effectiveness is a complex matter with no universally applicable prescriptions. It is often defined in terms of goal achievement – a school, or any other organization, is effective in so far as it fulfils its goals or objectives. This raises the problem of organizational goals – how far do schools and their staff have agreed and realistic goals which they attempt to achieve in practice?
>
> (Preedy, 1993, p.1)

Staff development, professional development, personal and individual development are terms which are sometimes used interchangeably. *Institutional development* is more obvious; it refers to initiatives designed to develop the organisation as a whole, based on the needs perceived by senior management. It represents a 'top-down' approach, involving organisation-wide initiatives to which individuals conform. This can be a manifestation of *staff development*, involving the training of individuals in the skills and techniques seen as necessary for pursuing the aims of the institution. *Professional development* is used in a broader sense, frequently encompassing 'all types of learning undertaken by teachers beyond the point of initial training' (Craft, 2000, p.9). Generally this refers to the development of pedagogic knowledge and subject expertise with a view to the enhancement of student learning; it may also be related to career development and promotion prospects.

Personal development, on the other hand, may involve the development of abilities that would be useful to the individual in a variety of situations.

For example, Butcher et al. (1997) identified four such 'meta-abilities': cognitive skills, self-knowledge, emotional resilience and personal drive. *Individual development*, although frequently used interchangeably with personal development, is here considered to be an approach that follows the interests of the individual, interests that have no obvious bearing on the role in the workplace.

In this book we argue that it is personal and individual development that is increasingly losing ground against organisational needs. Yet, as Butcher et al. believe, personal development that offers increasing self-knowledge and improvement of meta-abilities provides the fundamental basis for organisational development, as it encourages versatile, thinking professionals. Individual development, as defined above, would also seem irrelevant to organisational needs, but the width of experience and fresh perspectives gained can increase the flexibility of individuals and hence the capacity for change in an organisation.

Inevitably, any discussion about the balance between the needs of the individual and the organisation results in a debate about the role of head teachers or departmental heads, as integration of the two is a key management issue. Several of the chapters in this book explore the skills and personal attributes needed for the effective leadership of the complex organisations that schools and colleges represent. As Drucker (1988) argues, effective organisations are those that remain fully aware that the quality of management support has a direct influence on the performance of individual staff and in consequence, the contribution that these staff make to the organisation.

Chapters 2 and 3 begin by looking at the growth of 'managerialist' cultures in schools and further education respectively, and the effect that this has on the professionalism of teachers. In Chapter 2, Richard Pring traces the change in the balance of power and control between the state and the professional in education over the last forty years, from the professional as 'all powerful', through the 'consumer choice' of the 1980s and 1990s to the introduction of performance related pay. Professional independence has gradually been eroded, aided by a series of white papers which have resulted in a new 'managerialism'. Thus, as he indicates, the language of education has become the language of business, with inputs and outputs, performance indicators and audits. The language of educational practice has been redefined, together with the moral context in which education takes place. Pring points out that the greater management control now exercised by government is a major, unrecognised shift which profoundly affects the nature and scope of continuing professional development. The question arises as to whether effective continuing professional development is possible within such a centrally controlled system.

Teachers Meeting the Challenge of Change, DfEE (1998) sets out a model of the teacher, in the form of National Standards. These, he argues, have resulted in a restriction in what we mean by education, and a consequent shift in what is meant by professional responsibility, professional judgement and professional development. What was defined as professional, in terms of personal development, is lost in this more limited picture of the teacher.

Whilst the impact of the notions of competence and accountability are visible in all educational institutions, there is no sector so much affected by change, both in financial terms and management control, as further education (FE). Since the incorporation of FE colleges as a result of the 1992 Further and Higher Education Act, they have had to adapt to a series of dramatic changes. Rapid shifts in emphasis, in expectation and outcomes on the one hand, and on styles of teaching and the diversity of client groups on the other, have seen the sector struggle to survive in the face of competition. This competition has been with overlaps of interest – schools and higher education – and more significantly, competition between individual institutions. FE staff have therefore been required to develop different skills, and the way that staff development is managed has also changed. In Chapter 3, Rachel Brooks gives an account of the changing emphasis of thinking about staff development and the demands of institutions in this volatile climate. She describes the changes in FE staff development from the introduction of formal staff development policies in the 1970s, through curriculum-based development, to the recent introduction of sector-wide standards for FE teachers.

Although there is little evidence that previous staff development arrangements were successful in meeting either individual or institutional needs, Brooks argues that incorporation and the new FE sector standards have had a major impact on professional development, and resulted in significant changes in the way that development needs are identified. Like Pring, she argues that the growth of a business or 'managerialist' culture has exacerbated differences between strategic and individual goals. The greater articulation of strategic goals and 'mission statements' by managers appears to be leading to a greater tension between lecturers and managers. Some lecturers feel that their professionalism is being threatened by quality controls which emphasise conformance to prescriptive and quantifiable requirements. Thus, institutional needs have become aligned with 'managerialism', and the maximisation of 'output', while the individual needs and goals of teaching staff are identified with 'professionalism'.

However, Brooks suggests that there are ways of resolving this dilemma; instead of juxtaposing managerial and professional cultures, there is a possibility of finding ways to mediate between the two. She cites research which shows that middle managers in FE who have demonstrated strategic compliance in response to pressures from above can yet maintain professional values such as collegiality and student-focused care. Other research has identified areas where managerial initiatives can be harnessed to benefit professional groups as a whole, such as the shared evaluation of practice and mentoring.

In Chapter 4, Christopher Day examines the role played by Continuing Professional Development (CPD) in raising standards of teaching and learning. To be effective, developments in teaching and learning must be informed by an understanding of the ways in which teachers learn best. This in turn requires an understanding of teachers' professional lives and working conditions. Day's review of the current state of CPD finds short term instrumentalist 'training models' in place, frequently designed to ensure compliance with an externally initiated curriculum, or to meet demands for systemic improvement in teaching standards and student achievement. Other demands include quality audit and performance management systems such as Investors in People. These are necessarily concerned with organisational needs rather than individual, professional ones, and run the risk of further alienating overburdened teachers.

In the past, individual and organisational development needs have often been presented in an oppositional way. Managerial cultures have focused upon measuring the results of teaching and identifying key characteristics of 'good' teachers, resulting in a widespread downturn in morale. Research shows that teachers' professional development does not follow a smooth path from novice to expert; nor can they always be expected to learn solely from experience. Because of increasing and conflicting demands, engaging in systematic reflection is often not possible. Yet, reflective practice is recognised as being essential to effective teaching; without this, professional effectiveness may decrease over time. Day postulates that no one form of reflection is necessarily better than another, but that teachers should be encouraged to engage in different forms of reflective practice at different stages, perhaps reflecting their career cycle, resulting in a continuum rather than a hierarchy of reflective practice. Behaving as a professional involves reflection about action – it involves critical enquiry into moral and ethical issues as well as instrumental ones, in order to maintain a broad vision about one's work. Sustaining such 'moral purpose' requires support in the maintenance of a teacher's personal, social and intellectual health. These are issues which CPD currently fails to address, focusing as it does on knowledge and pedagogy.

Research has shown that there is a strong relationship between the quality of leadership and the prevailing learning culture of a school. Effective schools operate as 'learning communities' which seek to support the principles and practices of differentiation for teacher learning as well as for students. In the current system of devolved management, the head teacher is crucial in setting the vision for a broad and balanced approach to CPD within a culture that supports shared values, openness and trust. Day suggests that unless teachers themselves are 'healthy, motivated and enthusiastic', have a 'sense of personal efficacy' and are committed to student care as well as to achievement, it is unlikely that even those with the highest subject and pedagogical knowledge will really succeed. He considers that setting teacher development only within the context of institutional development underestimates the importance of teachers acting as 'active agents within their own worlds'.

The maintenance of teaching staffs' personal, social and intellectual health is a theme continued in Chapter 5, but from the perspective of further and higher education. Staff here have also perceived, with considerable unease, a change from a largely pedagogic orientation to one of increased managerialism. But research shows that they remain focused on the needs of their students. Julia Corkindale and Gillian Trorey, staff development co-ordinators in further and higher education respectively, present the findings of research carried out on organisational and individual perspectives of professional development within the two sectors. They suggest that the current focus on human resource management fails to recognise and cultivate the full professional potential of academic staff, to the detriment of the institution, individual members of staff and students. Staff feel excluded from executive decision-making, despite the considerable interest, expertise and knowledge that exists among them. Complex institutions need staff entitlement and empowerment to function effectively. It is easy to map out corporate objectives; it is harder to guarantee staff commitment. Corkindale and Trorey conclude that, as attempts to create a single organisational culture are not only unsuccessful, but also ineffective, further and higher education institutions must recognise the advantages of diversity and seek to develop internal policies through collaboration rather than imposition.

One suggested approach is to adopt an alternative model of employee-employer relationships: that of reciprocal contracting. Stemming from the same principles as 'psychological contracting' (Schein, 1978), reciprocal contracting emphasises the need for equity in this relationship. It implies a more teacher-centred epistemology and a need for more individual personal and professional development, tailored, as Day also points out, to the stages of one's 'life career' and working patterns. More complex than existing systems, its effectiveness will depend on the skill of individual managers; if carried out effectively, it has the potential to create more dynamic, intelligent 'learning organisations', using the wealth of existing expertise. In the end, teaching quality depends on this.

In Chapter 6, Catherine Scott and Steve Dinham review research that they have carried out over a number of years in Australia and other countries into the role of teachers and teacher satisfaction, which suggests that, for some staff, the need to consider career stages may be too late. They describe how teachers are increasingly being placed in a paradoxical situation. Widening responsibilities and increased expectations of teachers are set against mounting criticism and declining status. Many teachers are experiencing 'change fatigue' and feel less able to exert control over their professional lives. Many have reacted against this by reassessing their workloads and their commitment to professional development.

Scott and Dinham describe a phenomenon which they term 'retreating', whereby individual teachers, in a reaction to increased workloads and poor promotion prospects, progressively give up any extra-curricular activities. They point out that this results in a loss of the 'extras' that make schools so rewarding for teachers and pupils and usually enhance their reputation in the community. Their research showed a positive correlation between the length of time in the current school and teacher dissatisfaction; yet there were few opportunities to take a career break, sabbatical or other 'refreshing' activity. They suggest that the phenomenon of 'too long in one school' and a declining commitment to professional development go hand in hand. The resultant demoralisation represents a lost opportunity to share the fruits of experience with younger, less experienced teachers.

Scott and Dinham's research has also revealed that those teachers who are able to survive and are 'successful' in this climate are those who consistently reflect on their practice, and have formulated their own personal development plan, together with steps to put this into action.

However, these plans almost always showed a clear preference for professional development which was focused on the teaching of their subject discipline, whilst the training actually provided by employers was frequently concerned with systems, administration or school policy. They pose the question: is the 'average' teacher prepared to take charge of his or her professional development at a time of feeling overloaded and undervalued? The lack of trust in the professionalism of teachers and the concern over the use and misuse of educational standards is resulting in a move towards standardising and documenting as many aspects of the work of teachers as possible, in the name of 'quality assurance'. They predict that unless new approaches are found to support practising teachers, this de-professionalistion and consequent 'retreating' will continue.

In Chapter 7, Ros Ollin describes how competence-based qualifications, developed in the 1980s in response to the need to improve the skill levels and qualifications of the workforce as a whole, have resulted in a reconceptualisation of learning which has included modularisation, flexible delivery systems, new systems of assessment and accreditation and the notion of lifelong learning. The use of competence-based national occupational standards has subsequently been imposed onto other aspects of educational life, including that of professional development in schools, further and higher education and the health service, whilst educational organisations themselves have been encouraged to adopt national standards such as Investors in People and Total Quality Management. Ollin points out that national occupational standards could be seen by some as a means of exercising central control over disparate institutions.

She goes on to discuss the various criticisms of competence-based approaches to teacher development – that they focus on 'positivistic and minimalist' approaches to the 'complex and subtle processes of teaching', resulting in a de-professionalisation of the teacher's role. Now that these standards are compulsory for FE teachers, have they resulted in improved teaching and learning and more recognition for the role of the FE teacher? Or does the 'professional' status now awarded via the competence based route represent a 'debased view of professionalism', where teachers 'act in accordance with state requirements' instead of engaging in teaching and learning at a richer and more complex level?

The importance of effective leadership in promoting professional development is a theme that recurs throughout this book, in all sectors of education. What skills and personal attributes are required by heads, and how are they developed? In Chapter 8, Steve Belbin looks at the management of staff development in primary schools, based on his experience as a head teacher. He shows that, despite increases in funding for training, there will continue to be constraints on time and finances, especially in the smaller school. He describes a third dimension to the identification of priorities, that of external demands, or the 'set agenda'. The set agenda is one that emanates from government through the Department for Education and Skills. The very fact that the agenda is imposed from outside makes it somewhat problematic. Should schools give priority to their own needs (which may in any case have been identified by an external agency such as OFSTED) or to the latest government initiatives?

At the centre of this potential conflict are the head teachers. How do they cope with the expectations of those outside the school, and maintain a sense of external accountability on the one hand and responsibility for the development of their school and its staff on the other? Belbin argues that, under these circumstances, the needs of the school should be given priority, followed by those of individual staff. However, he suggests that it is possible to balance the needs of individuals and schools, by involving all those connected with the school in setting priorities via the School Development Plan. Advantages of this approach include staff feeling that they are being listened to, and a shared ownership of the strategic direction of the school. As a consequence, staff are more likely to align their own development needs with those of the school. There is a need for transparent and proactive staff development policies which, he argues, may not always give priority to the government's agenda. Examples of two schools, as case studies in the prioritisation of needs, are given, one reacting to a poor OFSTED report, by going back to the basics of teaching and learning, and the other, having secured these, concentrating on the development of individuals, in subject and leadership roles. This is an account of how the prerogative to remain positive can be handled.

In Chapter 9 Adrian Raynor continues the discussion of the role of the head teacher in an age of accountability and institutional concerns. Schools are assumed by policy makers to be hermeneutic institutions which can easily be turned round by dynamic leaders. Headteachers are assumed to have both power and responsibility; their role is crucial, but how is it learnt? The standards for the National Professional Qualification for Headteachers (NPQH) reflect an institutional approach to development which is likely to result in a standardised practice of headship. Should a school be viewed as a mechanistic organisation, based on the factory model, or as an entity that co-evolves with the changing environment?

Raynor considers the balance between institutionally-driven development and the personal development of heads and staff, drawing on his research into headship carried out over a three year period. He found that head teachers felt that the 'measured' outputs of the system, in terms of test and examination results, had been successful in ensuring a good balance in the curriculum, especially in primary schools. Teachers had developed a wider skill base, and attention to assessment and monitoring had risen. He considered that the professionalism of teachers had increased in these respects.

However, there were other serious consequences; heads feel that they no longer have a voice in curriculum matters, and that the degree of professional judgement they can apply is drastically lessened, with a consequent reduction of creativity in the curriculum, both at the level of the school and the individual teacher. The result is that heads, whilst wishing to keep the rigour of the national curriculum, also feel they must encourage teachers to rethink what they are really doing in teaching children. Central prescriptions cannot take into account the nuances of context that teachers experience.

Raynor's research shows that the suppression of creativity in the classroom is becoming more apparent. He suggests that the creativity of teachers needs to be encouraged, in their ability to respond appropriately to the needs of their students. It is the nature of classroom interaction to be complex. Much of the teacher's skill is intuitive rather than deliberate. Creativity results in complexity, and complex organisations are better able to respond to their external environment. Promoting complexity promotes creativity, and is a key aspect of the head's role. Head teachers, like other managers, rarely deal with discrete, single events but rather with interconnected ones. Handling complexity is central, as Raynor points out:

> Shaping multiple forces, fitting chance events into a wider picture and seizing opportunities as they occur demand cognitive abilities that go beyond rational techniques, procedures and deterministic planning.

The unique qualities of each school and the complex interplay of factors are central to headship. Therefore, while technical and competence-based development is required for head teachers, personal factors, such as the development of cognition and self-knowledge, are fundamental to handling complexity and to increasing the strategic fitness levels of schools.

Head teachers and others concerned with the improvement of institutions need as much information as possible on which to base their decision-making. One of the most pervasive phenomena of our time is the amount of information about schools that is now available. Every aspect of performance is scrutinised, from exam results to maintenance costs. Such a plethora of information has an impact on head teachers in particular. How much of this information should they share with their staff, school governors and parents? One important form of institutional information is the school profile, which includes statistics on attendance (pupils and staff), pupil staff ratios, proportion of free school meals, maintenance costs, teachers' staff development records and so on. These profiles are both descriptive and used to measure achievement of targets. They could be a useful source of information for individual and institutional development.

In Chapter 10, Cedric Cullingford and Helen Swift present research that explored the reactions of head teachers to their school profiles and the ways in which they planned to use them. In principle, the heads welcomed the information, since it helped them understand their schools' needs and identify specific areas in which to develop and support staff. However, all heads were concerned about other people having access to the information. Other people included their own staff, school governors and parents. They feared a potential misuse of the information; that it could become a weapon against which they felt defensive. This contradicts the 'open' approach that many heads, especially those of primary schools, advocate.

Cullingford and Swift point out that the detailed information provided in the School Improvement Initiatives and the comparisons against similar schools provides an ideal opportunity for schools with similar profiles to learn from each other and co-operate in improvement initiatives. Yet, the tension between the possibility of learning new approaches and the competitive climate generated by the profiles themselves has inhibited any mutual collaboration.

Much of this book is concerned with the tensions between the needs of the institution and the personal development of individuals within it; what happens when there is a whole school policy devoted, say, to democracy, not just as a theory, but as a practice? Is it possible to create an environment which retains the demands of the National Curriculum and external accountability and yet demonstrates some of the principles intended to enhance the lives of everyone in the school? One current example of this is 'citizenship'. A case study looks at an institutional initiative, a school with a commitment to education for citizenship and which has developed a policy which is designed to involve all staff, and consequently, their students.

Chapter 11, based on research by Christopher Greenfield, attempts to define the concept of the ethos of schools as official policy. It raises the question of whether schools are there to promote social values, and who is responsible for them. Can schools teach citizenship by example, not just as a subject, but as a whole school policy? To explore this, a school that had a policy to inculcate democratic values by involving all staff and students was studied. Managers, teachers and pupils were interviewed. The policy looked good, and was strongly promoted by the school management team. The teachers, however, felt muddled and equivocal, while the pupils felt wholly excluded, appearing unaware of the exisitence of a policy that was intended to involve them. The research showed that, even with the best intentions, creating a school initiative and institutional policy which involves individual and whole school development is easier said than done at the present time.

Another initiative intended to be holistic and inclusive is that of sustainable development education. This is an approach to learning that should be led rather than managed, and must be allowed to evolve in a self-organising fashion. Where does such leadership come from? In Chapter 12, John Blewitt takes a regional initiative on sustainability, designed to involve individuals and institutions, as a starting point. The initiative focused on the development of 'leaders', that is, individuals who would influence and change institutions in order for them to operate according to sustainable development principles. Analysing the requirements of this showed how difficult it is to achieve. As Blewitt, and several other contributors to this book have pointed out, in complex organizations institutional strategies are most effective where 'implementers become formulators', where people at all levels are able to influence the evolution of the organisation. To become a genuine 'learning organisation', all members must understand the 'flows and influences' that affect it, and each member should be able to take a lead in responding intelligently and creatively to these influences. There are parallels here with natural ecosystems.

Consequently, any leadership programme must encourage leaders to recognise that innovation from below is something to be nurtured and not controlled. Innovation will require leaders to address challenging situations in such a way as to integrate learning and apply it creatively and reflexively to other situations. The task is to fully embed sustainable development education values in the culture, consciousness and practice of all sectors of education. This style of leadership, articulating ecosystem norms and values, could become part of an individual's continuing professional development or an aspect of an organisation's strategic staff development programme. Leadership development in general is already a major issue for senior managers in most educational institutions.

The last chapter reflects on the themes of the book as a whole. The culture of the age is clear, of centralisation and control, leading to accountability and measurement. These have clear effects on the traditional notions of professional development and on individuals. Yet there is a growing re-awakening of the notion of institutions as consisting of the people within them. Whilst the 'manager' is recognised as the most effective and influential source of change, the assumption that all depends upon the centre can have dire results. More sophisticated notions of professional development are suspicious of 'cheap' competencies and recognise the complexities of individual interactions. An interrogation of underlying cultural notions reveals that professional development is a starting point, is central rather than an afterthought.

In drawing these chapters together, from researchers and practitioners from all sectors of education, in the UK and elsewhere, we have been surprised by the consistency of the messages, the views and opinions held, even given the focus of the book – the importance of effective leadership, the need to harness the considerable expertise of staff in engaging them in organisational development in order to align their own needs with the institution. Judging from the perceptions of staff in this book, they remain an under-utilised resource.

And what of the future? The problem will still remain of how any development review system can serve the competing interests of the organisation and its employees, as long as they continue to be competing. Perhaps there should be increasing efforts to find out what employees see as their interests so that these can be harnessed? As Bratton (1999, p.371) points out, 'Many UK organisations are beginning to accept the importance of utilizing and developing the potential of their employees as a means of enhancing competitive capability'. Will education follow business in this respect?

> ... the key issue will be the extent to which organization policies and practices facilitate the use of skills and the development of employee potential ... Employee talent will only be retained if organisations are able to provide work which is sufficiently challenging and opportunities for development that meet

> their aspirations. Of particular importance in the future will be the capture of knowledge that is generated by learning and the management of such knowledge ... The learning organisation may be a difficult idea to grasp and implement, however there will be greater effort and growing sensibility to how and where learning takes place in organisations and how knowledge can be generated collectively. (Bratton, 1999, p.372)

References

Bennett, N., Crawford, M. and Riches, C. (1992) Managing Educational Change: the centrality of values and meanings. In Bennett, N., Crawford, M. and Riches, C. (Eds.) *Managing Change in Education: Individual and Organisational Perspectives.* London: Paul Chapman.

Bratton, J. (1999) Back to the Future. In Bratton, J. and Gold, J. *Human Resource Management: Theory and practice*, pp.367-376. London: Macmillan Press.

Butcher, D., Harvey, P. and Atkinson, S. (1997) *Developing Businesses through Developing Individuals.* Cranfield: Cranfield School of Management.

Craft, A. (2000) *Continuing Professional Development: a practical guide for teachers and schools.* London: Routledge Falmer.

DfEE (1998) *Teachers: Meeting the Challenge of Change* – a summary. London: DfEE.

Drucker, P. (1988) *Management.* London: Pan Books.

Hewton, E. (1988) *School Focused Staff Development.* London: Falmer Press.

Midwood, D. (1997) Managing Staff Development. In Bush, T. and Midwood, D. (Eds.) *Managing People in Education*, pp.186-202. London: Paul Chapman.

Preedy, M. (1993) Introduction. In Preedy, M. *Managing the Effective School.* London: Paul Chapman.

Schein, E. H. (1978) Career Dynamics: Matching individual and organizational needs. Reading, Massachusetts: Addison Wesley.

Sergiovanni, T.J. (1997) Organizations or Communities? In Harris, A., Bennett, N. and Preedy, M. (Eds.) *Organizational Effectiveness and Improvement in Education*, pp.231-238. Buckingham: Open University Press.

2 Performance Management and Control of the Professions

RICHARD PRING

Introduction

The last few years have seen quite radical changes in the management of public services, and thereby of the professions within those services. These changes reflect not only a change in control, but also a reconceptualising of what it means to manage them. This is reflected in a new language, a new way of conceiving the relationship between the government and the professional, and a new ethical dimension to professional activity and responsibility. In this chapter, I wish to develop the argument through the particular case of teaching. But in essence the story is much the same in medicine, nursing, social work and other professional areas within the public services – a change of balance of power and control between a greatly increased central administration and diminished professional bodies, reflected in a rarely articulated but powerful system and language of accountability.

The Changing Nature of Public Services

When I entered the civil service in 1962, there was a relatively clear distinction to be made between the role and expertise of the public servant and that of the professional adviser. The public (or civil) servants would not claim expertise in the substantive elements of the service they were administering. Rather did their expertise lie in making the machinery of government work – in providing the necessary funding for that service, in ensuring that there was adequate recruitment of the professionals, in providing the legal or regulatory framework within which those public services (education, health, social security, the police, etc.) might operate most effectively. It was not the job of government to say what exactly should be done or how it might be carried out. That was a job for the professionals.

The professional, therefore, exercised immense power. In education for instance, the Secretary of State would have instant access to the 'professional view', given by the Chief Inspector. The inspectorate (*Her Majesty's Inspectorate*, thereby emphasising their independence of government) were a body of about 450, covering the whole country, acting as the 'ears and eyes' of government certainly, but gathering the evidence about the state of education both locally and nationally which would inform the judgements of the chief and staff inspectors as they advised government on educational policy. Great care was taken to say only that which was justified by the evidence gathered. In the 1970s, for example, the annual reports on local education authority expenditure were hard hitting, comprehensive accounts of the state of our schools in relation to the resources made available.

The post-war period was characterised by this clear separation of government from the substance and control of the professional service offered. Thus, Dr Marjorie Reeves, Emeritus Fellow of St Hugh's College, Oxford, recalls her conversation with the Permanent Secretary, John Maude, when in 1947 she was appointed to the Central Advisory Committee for Education (England). In answer to her question concerning the responsibilities of the Advisory Committee, Maude replied that it 'was to be prepared to die at the first ditch as soon as politicians try to get their hands on education'.

When, in 1962, the Ministry of Education established a Curriculum Study Group, there was an outcry from the teachers and the local authorities. They protested at the encroachment of government into what the Minister of Education referred to as 'the secret garden of the curriculum'. Gould (General Secretary of the National Union of Teachers) thoroughly objected to the unilateral intervention of the ministry in an area which had by most been recognised as the teachers' professional concern. Alexander (Secretary of the Association of Education Committees) saw in the initiative a bid to alter existing power relations (Simon, 1991). Quickly the government retreated and established instead, in 1964, the Schools Council for the Curriculum and Examinations – the majority of whose membership were teachers. The job of the Council was curriculum research and development with a view, not to dictating what should be taught or how, but to informing professional judgement.

Perhaps the 'philosophy' underpinning the Council was best expressed by its architect and first joint secretary, Derek Morrell, a quite exceptional career civil servant. The purpose of the Council was:

> to democratise the processes of problem-solving as we try, as best we can, to develop an educational approach appropriate to a permanent condition of change. (Morrell, 1967, p.12)

Such a democratic approach was seen to be essential because the direction and consequence of change were unpredictable and because there was decreasing consensus over the values which should direct that change:

> Jointly, we need to recognise that freedom and order can no longer be reconciled through implicit acceptance of a broadly ranging and essentially static consensus on educational aims and methods. (ibid., p.13)

Hence, teachers and their professional advisers were in the forefront, not only in determining the means to achieve certain ends, but also in questioning and reshaping the ends or educational purposes themselves. Essential to such questioning was a professional forum (with its regional and local outposts) supported by research and development, which debated the very values and purposes themselves.

But the Schools Council survived less than 20 years. That period coincided with a growing suspicion of professional knowledge and power and by an increasing encroachment of government on territory previously controlled by the professionals. The Fulton Report on the civil service, published in 1968, questioned the continued role of the civil servant as the 'intelligent amateur'. There was a need for greater expertise, a more proactive involvement in the services administered. In education, the retreat over the Curriculum Study Group was to be temporary only. The investment in education and training was too great to be left unaccountable. There were too many examples of professional failure, one notable example being what came to be known as the Tyndale Affair (Auld Report, 1976). The need to raise standards of performance was too pressing to be left to the professionals, given the increasing economic competition from abroad.

The 1980s, therefore, saw a dramatic shift in the balance between the government and the professionals. The Schools Council was closed. The inspectorate was decimated. A range of legislation (culminating in the Education Reform Act of 1988 which established a national curriculum and national assessment) restricted the scope for professional judgement, gave central direction to educational change and reformed the governance of schools accordingly. The Chief Inspector became a political appointment.

However, these quite radical changes in balance between state and professional in education were a reflection of the reform of public services more generally – initiated, though by no means shaped, by the 1968 Fulton Report on the civil service – requiring a different approach to public administration.

These changes in balance came to be directed, certainly within the Conservative administration from 1979 onwards, by a 'neo-liberal' trust in market forces. The emphasis lay in 'consumer choice', in contrast with professional expertise. Hence, the national system of assessment and the regular and systematic reports by the newly formed Office for Standards in Education (OFSTED) provided the public data on which parents would be able to exercise choice of schools. Money would follow those choices. Unpopular schools would wither, popular ones flourish. But, of course, such choice would be exercised within a highly regulated framework of a centrally controlled curriculum.

Although on the surface little seems to have changed under the Labour administration with regard to the inherited arrangements (centralised curriculum, national assessment, regular inspections, league tables based on performance criteria), faith in the market no longer prevails. Instead, the same arrangements are now seen to be essential to the increased emphasis upon accountability to government which provides the money and which takes on a much greater degree of responsibility for defining standards and for ensuring performance improvement according to those standards. Thus, the 1998 School Standards and Framework Act sets the framework within which the government is able to determine the standards by which schools and their teachers are to be judged, and the targets which need to be met if those standards are to be achieved. Hence, there is a much greater control over public service through a range of measures, the latest (in education) being 'performance related pay'. Thus, arrangements previously devised to support market choice are now employed to ensure greater management control and manipulation by government. This is a quite major, and often unacknowledged, shift which affects profoundly the nature of, and scope for, continuing professional development.

This change in the management of public services is explained in a series of government White Papers from HM Treasury and the Cabinet Office: *Modern Public Services in Britain: Investing in Reform* (1998, Cm 4011); *Public Services for the Future: Modernisation, Reform, Accountability* (1998, Cm 4181); *The Government's Measures of Success: Output and Performance Analyses* (1999); *Modernising Government* (1999,

Cm 4310) – and many others. This is important to note. Too often the recent developments in education which affect profoundly the role of the professional and of professional development and which I shall describe in detail in the next section, are not seen within this wider context. Furthermore, what is sometimes referred to as 'new public management' is fairly widespread in the world at large (see, for example, McKevitt (1998) on developments in Australia and New Zealand, and Osborne and Gaebler, (1992) on the United States).

The principles underpinning this new approach to management have been identified by Foster & Plowden, quoted by Faulkner et al. (1999) as including:

- separating purchasing public services from production
- serving consumers rather than bureaucratic political or producer interests
- using market pricing rather than taxes
- where subsidising, doing this directly and transparently
- extending competition
- decentralising provision
- empowering communities to provide services
- setting looser objectives, and controlling outputs rather than inputs
- bringing about deregulation
- prevention of problems, rather than cure, through planning.

In the educational service, we see these principles applied to different degrees and in different ways: different 'producers' of public services such as professional development and inspection (including private businesses) bidding for custom of schools; the more explicit statement of the 'consumer's' rights (see for example the Code of Practice in the Department for Education and Employment Consultation Paper, *Professional Development*, DfEE, 2000); the process of bidding for custom, as in institutions' (universities' as well as private providers') proposals to provide professional development, where cost as well as quality is taken into account; and so on.

Most significant, however, is the 'public service agreement' whereby funding is provided, ultimately by the Treasury to the Department of State concerned, and then 'cascaded down' to the ultimate providers of the service. Thus, in education, targets in terms of outputs are established centrally (for example, the proportion of 16 year olds who will gain five

GCSEs at A to C) and 'cascaded down' to local authorities who incorporate these into their development plans, which themselves 'cascade down' to the schools, who also have development plans to be approved. Of course, there is a further tier of 'cascading' as the schools' development plans are cashed out in terms of the expected performances of individual teachers. In this way the government determines the standards and sets the targets, but assigns responsibility for achieving those targets to the local authorities, the schools and the teachers – what Mark Freedman refers to as 'imposed contractualism' (Faulkner et al. 1999). And the rewards or punishments are provided in terms of funding – and teachers' pay.

Reforming Teachers' Pay

In their book *Paying Teachers for What They Know and Do*, Odden and Kelley (1997) argue that the traditional way of paying and rewarding teachers is simply out-dated. It reflects a view of management which has been abandoned elsewhere in private, public and voluntary services. And it is partly responsible for the comparatively low pay of teachers, especially after several years of service.

That 'traditional way' is for teachers to be placed on a single salary schedule, albeit with some compensation for extra responsibilities. Thus, teachers, from the moment they join the profession, can expect a predictable progression up the scale or schedule until they reach the 'ceiling' – irrespective of merit, hard work, or need. Indeed, further progress in terms of salary would require leaving the classroom for a more administrative responsibility. According to Odden and Kelley, this ill-serves the recruitment, retention, morale and incentives of teachers. Moreover, it reflects a rather hierarchical view of school management. By this is meant that, in such a system of 'teacher compensation', there is a clear division between those whose job description is to manage the school and those (on the single salary schedule) who are managed.

By contrast, management and compensation in other employments reflect much more what the employees can do and have achieved in terms of devolved responsibility and remuneration. Management is 'flatter', employees or teams of employees receive due recognition for their efforts and successes, and their proven professionalism is recognised in the assumption of greater responsibility for practical and strategic decisions.

Odden and Kelley argue, therefore, that teaching should be rather like that: greater recognition, through an appropriate funding mechanism and through the devolving of management responsibility, of what teachers can do and have achieved. There is, in their view, an urgency to move in that direction because:

> the tax-paying public, the business community, and policy-makers still pressure the education system to produce results and to link pay – even school finance structures, more broadly – to performance. (op. cit., p.11)

The pressure arises from the felt need to raise standards, to improve 'productivity' in relation to these standards, and to hold teachers accountable (both positively where they have succeeded and negatively where they have failed) for their professional work.

To enable this to happen, there needs to be much greater precision in what teachers are expected to achieve – productivity targets, if you like. But this in turn requires the setting of reasonable targets – the clear statement of what good teachers of subject X and level Y should be able to achieve. And there should be the continuing professional development to enable teachers achieve these targets. There must be an investment in training.

In anticipation of this shift in the management of schools and the compensation of teachers, the National Board for Professional Teaching Practice (and other professional organisations in the USA) have spelt out in much detail what these targets, within specific subjects and for specific age-ranges, should be.

The position is clearly summarised by Odden and Kelley:

> Shifting pay increments from years of experience and loosely related education units to more direct measures of professional skills and competencies, adding a mechanism that undergirds the need for ongoing training and assessment of instructional strategies, and perhaps adding group-based performance bonuses are compensation changes that could reconnect how teachers are paid with the evolving strategic needs of new school organizations, calls for teacher professionalism, and the core requirements of standards-based education reform. Providing salary increments for teachers who are certified by the NBPTP as accomplished expert teachers, a policy increasingly adopted by states and districts, is a direct competency-based pay element and represents specific movement on teacher compensation reform. (ibid.)

Odden and Kelley's argument has been influential both within and outside the United States. Certainly it has had a profound effect upon the British

Government which has been advised by Odden and which is now swiftly introducing 'performance related pay' to schools in England and Wales. The government Green Paper, *Teachers Meeting the Challenge of Change* (DfEE, 1998), followed by a 'technical consultation document' on pay and performance management, and a further consultation document, *A Fast Track for Teachers* (DfEE, 1999) all spell out the policy which is being implemented at speed. The proposals might be summarised as follows, starting with the words of the Secretary of State for Education and Employment:

> Part of this investment (in education) is for a new pay and award structure for the teaching profession ... the present pay arrangements reflect a different era. They do not sufficiently reward good teachers for excellence in the classroom. Many teachers reach a scale point beyond which they cannot progress, however good they are, unless they take on management responsibilities. (DfEE, 1998, p.8)

As, indeed, with Odden and Kelley, this changed pay and reward structure is connected positively with a 'new vision of the profession', including professional development. The details of this 'new vision' can be summarised as follows:

(i) *Better rewards for teachers*. There will be two pay ranges for classroom teachers, with a 'performance threshold' at the end of the first range. 'Crossing the threshold' will depend on 'assessment of performance against agreed objectives'. Thereafter, annual assessments of performance, reflecting 'new professional expectations', will determine the speed with which teachers progress or do not progress up the second pay range. Furthermore, consistent with the recognition of team work in any successful organisation, there will be a School Performance Award Scheme for successful teams of teachers and whole schools, in recognition of yearly improvement and 'high results'.

(ii) *Improving leadership*. Extended pay scales will reward 'strong and effective leaders' (headteachers and their 'management teams', including 'advanced skills teachers'), though with 'fixed-term contacts' to link rewards to the achievement of agreed objectives. 'Fast track teachers' will be identified early (even before or during their training) and given supplementary contracts, incentives and professional development to help them on their way to leadership.

(iii) *Better skills and staff development.* Progression up the pay scales will be supported by a contractual duty for all teachers to keep their skills and subject knowledge up to date, together with an appropriate qualifications framework, a 'Code of Practice' for providers of professional development and a new inspection programme to ensure 'value for money'.

(iv) *Initial training.* More flexible routes into teaching (employment-based, related to diagnosed needs for specific competencies, school led) will emphasise performance and practical skills, and will require nationally set standards of teaching competence and of performance in numeracy, literacy and information technology.

Professional Development

According to Odden and Kelley, rewarding performance (and punishing non-performance or failure) makes sense if, following regular appraisal, there are opportunities for teachers to obtain the professional competencies necessary for performing according to standard or meeting the 'output targets'. Therefore, the DfEE has produced a further consultation document on professional development – such development being defined in terms of what makes a good, and progressively better, teacher within a framework of professional development (DfEE, 2000). Such a definition is based upon the research commissioned from Hay/McBer (2000). Let me, therefore, summarise briefly what Hay/McBer have to say about the effective teacher. From a wide and systematic gathering of evidence (questionnaires, interviews, observations, etc.) the researchers provided a 'model of effective performance'. This consisted of 16 characteristics split into five groups concerned with professionalism, capacity to think analytically and conceptually about teaching, planning and setting expectations, leadership qualities, and the capacity to relate to others.

In many respects, this is a valuable piece of research, and can, and no doubt will, serve as a useful document for continuing professional development. But (and here I anticipate what I shall say later about the nature of and scope for professional development within the more centralised management of public services) the model of the effective teacher (in terms of skills, knowledge and qualities) is set out in terms of the National Standards determined by the government. It provides the basis on which teachers are to be assessed for progression through the main professional grades, through the new 'performance threshold' and beyond, into the Advanced Skills Teacher grade, and thence to those of senior management and leadership.

Therefore, the Secretary of State, in his introduction to the consultation paper on professional development, feels confident in saying that 'professional development is all about making sure that teachers have the finest and most up-to-date tools to do the job' (DfEE, 2000). Professional development is about equipping teachers (giving them the knowledge and skills – and personal qualities, where possible) to 'deliver' improvement in schools and to raise standards (by which is presumably meant performance according to agreed standards).

The framework within which performance is measured according to standards (where output targets are to be defined) is comprehensive: at the levels of initial training (where already many detailed standards have been defined and against which training institutions have been assessed), of newly qualified teachers, of the main career threshold, of subject leadership or middle management, of advanced skills teacher, and of school leadership (heads and their deputies). Although the document states that 'schools and teachers are best placed to know what development activities will meet these particular needs and raise standards of teaching and learning in their school' (N.B. not the universities which are the traditional inservice providers), such professional responsibility is confined to the *means* of achieving the ends, to the *tools* of efficiency and effectiveness, not to the deliberation over the educational values and purposes themselves. These alues and purposes have, as it were, have been cascaded from above. To help with the professional re-equipping, opportunities will be given to help teachers – including an extra school-based inservice day for the introduction of performance related progress and small bursaries to subsidise the costs of professional development.

However, what is remarkable about the consultation paper and about the Hay/McBer research into teaching upon which it leans, is that there is no account given of education. The professional development of professional educators assumes that what it means to educate someone (anyone – irrespective of social context or individual aspirations and capacities) is uncontroversial – and, indeed, is clearly established in the nationally established targets, though refined or tweaked occasionally as problems or new needs become apparent (as in the recent requirement, reflected in the requisite targets, for citizenship education).

However, education is a 'contestable concept' in many ways. There is no consensus within society on what is to count as an educated person; the link between social and economic needs, on the one hand, and individual needs, on the other, is complex and varied; the struggle to make sense or to find value in life will not be uniform. And the recognition of this was reflected in Morrell's establishment of the Schools Council and in his recognition of the role of teachers, in their professional capacity, to deliberate the ends and purposes of their teaching (the values which these embodied) as well as being equipped with the tools for reaching the ends.

On the other hand, the new management of public services, the central setting of targets, the cascading of these targets eventually to individual teachers no longer has room for that. As Faulkner et al. (1999) argue (albeit in the context of the administration of public services more generally):

> Judgements which professional public servants have made, or could reasonably be expected to make, on a basis of their own authority, experience and expertise, are increasingly becoming matters of departmental guidance, ministerial direction, or even statutory duty. (p.4)

There was to be, and is, little scope for professional judgement in the establishment of standards or targets. All the wisdom is at the centre – in the hands of government. In this we see, I believe, a necessary restriction of what we mean by education, and thus a shift in what is meant by professional responsibility, professional judgement and professional development. This is reflected in the changed language of education as it is encompassed within the new management of public services.

The Language of Education

How we see the world depends upon the concepts through which experience is organised, objects identified as significant, descriptions applied and evaluations made. The choice of metaphor changes our vision of what is important or how a situation is to be understood or what is to count as an appropriate assessment. The Odden and Kelley proposal, in particular its implementation by government, assumes a distinctive language through which to describe, assess and evaluate an 'educational practice' and thus the professional engagement within it. Such a language draws upon new metaphors, and through these metaphors the concept of a profession changes. Professional judgement and development take on different meanings. Teachers and 'their managers' perceive what they are doing differently. What previously was seen to be of significance to professional development is frequently demoted to the trivial and irrelevant.

The danger might be illustrated as follows. The Permanent Secretary responsible for implementing these changes in Britain, in giving an account of the nature and purposes of policy changes, said that we must 'think in business terms' – and thus draw upon the language and practices of the business world. That means that we look at those changes, as engineered by government for the improvement of standards in schools, as a 'quality circle' in which one defines the product, identifies the means for producing that product, empowers the deliverer, measures the quality, empowers the client, and develops partnership between the clients, the deliverers and the managers of the system such that there might be a continuous review of targets and means for achieving those targets. The 'product' is defined in terms of a detailed, outcomes-related curriculum. The 'process' (or 'means' for reaching the targets) is spelt out in terms of 'effectiveness' in the production of this 'product'. The changed management structures 'empower the deliverers' of the 'process' to satisfy the needs of the respective 'stakeholders'. The 'measurement of the quality' of the 'product' is provided through a detailed assessment (a 'testing against product specification'). 'The empowering of the clients' comes about through the creation of choice, which is achieved through the availability of public data on effectiveness and through competitiveness amongst the 'deliverers of the product' so that the clients can exercise choice. And 'partnerships' are created for 'stakeholders', 'deliverers' and 'clients' to work together in developing the 'effective processes' for producing the 'product' (which is generally defined by someone external to the 'process'). The management of the whole process is conducted by what Mark Freedland (quoted in Faulkner et al., 1999) refers to as 'imposed contractualism' – the cascading down from above of 'productivity targets'.

The language of education through which we are asked to 'think in business terms' – the language of inputs and outputs, of value-addedness, of performance indicators and audits, of products and productivity, of educational clients and curriculum deliverers – constitutes a new way of thinking about the relation of teacher and learner. It is a way of thinking which was non-existent until comparatively recently. It employs different metaphors, different ways of describing and evaluating educational activities. But, in so doing, it changes those activities into something else. It transforms the moral context in which education takes place and is judged successful or otherwise.

The effect of this new language is not a matter for empirical enquiry alone, for that which is to be enquired into has become a different thing. So mesmerised have we become with the importance of 'cost efficiency', 'value for money', 'productivity' and 'effectiveness' that we have failed to see that the very nature of the enterprise – of an 'educational practice' - has been redefined. Once the teacher 'delivers' someone else's curriculum with its precisely defined 'product', there is little room for that *transaction* in which the teacher, rooted in a particular cultural tradition, responds to the needs of the learner. When the learner becomes a 'client' or 'customer', there is no room for the traditional apprenticeship into the community of learners. When the 'product' is the measurable 'targets' on which 'performance' is 'audited', then little significance is attached to the 'struggle to make sense' or the deviant and creative response.

Indeed, the metaphors taken from management do not seem to embody values other than those of efficiency and effectiveness. It is as though (within the discourse of management) there are two quite different sorts of debate: that which concerns the efficient means to the attainment of clearly defined targets, and that which concerns the targets towards which we should seek to be efficient. The result is a language of 'ends' and targets established outside the process of being educated - the endless lists of competencies, the 'can dos' which might be objectively measured, the professional skills on which teachers are to be assessed if they are to progress up the 'salary schedule'. 'Education', then, becomes the means to achieve these ends, and it is judged essentially by its effectiveness. If it is not effective, then it should adopt other 'means', based on the kind of research which relates means to ends - that is, what the teacher does, to what the learner can produce as a result. 'Means' are logically 'separated' from the 'ends', and the quality of the 'input' is measured simply by reference to the success or otherwise of the 'output'.

Think, however, in terms of a different set of metaphors. Oakeshott (1972), in his essay *Education: its engagement and its frustrations*, speaks of education as the introduction of young people to a world of ideas which are embodied in the 'conversations between the generations of mankind'. Through that introduction the young learner comes to learn and appreciate the voices of poetry, of philosophy, of history, of science. There is an engagement with ideas, a struggle to make sense, a search for value in what often appears dull and mundane, an excitement in intellectual and aesthetic discovery, an entry to a tradition of thinking and criticism. As in all good conversations (especially one where there is such an engagement with ideas and where the spirit of criticism prevails), one cannot define in advance what the end of that conversation or engagement will or should be. And, indeed, the end is but the starting point for further conversations.

Teaching, therefore, becomes a 'transaction' between the teacher and the learner in which the teacher mediates the different voices to those who are seeking to take part. That conversation between the generations, embedded within literature, drama, oral traditions and narratives, artefacts, social practices, works of art, etc., speak to the needs and aspirations of the young people, but at different levels and in different ways. The art and skill of the teacher lie in making the connections between the *impersonal* world of what is bequeathed to us in libraries, etc. and the *personal* world of the young people, thereby creating an *interpersonal* world of informed and critical dialogue. The fruit of such efforts will be reflected in thoughts, beliefs and valuings which are diverse, unpredictable and sometimes slow to mature.

Different metaphors, therefore, provide different understandings of an 'educational practice'. Business metaphors make possible a management of that practice in terms of 'targets', 'productivity', 'effectiveness', 'professional competence', 'professional appraisal', 'client choice' within a 'market setting', which the metaphor of 'conversation' does not. Indeed, the business metaphor provides the framework of management control, as 'targets' are 'cascaded' from above, and as pay is related to the achievement of those targets. But such business terms provide an impoverished vocabulary for that transaction between teacher and learner as both engage with the richness of the ideas which we have inherited and through which we struggle to make sense of the physical, social, moral and aesthetic worlds we inhabit. The engagement between teacher and learner, as they endeavour to appreciate a poem or to understand a theorem or to solve a design problem or to test out a favourite theory or to resolve a moral dilemma, is both the means and the end. For, as the philosopher Dewey argued, the so called 'end' becomes the 'means' to yet further thinking - the pursuit of yet further goals. But that is probably why Dewey for so long was on the index of forbidden books in teacher training - a different language from that of management and control (Dewey, 1916).

Professionalism and Professional Development

'Professional' is a very elastic term and no one definition can quite capture its quite complex usage. Footballers and second hand car salesmen refer to themselves as professionals, thereby hoping to improve their status in the eyes of the public.

But such improved status is parasitic upon certain general, if ill-defined, expectations of a member of a profession. These might be summarised as: the possession of expertise as a result of training and experience; some element of self-regulation in terms of accountability, discipline and membership; and ethical standards in terms of service to the public. In the case of the last criterion, the *professional* teacher would provide advice and help to the young learner on the basis not of self interest or profit, but of the assessed needs of the learner. In the case of the first criterion, the *professional* teacher would claim expertise not simply on the best available ways of attaining some goal, but on the capacity to deliberate about the goals themselves. Indeed, the transaction between teacher and learner is, more often than not, a deliberation about values, an engagement with 'the best that has been thought and said', an exploration of what is really worthwhile. To reduce such a transaction to the delivery of someone else's targets demeans the professional role as has been exercised by able and committed teachers.

Odden and Kelley argue, as does the British Government, that 'performance related pay', supported by a detailed analysis of the relevant skills and competencies, enhances rather than diminishes the professional nature and stature of teachers. In a sense it does. The competent classroom manager might be said to be more professional than the incompetent one. But at the same time it is a limited notion of 'professional'.

An educational practice is a transaction between a teacher and a learner within a framework of agreed purposes and underlying procedural values. Such a transaction respects the learning needs of the learner on the one hand, and on the other, mediates those aspects of the culture which are valued and which meet those needs. Such aspects include a tradition of literature and literary criticism, the narratives picked out by history, the understandings of the physical world embodied within the different sciences, the appreciation of the social worlds reflected in the arts. And, of course, such traditions, narratives, understandings and appreciations are by no means static. They are the product of deliberations, arguments, criticisms within and 'between the generations of mankind'. Many teachers – of

English, say, or of science – see themselves as participating in such a tradition, indeed as its custodians. They speak from a love of their subject and wish to convey that. They believe that the understanding enshrined within that tradition is important to the young people as they seek a deeper appreciation and knowledge of their lives and of the challenges within them. The teachers want, as it were, to bring the young people on the 'inside' of those traditions. Hence, it would be wrong to characterise such teaching activities by reference to some 'products' or set of 'targets' logically disconnected from the activity of teaching itself. The goal, aim, value or purpose is embodied within the practice. One might refer to an 'educational practice' as a particular form of life, a way of thinking, a mode of valuing, into which the learner is being invited or even seduced.

The role of the teacher in such a practice requires deliberation about the aims to be fulfilled in teaching this or that to these particular learners, as much as it does the best ways of achieving these values or aims. The teacher is constantly deliberating and making judgements about the value of what is taught as well as the effectiveness of a particular method. Such a way of seeing an educational activity is to be contrasted with one in which an activity is geared simply to the production of something else – something only contingently or even arbitrarily connected with the activity itself. In pursuit of imposed targets (against which teachers are to be assessed) professional judgement is increasingly limited to deciding upon the most efficient means to the achieving of those targets. Hence, the perceived poverty of those assessments of teacher performance which reduce professional judgement of teachers, immersed in their respective disciplines which they seek to communicate to the students, to the lists of competencies through which limited targets are reached.

Elliott (1991) illustrates this theorising about practice from the Ford Teaching Project which he directed and which involved over 40 teachers in 12 schools. The issue they were addressing was that of methods of teaching which promoted pupil enquiry and discovery. Pupil enquiry and discovery were an alternative mode of learning from that which normally prevailed in classrooms. What starts off with an aspiration, a rather general idea, certain educational values, needs to be translated into a set of practices. And these practices need to be examined critically in the light of those values. Do they, in fact, embody or make sense of the original aspiration? How far do they depend on classroom organisation or previous experience? Do these practices have unintended and unacknowledged effects on the rest of the curriculum? By sharing the problems, the questions and the tentative conclusions, the teachers were able to build up a body of *professional* knowledge, tentative perhaps, but knowledge which had withstood critical questioning. This professional knowledge was developed through the collection of relevant data, the interpretation of this data, the critiquing of the interpretation in the light of the evidence, the reflection upon the values which were implicit within the practice. Thus, there is a constant interpretation, testing, re-interpretation, critical scrutiny, moral reflection – an ongoing process which feeds into and is put to the test in the teaching.

This sense of the teacher as a professional – deliberating about the value of proceeding in this way rather than that or about the most appropriate way ahead for particular students – is lost in the more limited picture of the teacher, assessed according to the preordained performances required by those who set the targets. Indeed, this capacity for moral deliberation and for professional judgement about the relevance of general theoretical knowledge to the peculiarities of particular circumstances is interestingly omitted from the Hay/McBer research, on which the current conception of professional development depends.

Conclusion

In this chapter I have briefly outlined a changing view about the management of public services – and thus about the relation of such management to professional practice. The change is:

- from a management which provided the framework only, leaving very largely the professionals to determine the nature of the service offered
- through a management which sets the rules and framework within which a more market driven shaping of public services was to emerge (thereby diminishing the professional role of the teacher)
- to a management which set the 'targets' and exercises control through the reward or retribution of the performance of those employed to deliver those targets.

A new management-speak reflects this quite radical shift in the management of public services – a language of target setting and outcomes, productivity and performance indicators, inputs and value addedness, customers and service delivery.

I have used the particular example of teaching and of the changed relationship between the profession of teaching and central government to illustrate and to develop the thesis. But the philosophy or management theory which lies behind these changes extends far beyond the organisation of education. It embraces more generally the management of public services as such and thus of other professions – those of medicine, nursing, social work, the police and so on. Indeed, it would be useful to see more detailed accounts of the changes in these other areas. The main point is that there has been a quite radical shift in the relation of government to public services and thus to professions, and this has been made possible in a radical change of language through which those services are described.

This language, and the understanding of management and control which it reflects, transform our understanding of 'educational practice' (and of other practices) and thus of the professional role of those who engage in and are responsible for such practices. That shift in role (and thus in our understanding of professional judgement and of professional development for exercising that judgement) is best reflected in that changed vision of education and of the teacher, illustrated by Morrell's defence of the teacher and the educational community on the one hand, and the DfEE's recent accounts of the profession of teaching on the other. In the former, education and thus teaching is a social practice within a tradition of deliberation about values (through literature, the humanities, the arts, the practice of the sciences). To that extent, the profession of teaching was a custodian of those values, of (if you like) those moral purposes and practices. In the latter, education and thus teaching are more narrowly confined to those practices which most effectively produce the targets established outside the educational community and tradition. The control, direction and nature of professional development changes accordingly – and the role of higher education necessarily is diminished.

References

Auld Report (1976) *William Tyndale Junior and Infants School Public Enquiry*, a report to Inner London Education Authority.

Dewey, J. (1916) *Democracy and Education*. New York: The Free Press.

DfEE (1998) *Teachers: Meeting the Challenge of Change, A Summary*. London: DfEE.

DfEE (2000) *Professional Development*, Consultation Paper. London: DfEE.

Elliott, J. (1991) *Action Research for Educational Change*. Milton Keynes: Open University Press.

Faulkner, D., Freedland, M. and Fisher, E. (1999) *Public Services: Developing Approaches to Governance and Professionalism*. A Report of a Series of Seminars, St John's College, Oxford.

Hay/McBer (2000) *Raising Achievement in our Schools: Models of Effective Teaching*, interim report to DfEE, Hay Group.

McKevitt, D. (1998) *Managing Core Public Services*. Oxford: Blackwell.

Morrell, D. (1967) *Education and Change*. Lecture 1: The Annual Joseph Payne Memorial Lectures, 1965-6. London: College of Preceptors.

Oakeshott, M. (1972) Education: Its Engagement and Its Frustration. In Fuller, M. (Ed.) *Michael Oakeshott and Education*. Yale University Press.

Odden, A. and Kelley, C. (1997) *Paying Teachers for What They Know and Do*. California: Corwin Press.

Osborne, D. and Gaebler, T. (1992) *Re-inventing Government: How the Entrepreneurial Spirit is Transforming the Public Sector*. Massachusetts: Addison Wesley.

Simon, B. (1991) *Education and the Social Order 1940-1990*. London: Lawrence & Wishart.

An early draft of this paper was presented at a conference of the ESRC Centre for Skills, Knowledge and Organisational Performance in Oxford. The author wishes to thank the Centre for the opportunity given and the criticisms received.

3 The Individual and the Institutional: Balancing Professional Development Needs Within Further Education

RACHEL BROOKS

Introduction

In their study of the Further Education (FE) sector, published in 1986, Cantor and Roberts outlined three overlapping phases through which professional development had passed. These were the introduction of formal staff development policies in the 1970s; curriculum-based staff development; and finally, in the late 1980s, the introduction of systematic staff development based on external funding from the local education authorities. Over the last 15 years, two additional phases can be identified. The first resulted from the incorporation of FE colleges, introduced by the 1992 Further and Higher Education Act. Under this legislation (which came into effect in April 1993), local education authorities' responsibility for FE colleges was removed. Instead, the colleges became state-supported corporations financed largely through the Further Education Funding Council (FEFC), responsible directly to the Secretary of State for Education (or, in the case of Welsh colleges, the Secretary of State for Wales).

The introduction of sector-wide standards for FE teachers in January 1999 by the Further Education National Training Organisation (FENTO) signals the latest phase. These standards are intended to inform the initial training and continuing professional development of staff involved in teaching and learning in FE and to assist institution-based activities such as recruitment, appraisal and the identification of training needs (FENTO, 1999). The standards will also underpin the move towards ensuring that all new FE staff hold or are working towards a recognised teaching qualification appropriate to their role. Historically, there has been no minimum level of qualification for FE teachers, although the proportion of staff with a teaching qualification has shown a steady increase from around 43% in the mid-1970s, to 53% in 1985 and 60% in the mid-1990s (Guile and Lucas, 1996). The latest figures suggest that 83% of teaching staff hold a teaching qualification, together with 33% of staff who work in a 'supporting' role (FENTO, 2000).

There is little evidence that professional development programmes were consistently successful in ensuring that both individual and institutional needs were met in any of the first three phases. However, it will be argued in this chapter that the balance between individual needs and institutional needs within staff development was altered as a direct result of incorporation in 1993 and the significant curriculum changes introduced in the late 1980s and early 1990s (in particular, the introduction of National Vocational Qualifications in 1987 and General National Vocational Qualifications from 1992). These had a direct impact upon professional development programmes and led to significant changes in the prioritisation of need. Although little empirical research has yet been conducted on the impact of the FENTO standards, some of the literature exploring the possible consequences for the 'latest phase' of professional development will be discussed in this chapter.

Diversity within the FE Sector

Traditionally, professional development within the FE sector has operated on an ad hoc basis, with the quality of staff and their training left largely for the market and individual colleges to determine (Lucas and Betts, 1996). Although incorporation has exerted similar types of pressure on most FE colleges, empirical studies have highlighted a continuing diversity, both in terms of policies and practices in these areas (Martinez, 1994; Cantor et al., 1995) and in the percentage of the college budget devoted to staff development and training (Lucas and Betts, 1996). Prior to incorporation, the average level of targeted funding for staff development was 1%. In 1996, the average was still about the same but with a variation from 0.33% to 2% between colleges (op.cit.).

Although some steps are being taken to reduce this diversity, such as the introduction of the sector-wide FENTO standards, the considerable and enduring differences between colleges make generalisations about the sector problematic. Thus, while this chapter presents a substantial body of evidence that suggests institutional needs have often been given priority over the individual needs of FE staff, this has not necessarily been the case in all colleges. Indeed, studies have shown how, in some cases, professional development programmes have succeeded in meeting both sets of needs, while a small number have suggested that some colleges may have prioritised individual needs over institutional ones. This is discussed in greater detail below.

The Prioritisation of Institutional Needs

In some FE colleges, in the years immediately following incorporation, professional development was marginalised, as managers attempted to reorient their colleges along market lines (Lucas and Betts, 1996). Thus, during this period, the tension, if any, seemed as much between staff development and other activities as between institutionally-driven professional development and more individually-focused programmes. Although this decline was temporary and not prevalent throughout the sector, there is evidence that, even today, many general aspects of staff development are still not well developed, such as mechanisms for evaluating development and training activities (FEFC, 2000). Nevertheless, numerous studies over the last decade have demonstrated the ways in which institutional needs have been prioritised in FE colleges, often over the personal development needs of members of staff.

In seeking to explore the reasons for this imbalance, studies have focused on several factors. By far the greatest body of work has explored the growth of a business or 'managerialist' culture within the FE sector, as a result of incorporation, and argued that this has exacerbated, if not created, differences between strategic and individual goals while serving to privilege the former. Ostensibly, managerialism was introduced as a rational process to increase efficiency and professionalism within the sector. As part of this, reconstructing professionals:

> as managers of reform [was] of strategic importance to the implementation of market and managerial initiatives in education.
>
> (Gleeson and Shain, 1999, p.466)

It is not unrealistic to assume that specific professional development needs can be common to both institutions and individuals: that the needs of an individual member of staff, or staff group, can also be held by the college as a whole. This presupposes a set of common goals, which both the individual and the institution are working towards. Empirical evidence suggests, however, that over the past decade goals at the two levels have increasingly diverged, with a tendency for teachers and managers to display polarised identities, in defence of either pedagogy or management interests (Gleeson and Shain, 1999). In this way the objectives (and thus the institutional needs) of the college as a whole have become aligned with 'managerialism', while the goals and development needs of teaching staff have become identified more closely with 'professionalism'.

A possible explanation for this increasing divergence is that it is a result of a clearer articulation of strategic goals, brought about by the process of drafting mission statements, policy documents, materials for inspection and marketing information. This hypothesis assumes that people at different levels of the organisation held different goals and objectives prior to incorporation, but that these were largely masked. If this is the case, the process of making existing differences explicit can be viewed as an improvement on what went before.

However, a more plausible theory, based on the available evidence, is that the increasing divergence has been brought about by an actual realignment of college goals - in accordance with the new environment in which FE colleges now have to operate, namely, national inspection, targets for retention and achievement and emphasis on measurable performance outcomes. In this interpretation, there is no longer any congruency in goals at different levels of the organisation (and thus neither in development needs) and furthermore, the term 'professional development' is itself interpreted differently by different members of staff. Some have suggested that amongst managers it is no longer understood solely as a means of encouraging learning and reflective practice, but as a tool to monitor performance in line with centrally determined goals (Avis, 2000; Bathmaker, 2000). This interpretation is supported by Gleeson and Shain's (1999) research which suggests that there has indeed been a struggle over meaning and identity in the FE workforce; that within the sector there are competing visions and cultures, and that these are intimately connected to wider social and economic change.

Other research has shown how these tensions have been played out in practice. Randle and Brady's (1997) study of 'Cityshire' college, for example, explored the development of what they call the 'new managerialism' and the impact this exerted on professional control within the college. Lecturers felt that their professionalism was threatened through new quality controls which emphasised conformance to prescriptive and quantifiable requirements only, and which placed emphasis on materials used in teaching rather than on the quality of interaction in the classroom. Summarising their findings, Randle and Brady claim that:

> Traditionally, staff and managers aspired to a common set of educational values, encompassing the notion of professional expertise and some discretion in the design, delivery and assessment of provision ... [This is] being replaced by a new type of manager primarily concerned with resource management, particularly financial resources. (Randle and Brady, 1997, p.232)

Although they make no direct reference to professional development, it seems likely that the shift in values, which they argue has permeated throughout college life, would be reflected in development programmes.

A study focusing on the impact of managerialism on staff development and training was conducted by Elliot and Hall (1994). They argue that the need for managers to be able to respond quickly to changes in policy and to competition with other colleges gave rise, in many colleges, to 'human resource management' in place of personnel management. This was predicated on a more strategic approach to staff planning and development, making it easier to manipulate the allocation of staff to particular vocational areas. Elliot and Hall suggest that while staff development is likely to be highlighted and achieve greater prominence under this new system, it will be used as a means of widening staff competence to meet institutional needs, and that 'multiskilling' of staff will be prioritised in order to maximise 'output' (p.7). An in-depth investigation of ten FE colleges conducted by the International Centre for Research on Assessment (ICRA, 1995) revealed similar trends. The majority of the colleges in the study had boosted their staff development budgets after incorporation in an attempt to make human resource development a central 'plank' of the college ethos. However, all colleges had tightened up their procedures for staff to apply for funding, with the two most important criteria being support for the priorities of the college's strategic plan and the cost-effectiveness of the staff development activity:

> even very short courses and conferences must be justified through application forms or questionnaires and must carry the approval of the line manager and in many cases the staff development manager. (ICRA, 1995, p.8)

Nevertheless, within this overall orientation there were considerable differences between the ten colleges in the study. In four of them, the staff development manager had established tight control over professional development programmes and they were geared very closely to the college's overall strategic objectives. In the other six:

> whilst external demands and limited budgets reduced opportunities, individual lecturers or teams of staff were more likely to initiate staff development activities. (ICRA, 1995, p.14)

Not only has increasing managerialism affected the type of staff development activity that can be undertaken by staff, there is also evidence that it has served to determine the way in which such activities can be delivered, largely as a method of containing staff development budgets; staff have been encouraged to use cheaper forms of provision and discouraged from enrolling on a course if another member of staff has already embarked upon it (Shorter, 1994; ICRA, 1995).

The increasing importance of strategic or institutional objectives in determining the development activities of individual members of staff has been implemented through the assessment and appraisal of staff as well as through a tightening of the criteria to apply for development programmes. The latest inspection report from the FEFC (2000) states that in most colleges 'there are effective arrangements to appraise and develop full-time staff' (p.40). However, others have argued that appraisal is not primarily a tool for staff development but an apparently benign process through which those in higher positions monitor others. Avis (1996), for example, claims that:

> To the extent … that appraisal may be used to separate individuals from their working environments and constrains, to control their rewards and to elide their personal development needs with those of the organisation, it may work against the interests of the professional group. (Avis, 1996, p.601)

Differential Impact on Different Groups of Staff

Although similar 'managerial' changes have been introduced throughout the public sector over the past decade, a number of researchers maintain that FE teachers have been particularly vulnerable to such pressures as they lack a strong professional identity. FE staff are traditionally recruited from a wide range of backgrounds and Robson (1998) argues that there are certain incentives for them to maintain their previous occupational allegiance - to ensure credibility as vocational teachers. This results in many different cultures coexisting in the FE workplace and militates against the formation of a clear professional identity for the group as a whole. Robson goes on to claim that:

> The existence of dual professional identities amongst many of its staff should be a source of strength, both for the individual and the sector as a whole, but the official failure to support the development of a full professional identity for the FE teacher, the prioritising (both officially and unofficially) of the first occupational identity, at the expense of the second, has resulted in anomaly and confusion. (Robson, 1998, p.603)

While it can be argued that this diversity rendered FE staff more vulnerable to managerialist change than professionals working in other areas of the education system, it also ensured that the changes did not impact in any uniform way across the sector: different groups of staff were affected in different ways. Nor was the impact determined entirely by job title or part-time/full-time status. Gleeson and Shain (1999) found considerable differences between middle managers in the way they responded to the pressures from above and below. They characterised the different groups of managers as 'willing compliers' (those who were deeply committed to the FE institution and its corporate image), 'unwilling compliers' (those more sceptical and disenchanted with the new FE ethos) and 'strategic compliers' (pragmatists who were able to reconcile professional and managerial interests) and sought to explain these differences by drawing on the characteristics of individuals and their social location.

This typology assumes a degree of agency on the part of the middle managers: they were able to decide how they would respond to the different pressures they faced. Other groups of staff, however, have had fewer options in their responses to managerialist change in general, and professional development opportunities in particular. Part-time staff have historically been neglected in colleges' staff development programmes (Hopkins, 1989; Bryning, 1991; Elliot and Hall, 1994). However, the increasing use of part-time lecturers in recent years has accentuated the needs of this particular group of staff. In 2000, the FEFC reported that around 26% of full-time equivalent teachers in inspected colleges were not full-time members of staff, and in 19 colleges the figure was 40% or more (FEFC, 2000). Indeed, there are now more part-time than full-time teachers working in the sector and, in some colleges, part-time staff teach a higher proportion of lessons than their full-time colleagues (op.cit.). The findings from research are unequivocal: throughout the sector part-time staff receive much less professional development than their full-time colleagues. Lucas and Betts (1996) found that many colleges do not provide any training or development opportunities for part-time staff if they are employed for fewer than a specified number of hours per week, often between eight and ten, while the FEFC (2000) notes that 'insufficient attention is given to ensuring that part-time staff are effectively supported by training' (p.40) and recommends that colleges:

> ensure that all the staff they employ are able to take full advantage of development opportunities and support services ... targeted funding to help colleges tackle these issues should be of highest priority. (FEFC, 2000, p.4)

Although the relative disadvantage of part-time lecturers, in terms of professional development, when compared to their full-time colleagues is not new, the increasing use of such staff to increase the flexibility of the workforce has largely been brought about by incorporation and the need to be able to respond quickly to national and local changes (Lucas and Betts, 1996; FEFC, 2000).

However, some staff have benefited from changes since incorporation. Prior to 1993, professional development in the FE sector focused almost exclusively on the needs of teaching staff, while support staff received very little training or development (Cantor et al., 1995). Since then, most colleges have moved towards a whole-staff approach and both teaching and non-teaching staff are generally included in the staff development programme (ICRA, 1995). This is partly due to the 'blurring' of boundaries between the two groups of staff (Spours and Lucas, 1996), but also to the new autonomy of colleges: previously, the grants available from the local education authority for staff development were restricted to teaching staff only. Managers have also benefited from extensive training as part of a general shift from curricular staff development to management development (op.cit.).

The Impact of Competence-Based Qualifications

A second strand in the literature exploring the balance between individual and institutional needs focuses on the growth of competence-based qualifications especially National Vocational Qualifications (NVQs), for both FE staff and students which were introduced in the late 1980s. The award of this type of qualification is based upon the competencies which students demonstrate as outcomes of their training rather than upon a specific syllabus or period of time spent engaged in a programme of learning (Jessup, 1991). These qualifications achieved prominence in the UK through a series of government white papers introducing a new training policy which emphasised competence as its necessary outcome (Tuxworth, 1989; Norris, 1991). In particular, the 1986 white paper, *Working Together - Education and Training* (GB Parliament, HoC, 1986) called for the reform and modernisation of vocational training through a structure of recognised qualifications based on competence and matched to the needs of modern employment.

A number of studies have described the advantages that a competence-based approach can bring to both initial teacher training and other types of professional development in FE. Several authors have highlighted the clarity associated with competences, the clear statements they provide of the skills that need to be demonstrated, the criteria used for assessment and the recognition given to prior achievement (Last and Chown, 1996; Whitty and Willmott, 1991). It has also been argued that they can contribute to making professional practice in education more transparent and clarify the expertise that is required of teachers (Hodkinson, 1995). This, Robson (1998) maintains, may help to delineate the boundaries of a 'further education lecturer job' and, as a result, emphasise the 'professional' nature of work in the sector.

However, the limitations of the competence-based approach are also clear. Much of the literature focuses on the narrowness of its approach and its failure to address certain important aspects of professional practice in FE such as theoretical knowledge and understanding (e.g. Ashworth, 1992), the ethical principles which underpin practice as an FE teacher (Chown, 1996) and the ability to make autonomous and pragmatic judgements (Chown, 1996; Elliott, 1996). Chown claims that the competence-based approach seems:

> unable to cope with the fact that a vital part of teaching is the complex process through which teachers draw on different types of knowledge from a range of

> domains and decide what to do in rapidly changing, unpredictable circumstances.
> (Chown, 1996, p.143)

Similarly, Ecclestone (1993) argues that lecturers and education managers within FE should be entitled to a more professional and academic training 'if they are to deal effectively with the increasingly complex situations they face' (p.89). The failure of competence-based qualifications to engage with these more complex aspects of teaching has largely been explained by their 'pre-occupation with observable phenomena' (Elliott, 1996, p.21) and the assumption that all knowledge can be observed, and thus assessed, in use.

It has also been argued that in addition to failing to capture the complexity of the FE teacher's work, competence-based qualifications have served to push forward institutional objectives at the expense of the individual needs of staff. Several of those interviewed as part of an in-depth study of ten FE colleges (ICRA, 1995) claimed that:

> The standards approach to staff development [i.e. competence-based] was not satisfying enough for staff. A senior manager said that NVQs were seen by staff in the college as simply the accreditation of existing practice, 'of what is done well already, of what they know they can do'. He argued that staff were more interested in mechanisms for improvement, and in moving forward from their existing knowledge, skills and understanding.
> (ICRA, 1995, p.23)

Taking this argument further, Edwards and Usher (1994) suggest that competence-type professional development programmes are a way of imposing self-discipline and self-regulation on individuals so that they conform to what is required. Indeed, Bathmaker (2000) argues that if the FENTO standards are applied in the form of competence units, they:

> might offer an easy way to meet institutional monitoring and assessment requirements ... but fail to stimulate the development of imaginative and creative professionals who can be flexible and responsive in a rapidly changing environment.
> (Bathmaker, 2000, p.19)

Resolving the Tension?

It has been argued in this chapter that the change in curricular focus to competence-based qualifications for both FE students and staff, and a growing managerialism throughout the sector have served to privilege institutional needs over those of individual members of staff. Various suggestions have also been made as to why these individual and institutional needs might differ, drawing on research which has contrasted a prevalent 'professional' culture amongst lectures with a 'managerialist' culture imposed as a result of incorporation. Much of the work in this area emphasises the negative consequences of such trends for the profession. However, it can also be argued that the prioritisation of individual over institutional needs can be equally problematic. There is evidence that, prior to incorporation, some staff development programmes were similarly failing to marry individual and institutional needs. For example, McAleer and McAleavy (1989) discuss a series of action research projects conducted by FE teachers studying for a BEd degree. As part of this programme, they were required to implement and evaluate changes designed to bring about an improvement in practice. Although the degree may have satisfied the intellectual needs of the individual participants, McAleer and McAleavy demonstrate that the action research projects had little effect on policy and practice due to the failure (of participants, teachers and, ultimately, the qualification itself) to recognise the specific characteristics of the institutions in which the participants worked. Similarly, there have been criticisms that secondments (for example, to relevant industrial employers) taken by FE staff have been poorly integrated into the life of some seconding institutions (Lewis, 1991). Lewis argues that while such development activities often succeeded in fulfilling individual needs, their potential contribution to the college as a whole was frequently not realised. Failure to match institutional and individual needs is not, therefore, unique to the FE sector of the 1990s and beyond.

It would thus seem unwise to view the period prior to incorporation as a 'golden age' for the FE sector, when individual and institutional needs were well aligned. Instead, it may be more fruitful to look forward and consider whether the well-documented tensions can be resolved. Avis (2000) points out the need to recognise that models of teaching and learning are never 'innocent', that 'they derive from particular socio-economic contexts and construct teachers and learners in particular ways' (p.54). It has also been asserted that the increasingly managerial focus of the education system implies consensus over both the end products and the means by which to reach them, ignoring the ideological nature of teaching and learning (e.g. Bartlett, 2000). These differences in approach suggest that greater clarity is needed within FE about the aims and objectives of both institutions and individuals, together with a more constructive dialogue about their respective development needs. Avis alludes to something similar in his discussion of 'an engaged and dialogic practice' (p.38). By this he means that FE staff need to work with a flexible understanding of learning outcomes, recognising both the open-ended nature of learning and the need for flexibility.

Furthermore, Gleeson and Shain's (1999) work indicates that it may be misleading to think of two diametrically opposed cultures and sets of development needs within FE as some have claimed. Instead of juxtaposing managerial and professional cultures, they argue that the values of professionalism can be reworked and are subject to social, political and cultural definition. Thus, a majority of the middle managers in their study:

> adopted an approach of strategic compliance in dealing with pressures from above and below while, at the same time, maintaining a commitment to educational and other professional values in support of student care and collegiality. (Gleeson and Shain, 1999, p.488)

This suggests that both managers and lecturers within the FE sector may be able to find ways to mediate between the two cultures, fusing individual and institutional development needs.

Indeed, other researchers have identified specific areas of staff development in which managerial initiatives can be harnessed to benefit the professional group as a whole. Robson (1998) points to a shared need for internal and external evaluation of practice, while Bostock (1997) argues that inspection, although an important driver of 'managerialist' change, can lead to positive change for FE professionals. She describes research in a further education college that sought to identify deficiencies in the training and development of part-time staff. This had been prompted by an FEFC inspection that had highlighted a lack of appropriate training and support for this group of staff. In this way individual needs became those of the wider institution. Similarly, Hankey (1999) maintains that a peer mentoring scheme, introduced as part of wider college initiatives to improve the quality of teaching and learning and to improve self-assessment, empowered teachers by offering them a more active part in the process of review, and encouraged them to become agents of change within the organisation. A number of case studies of secondments by FE staff have also sought to demonstrate how personal and institutional objectives can be fused together effectively. Although two of these describe activities pursued prior to incorporation (Lewis, 1991; Levene, 1992), there is also evidence that, in some colleges, such projects have continued under a more managerial culture. Robinson et al. (1996), for example, claim that management has played a central role in ensuring that secondments remain targeted and focused. They describe a scheme in which staff are released to conduct action research within the college and assert that, in addition to meeting individual development needs, an important component of each research project is:

> the need to generate credible findings, make recommendations which can feed into institutional decision-making structures and contribute to wider academic debate. (Robinson et al., 1996, p.25)

While such evidence suggests that congruence of goals and needs is possible and that a managerial culture can, in some cases, operate to further professional values, the research base on which these types of arguments are predicated is not strong. The majority of the studies reported above are case studies of individual institutions, often linked to specific action research projects. These are extremely useful in providing examples of 'what may be' (Schofield, 1993, p.213), and give some indication of the diversity of provision amongst FE colleges, but they rarely engage in discussions of their typicality across the sector as a whole. Theoretical discussions in this area are plentiful, and have generally emphasised growing tensions between the individual and the institution. To assess whether it is really possible to resolve this tension, more wide-ranging and larger scale empirical work is urgently needed.

References

Ashworth, P. (1992) Being competent and having 'competencies'. *Journal of Further and Higher Education* **16** (3), pp.30-38.

Avis, J. (1996) The Enemy Within: Quality and Managerialism in Education. In Avis, J., Bloomer, M., Esland, G., Gleeson, D. and Hodkinson, P. *Knowledge and Nationhood: Education, Politics and Work.* London: Cassell.

Avis, J. (2000) Policing the Subject: Learning Outcomes, Managerialism and Research in PCET. *British Journal of Educational Studies* **48** (1), pp.38-57.

Bartlett, S. (2000) The Development of Teacher Appraisal: a recent history. *British Journal of Educational Studies* **48** (1), pp.24-37.

Bathmaker, A. (2000) Standardising Teaching: the introduction of the National Standards for Teaching and Supporting Learning in Further Education in England and Wales. *Journal of In-Service Education* **26** (1), pp.9-23.

Bostock, A. (1997) The integration and support of part-time staff within a college of further education. *NASD Journal* **37**, pp.17-27.

Bryning, P. (1991) Part-time teachers' perceived training needs. *Journal of Further and Higher Education* **15** (1), pp.17-19.

Cantor, L. and Roberts, I. (1986) *Further Education Today: A Critical Review* (Third edition). London: Routledge and Kegan Paul.

Cantor, L., Roberts, I. and Pratley, B. (1995) *A Guide to Further Education in England and Wales*. London: Cassell.

Chown, A. (1996) Post-16 Teacher Education, National Standards and Staff Development Forum: time for openness and voice? *British Journal of In-Service Education* **22** (2), pp.133-50.

Ecclestone, K. (1993) Mastering the job? *Education* **182** (5), p.89.

Edwards, R. and Usher, R. (1994) Disciplining the Subject: the power of competence. *Studies in the Education of Adults* **26**, pp.1-14.

Elliot, G. (1996) The Assessment and Accreditation of Lectures in Post-Compulsory Education: a critique of the use of competence-based approaches. *British Journal of In-Service Education* **22** (1), pp.19-29.

Elliot, G. and Hall, V. (1994) FE Inc. - business orientation in further education and the introduction of human resource management. *School Organisation* **14** (1), pp.3-10.

Further Education Funding Council (2000) *Quality and Standards in Further Education in England 1999-2000. Chief Inspector's Annual Report*. FEFC.

Further Education National Training Organisation (1999) *Standards for Teaching and Supporting Learning in Further Education in England and Wales*. http://www.fento.org/staff_dev/teach_stan.html.

Further Education National Training Organisation (2000) *Skills Foresight for FE, Phase 1 Report*. http://www.fento.org/res_and_dev/reports/skills-foresight-fe-phase1/skills&quals.html.

Gleeson, D. and Shain, F. (1999) Managing ambiguity: between markets and managerialism - a case study of 'middle' managers in further education. *The Sociological Review* **47** (3), pp.461-490.

Great Britain, Parliament, House of Commons (1986) *Working Together - Education and Training* (Cmnd. 9823). London: HMSO.

Guile, D. and Lucas, N. (1996) Preparing for the Future: the training and professional development of staff in the FE sector. *Teacher Development* October, pp.47-54.

Hankey, J. (1999) A staff development project: peer monitoring, self-assessment and reflective practice. *NASD Journal* **40**, pp.35-40.

Hodkinson, P. (1995) Professionalism and competence. In Hodkinson, P. and Issit, M. (Eds.) *The Challenge of Competence: Professionalism through Vocational Education and Training*. London: Cassell.

Hopkins, B. (1989) The staff development needs of part-time lecturers in an FE college. *Journal of Further and Higher Education* **13** (1), pp.3-10.

International Centre for Research on Assessment (1995) *Access to Training and Development for FE Staff, Report to the Employment Department*. London: Institute of Education.

Jessup, G. (1991) *Outcomes: NVQs and the emerging model of education and training*. Lewes: Falmer Press.

Last, J. and Chown, A. (1996) Competence-based approaches and initial teacher training for FE. In Robson, J. (Ed.) *The Professional FE Teacher, Staff Development and Training in the Corporate College*. Aldershot: Avebury.

Levine, C. (1992) A Model Secondment. *NASD Journal* **27**.

Lewis, P. (1991) Sandwell College - a perspective on industrial secondments. *NASD Journal* **24**, pp.10-14.

Lucas, N. and Betts, D. (1996) The Incorporated College: human resource development and human resource management - contradictions and options. *Research in Post-Compulsory Education* **1** (3) pp.329-342.

Martinez, P. (1994) Staff development in the FE sector. *NASD Journal* **31**, pp.3-9.

McAleer, J. and McAleavy, G. (1989) Action Research Paradigm for Individual Development or Organisational Change in Further Education? *Educational Management and Administration* **17** (14), pp. 214-224.

Norris, N. (1991) The trouble with competence. *Cambridge Journal of Education* **21** (3), pp.331-341.

Randle, K. and Brady, N. (1997) Further Education and the New Managerialism. *Journal of Further and Higher Education* **21** (2), pp.229-239.

Robinson, F., Such, C., Walters, C., Muller, D. and Stott, D. (1996) Researching in Further Education: an illustrative study from Suffolk College. In Young, M., Unwin, L., Howard, U., Hodgson, A.,

Robinson, J., Such, C., Walters, C., Muller, D. and Spours, K. *Colleges as Learning Organisations: the Role of Research* (Unified 16+ Curriculum Series No.12). London: University of London, Institute of Education.

Robson, J. (1998) A profession in crisis: status, culture and identity in the further education college. *Journal of Vocational Education and Training* **50** (4), pp.585-607.

Scofield, J.W. (1993) Increasing the Generalizability of Qualitative Research. In Hammersley, M. (Ed.) *Social Research: Philosophy, Politics and Practice*. London: Open University Press/Sage Publications.

Shorter, P. (1994) Sixth-Form Colleges and Incorporation: some evidence from case studies in the north of England. *Oxford Review of Education* **20** (4), pp.461-473.

Spours, K. and Lucas, N. (1996) *The Formation of a National Sector of Incorporated Colleges: Beyond the FEFC Model* (Working Paper No.19). London: University of London, Institute of Education, Post-16 Education Centre.

Tuxworth, E. (1989) Competence based education and training: background and origins. In Burke, J. (Ed.) *Competency Based Education and Training*. London: Falmer Press.

Whitty, G. and Willmott, E. (1991) Competence-based teacher education: approaches and issues. *Cambridge Journal of Education* **21** (3), pp.309-318.

4 Revisiting the Purposes of Continuing Professional Development

CHRISTOPHER DAY

Introduction

> Few axioms are more fundamental than the one that acknowledges the link between what happens to teachers and what happens to students … the idea of making classrooms into learning communities for students will remain more rhetoric than real unless schools also become learning communities for teachers. (Sergiovanni, 1996, p.42)

This chapter focuses upon the important part played by Continuing Professional Development (CPD) in raising standards of teaching, learning and achievement. It suggests that CPD which aims to raise standards of teaching and learning must be informed by an understanding of the ways in which teachers learn best, the organisational cultures most conducive to learning, a recognition of current conditions of teachers' work and an understanding of the ways in which teachers' professional and personal lives relate. Consideration of these clearly indicates a need for teachers, over a career, to engage in a range of learning experiences which match sometimes with organisationally defined needs, sometimes with individually defined and negotiated needs and sometimes with both. At present, however, the professional learning 'diet' remains largely limited for most teachers. Most CPD does not appear to be based upon a recognition of the complexity of teaching, nor demonstrate a commitment to supporting teachers' 'moral' purposes (Sockett, 1993) as an essential part of their professionalism or recognize the 'emotional labour' (Hochschild, 1993) and emotional intelligence (Goleman, 1995) which are fundamental parts of the teaching process.

Instead, narrowly conceived 'training' models designed to ensure effective compliance with externally initiated curriculum, assessment and teaching models predominate, and in many schools, performance management, quality audit and recognition systems such as Investors in People, essentially serve organisational rather than individual needs. These models run the risk of the further alienation of teachers who are already overburdened with bureaucracy.

The Current State of CPD

> Good teaching is not just a matter of being efficient, developing competence, mastering technique, and possessing the right kind of knowledge. Good teaching also involves emotional work. It is infused with pleasure, passion, creativity, challenge and joy … it is a passionate vocation.
>
> (Hargreaves, 1997, p.12)

Reporting on the findings of a recent Leverhulme-funded study of teachers' perceptions of the provision of CPD, conducted in four Local Education Authorities (LEAs), McMahon (1999) found that tensions between the two overall purposes of CPD - to promote school improvement or individual teacher development - had not been resolved. The evidence was that:

> teachers are keen to improve their knowledge and skills, although at any one time their learning priorities might differ from those of the school or government. (McMahon, 1999, p.104)

The introduction of site-based school management through which, in theory, 'need' and 'relevance' might be more accurately identified, had not, the research revealed, proved to be a success. Because resources were more thinly and unevenly spread, choice of CPD mode had diminished. For example, staff in rural schools had less access to higher education, and school networking had largely ceased. There were also wide variations within schools. Few professional development co-ordinators were allocated time to do their job, and the commitment of headteachers to CPD varied greatly. It was found that the bulk of the CPD budget was used for responding to external demands for curriculum reform and renewal. This meant that:

> individual development needs were neglected unless they were in an area that was designated a school priority. (McMahon, 1999, p.106)

The five non-contact professional development days were often not well used, and the content and level were often judged to be inappropriate. Overall, the quality of training was poor and:

> little or no attempt was made in any of the case study schools to identify and take account of teachers' preferred learning styles. (ibid., p.107)

Finally, most teachers' experience of CPD was of short training courses which were relevant to the immediate needs of the classroom. McMahon concluded that:

> It does not appear that the notion of individual teacher entitlement to training and development is being given serious consideration at national level ... so most decisions about who gets access to training will continue to be made at school level and this will disadvantage a number of teachers. (ibid., p.111)

Since this study was carried out, a number of initiatives have been put into place nationally which are designed to enhance opportunities for CPD. For example, the Department for Education and Employment (now the Department for Education and Skills) has produced a policy designed to extend professional development opportunities, by making available a limited number of short term secondments, classroom focused action research grants and teacher fellowships; the General Teaching Council is committed to enhancing teacher development as is the National College for School Leadership. All these potentially represent an increased investment in the well being of the teaching force. They do not, however, solve the problems highlighted in the study reported here, or the tensions between individual and organisational development needs. Indeed, many opportunities benefit only those in senior management roles, the instrumental implementation of government identified priority areas, or represent a linear 'career' oriented rather than 'professional development' oriented concept of growth. Hence the emphasis upon national competence standards at teacher, subject leader, head of department, aspiring heads, new heads and experienced head level.

However well meaning, these initiatives must be placed in the context of the broader 'standards raising' agenda which brings with it new, more frequent managerially driven systems of performance management, more competitive, diverse, career ladders and increasingly complex classroom management issues caused by changes in society's expectations. Whilst it may be argued that they are in part a belated recognition that teacher morale needs raising (in response to problems of recruitment and retention) and that conditions of service, such as increased intensification and high stress levels, need amelioration, they do not appear to target either learning preferences, the learning and change needs of individual teachers, or school and departmental cultures.

Time to Learn, Time to Reflect

> It has taken time since the difficulties and pessimism of the 1970s and early 1980s for the perception to be widely shared that the success of educational reforms, no matter how well they are conceived in principle, will only be fortuitous if the teachers who are actually responsible are not made an explicit and pivotal plank in these reforms. An uncommitted and poorly motivated teaching body will have disastrous effects for even the best of intentions for change. (OECD, 1989)

Teachers' voices are an important and still under-represented part of the debate on the nature, form and content of CPD. Writing about systemic reform in the province of Ontario, Canada, Ardra Cole suggests that perhaps the most persistent and poignant instances of teacher helplessness are within the context of formalised professional development (Cole, 1997, p.16) in which initiatives are for the most part, conceptualised, designed and delivered for teachers, not by them. The current situation in England and Wales is not unlike this.

One of the key recommendations of an American study conducted in 1996 by the National Foundation for the Improvement of Education was that 'finding time to build professional development into the life of the school through flexible scheduling and extended blocks of time when students are on vacation' (Rényi, 1998, p.71) was the teachers' primary concern. When teachers in England were asked about their professional learning preferences, including INSET (Harland and Kinder, 1997) their responses, too, pointed towards the need:

- for time to meet with colleagues from their own and other schools to discuss current issues and concerns
- to engage in curriculum development workshops which embodied the 'practicality ethic' (Doyle and Ponder, 1977)
- to learn from outside speakers and 'provider led' higher education programmes.

By far the greatest influences on their professional development, however, were their own experiences, beliefs and convictions and those of their colleagues.

We know from research that teachers do not follow a smooth, uninterrupted development trajectory from, for example, novice through to expert (Benner, 1984). They do not always learn from experience and that experience itself can be limiting to development (Britzman, 1991). We know also that they are influenced by:

- prior beliefs and personal values
- professional experiences
- the school and classroom contexts in which they work
- their personal relationships in and out of school
- other life circumstances e.g. health, changing educational policy climates, conditions of service. (Levin, 2001, p.22)

Because of changes in society such as the increased use of information and communications technology, policy reform and changes in the family circumstances of students, teachers also need to be responsive to external circumstance. Yet we know also that in order to survive in classrooms, teachers develop routines (Clark and Yinger, 1977) and are not naturally systematically reflective about their work - partly because of its 'busyness' and partly because interrogation of practice and its contexts can be threatening to self esteem and current practices, especially when organisational cultures are not supportive. That is not to suggest that they do not engage in reflection, but that to engage in systematic reflection of the kinds suggested in Figure 4.1 below is not always possible.

There is still some truth in the experiences, in Australia, of Sachs and Logan (1990) that:

> Rather than developing reflective practitioners who are able to understand, challenge and transform their practice, in-service education in its current form encourages the development of teachers who see their world in terms of instrumental ends achievable through the recipes of 'tried and true' practices legitimated by unexamined experiences or uncritically accepted research findings. (Sachs and Logan, 1990, p.479)

Figure 4.1 Kinds of reflection

<table>
<tr><th>REFLECTION TYPE</th><th>NATURE OF REFLECTION</th><th>POSSIBLE CONTEXT</th><th>CORE COMPONENT OF ALL REFLECTION</th></tr>
<tr><td>Reflection about action</td><td>Critical (social reconstructionist), seeing as problematic, according to ethical criteria, the goals and practices of one's profession.</td><td>Thinking about the effects upon others of one's actions, taking account of social, political and/ or cultural forces.</td><td rowspan="2">Intrapersonal, recognizing the self as contributing to social action, examining one's own behaviour in the context of personal values and emotions.

Thinking about the effects of one's own biography and feelings upon the management of classroom relationships.</td></tr>
<tr><td>Reflection on action</td><td>Dialogic (deliberative, cognitive, narrative), weighing competing claims and viewpoints, and then exploring alternative solutions.

Descriptive (social efficiency, developmental, personalistic), seeking what is seen as 'best possible' practice.

Technical (decision-making about immediate behaviours or skills), drawn from a given research/theory base, but always interpreted in light of personal worries, previous experience and employer expectations.</td><td>Hearing one's own voice (alone or with another), exploring alternative ways to solve problems in the broader school context.
Analysing one's performance in the professional role (probably alone), exploring reasons for actions taken.

Examining one's use of essential teaching knowledge and pedagogical skills in the classroom in relation to results-driven demands.</td></tr>
<tr><td>Reflection in action</td><td>Reactive, drawing upon experience, implicit knowledge.</td><td>Dealing with on-the spot professional problems as they arise.</td><td></td></tr>
</table>

There are three reasons why reflective practice is increasingly being recognised as essential to good teaching and having 'a central role in the learning life' of the effective teacher (Day, 1993, p.83). The first concerns the nature of teaching. The assumption is that since teaching and learning are complex processes and since there is not necessarily one right approach (Loughran, 1996), deliberating among competing versions of good teaching and recasting past understandings and current practices (Grimmett et al., 1990) are likely to lead to improvement. Without a capacity to evaluate assumptions, teachers will be more inclined to remain 'prisoners of (their) programs' (Argyris and Schon, 1976, cited in Day, 1985, p.137) and, as a result, their professional effectiveness, in circumstances which inevitably change over time, will be decreased. The second is that engaging in reflective practice is a means of helping individuals towards greater self-knowledge and self-challenge – 'a useful way of achieving personal development' (Johnston and Badley, 1996, p.5) through, for example, an analysis of the personal values and theories that underlie teaching. Finally (and here the link with action research becomes sharper), reflective practice is considered to be central to the growth of teachers as inquirers, who engage in collaborative research with others from inside and outside the school, in generating knowledge of practice rather than finding themselves as objects whose role is to implement existing theory in practice (Peters, 1985). However, research continues to reveal that there is a continuum of reflective practice that exists within the profession (Ebbutt, 1985; Day, 1999). Teachers may reflect in differing ways at different times. It is important, therefore, to recognise the impact of teachers' positions in their career and life cycle, and the effects of the organisational and cultural contexts in which they work, if opportunities for their professional growth are to be maximised (Day, 1993).

Essentially, reflection involves the participant in a *critique* of practice, the values which are implicit in that practice, the personal, social institutional and broad policy contexts in which practice takes place, and the implications of these for improvement of that practice. It is, then, about the past, the present and the future; it is about 'problem posing' as well as 'problem solving' (Mezirow, 1991, p.105), and it is essential for building and maintaining the capacity of all professionals whose work focuses upon the care and development of children, young people and adults – whether advantaged or disadvantaged – to maintain their effectiveness in changing circumstances. Because the reflective process is a dialectic between thought and action, theory and practice (Pedretti, 1990, p.325) it has been conceived as *praxis* through which change occurs:

> In praxis, the ideas that guide action are just as subject to change as the action itself. Therefore, only through a fundamental shift in our beliefs, values and feelings about teaching and learning, will we be effective in bringing about significant change in our practice. Creating a culture of critical reflection enhances our educative potential, and provides practitioners with opportunities to deconstruct conventional ... practices. (Carr and Kemmis, 1986, p.33)

What is particularly interesting in this perspective is that these authors introduce the notions of: i) a link between reflective practice and 'emancipation' from the limitations of 'conventional' practices, which implies the ability to exercise autonomy in developing a repertoire of practice; and ii) the necessity for 'fundamental shifts in beliefs, values and feelings' if change is to occur. Whilst this focus is an essential part of reflective practice, it does not recognise that change itself may be evolutionary or additive rather than radical or transformational, depending upon circumstance and disposition. Like other writers on reflection (e.g. Schoen, 1983), Carr and Kemmis do not pay enough attention to the importance of the emotional self (Goleman, 1995), preferring instead the high ground of rationality and cognition. So to engage in reflection creates opportunities for choices which relate to values as well as purposes, contexts and change. Whatever the orientation, however, its use presents possibilities for self-evaluation. It is:

> a model of a teacher who, given particular circumstances, is able to distance himself from the world in which he is an everyday participant and open himself to influence by others. (Day, 1991, p.49)

This model of the teacher as systematic inquirer is essential to the concept of 'reflective practitioner' and affects the nature of the research relationships between school teachers, university academics and those who shape policy.

Not all teachers are at a stage of readiness to engage in all of these reflective orientations. Indeed, the culture of the school in which they work may discourage them from doing so. However it is important that teachers engage in each of these forms of reflection during their career lives at times which are appropriate to the maintenance and development of commitment, knowledge, expertise and personal and professional health. This suggests a continuum rather than a hierarchy of reflective practice. The dilemma is which to choose and when. Reflecting about the action is a form of reflection which demands particular attention in current national contexts since it focuses upon tensions between policy and practice and the struggle for supremacy between different interest groups' definitions of 'professionalism' (see Hargreaves and Goodson, 1996 for a valuable discussion of different forms of professionalism). Behaving as professionals clearly involves reflection not only in and on, but also about the action – it involves critical inquiry into the moral, ethical, political and instrumental issues embedded in teachers' everyday thinking and practice. Reflection of this kind is a means for professionals both to exercise responsibility and accountability for the decisions that they make in their teaching and to maintain the broader perspectives of the inter-relationships between contexts, purposes, practices and outcomes which inform their views of what it means to be and grow as a professional.

My view is that no single form of reflection is necessarily 'better' than another, but that teachers must be involved in all during the course of a career. The different kinds of reflection may, therefore, be conceived as being parts of a *continuum of reflective practice,* rather than different levels in a hierarchy. However, if teachers want to avoid bureaucratic and technical conceptions of their role that have historically been given to them, and if they are going to become technically competent and reflective, then it is reasonable to suggest that they must seek to maintain a broad vision about their work and not just look inwardly at the efficiency of their own practices within externally imposed agendas, however well-intentioned they may be, if they are to maintain and build their effectiveness throughout their careers and maintain their vision of excellence in teaching in the face of multifarious challenge:

> Teachers cannot restrict their attention to the classroom alone, leaving the larger setting and purposes of schooling to be determined by others. They must take active responsibility for the goals to which they are committed, and for the social setting in which these goals may prosper. If they are not to be mere agents of others, of the state, of the military, of the media, of the experts and bureaucrats, they need to determine their own agency through a critical and continual evaluation of the purposes, the consequences, and the social context of their calling.
>
> (Zeichner and Liston, 1996, p.11)

Sustaining their 'moral purposes' (to make a positive difference in the lives of students) requires that teachers maintain, and are supported in maintaining, their psychological, personal, social and intellectual health. Much of the current CPD diet fails to focus on these as priorities, opting instead to assume that they are unproblematic, and that it is knowledge and pedagogy which require most attention.

The Complexity of Teacher Development over Time

Research shows that teachers' lives themselves may be subject to different phases of development:

Figure 4.2 Interrelated dimensions of teacher development

	6 participating in broad range of educational decisions at all levels	
→	5 contributing to the growth of colleagues' instructional expertise	← 5 preparing for retirement: focusing
4 autonomous/interdependent, principled, integrated	4 acquiring instructional expertise	4 reaching a professional plateau
3 conscientious, moral conditional dependence →	3 expanding one's instructional flexibility	← 3 new challenges and concerns
2 conformist/moral, negative, independence	2 becoming competent in the basic skills of instruction	2 stabilizing: developing mature commitment
1 self-protective, pre-moral, unilateral dependence	1 developing survival skills	1 launching the career
PSYCHOLOGICAL DEVELOPMENT (EGO, MORAL, CONCEPTUAL)	DEVELOPMENT OF PROFESSIONAL EXPERTISE	CAREER CYCLE DEVELOPMENT

(From Leithwood, 1990)

In the light of this, it is strange that governments opt to form frameworks for professional development which recognize only teachers' career development phases. Important though this managerialist perspective is, the reality is that within many 'career development' stages, for example as newly qualified teacher, subject leader, head of department, teachers will be at different phases of development with different levels of expertise, efficacy and commitment. All are likely at some point to experience 'stability', 'plateauing' and 'serenity or disenchantment'. Perhaps the most comprehensive, if complicated 'map' of factors which affect teacher development is that produced by Fessler and Christensen (1992) (see Figure 4.3).

In terms of CPD, then, teachers cannot be treated as a homogeneous group. Rather, each has competencies, professional attributes and personal qualities which will vary within and between the different phases and circumstances of their professional lives. The nature of good teaching, also, is that it is an emancipating rather than a controlling process. Development opportunities then, must be differentiated both in terms of content and process. One example of how this might be achieved (assuming supportive leadership and the aspiration of the organisation to be and remain a learning community) is through performance management systems which are part of an overarching system of staff (not school) development. This system must recognise the importance of attending differentially to the different components that make up the purposes, roles and responsibilities of the 'post-modern' professional of the twenty-first century, and enable individual teachers, in dialogue with colleagues and others, to enjoy a 'balanced' curriculum of continuing professional development which both challenges and supports. Such a system would not:

> be confined to matters of technical competence and personal, practical reflection about how best to deliver the means of an education that others have defined, but would be guided by moral and socio-political visions of the purposes which teacher professionalism should serve within actively caring communities and vigorous social democracies.
>
> (Hargreaves and Goodson, 1996, p.20)

Figure 4.3 Dynamics of the teacher career cycle

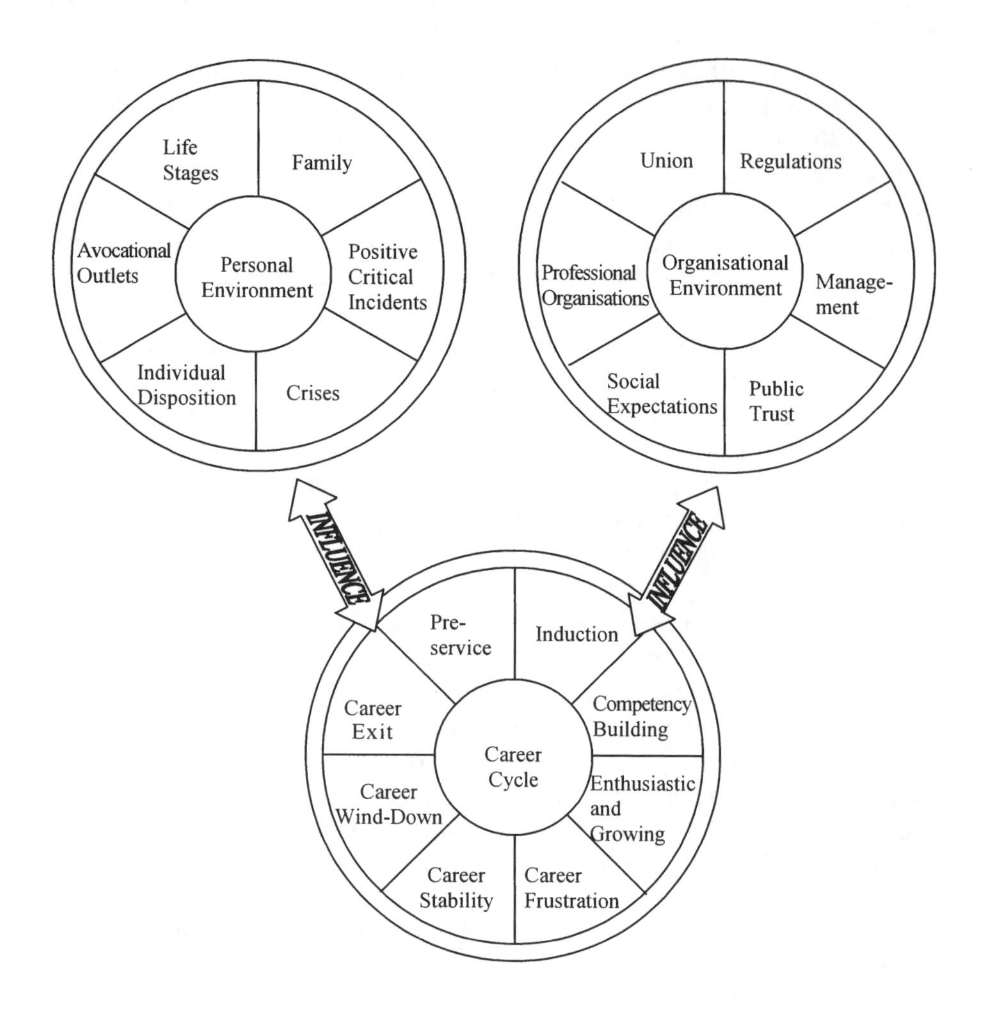

(From Fessler and Christensen, 1992)

The Conditions for Development: Range and Balance

There are valuable lessons here for those whose responsibility it is to promote teacher development:

- any comprehensive programme must attend to the classroom application of understanding, knowledge and skills – a simplistic 'learn-apply' model does not work
- feedback and ongoing coaching are essential components in the process of transfer
- the disposition towards and commitment to learning must be present in the teacher as lifelong learner
- the organisational culture must be supportive of collegial relationships - opportunities to learn through peer coaching and feedback require a school culture which facilitates ongoing collegial relationships and strong leadership, 'manifested in priority setting, resource allocation, and the logistics of scheduling on the one hand and substantive and social leadership on the other' (Joyce and Showers, 1988, p.91)
- resources must be targeted at long-term development, taking into account a balanced portfolio of learning needs (see Figure 4.4).

The problem is that over the last two decades in particular, in many schools the opportunities for a *balance* as well as range of CPD opportunities have reduced rather than increased. As budgets have become more limited and energy levels depleted, external pressures have ensured that, for all but the brave, resources are targeted at short term needs. Many teachers whose only experience is of learning how to deliver the National Curriculum (the post-1988 generation) might be surprised at the comments of more experienced teachers on the more complex needs which short term CPD cannot meet. They spoke through their learning biographies and interviews of the planned learning experiences which had been most significant for their development. One teacher wrote of the learning which resulted from attendance at a two-year part-time university postgraduate course:

> It challenged my attitudes and ideas subtly over two years ... my practice used to be very product based ... but now I can understand the child's work more and value it for what it is ... you get to a stage when you need to have your attitudes educated ... have opportunities to clarify your thinking ... not carry on doing the same old thing every day.

Figure 4.4 Orientations and benefits of career-long professional development planning

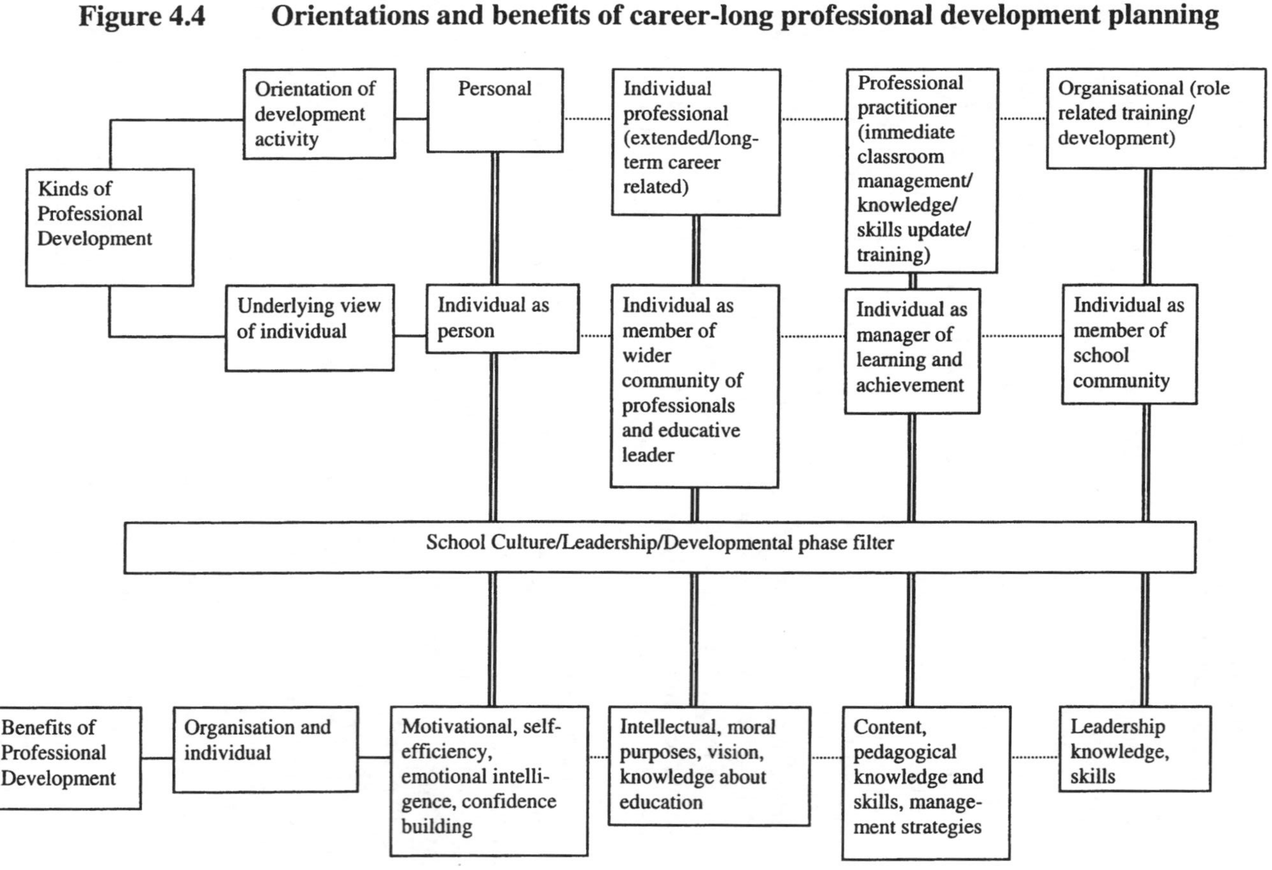

A second teacher attending a part-time university course had been 'transformed as a teacher', and was 'more able to support the needs of the children'. Another spoke of a part-time non-accredited extended course which had been:

> ... the start of my professional development ... that opened my eyes. I learned to look outside the classroom, how things were affecting the work inside the classroom ... management ... how schools are run ... and how the staff develop as a staff ... timing was quite critical.

Yet another had found that attendance at an intensive three-day residential course had 'transformed me as a teacher, opened up new ideas, ways forward, working with staff'. In addition to the needs met by short burst activities, these longer, more reflective and analytical in-depth learning opportunities had provided:

- Critical friendship - in-depth opportunities for sharing and building knowledge and skills over time in a supportive but challenging environment.
- 'Vision' needs - participants had been enabled to relate their experience of practice to theory, to reconsider critically their assumptions, predispositions and values (the 'why' as well as the 'how' and 'what' of teaching) and the contexts in which they taught.
- Skill development needs - they were able to develop new skills over time.
- Intellectual needs – they were able to engage in systematic reading which, 'otherwise I wouldn't do'.
- Personal needs - to build self-esteem, 'so important in these days when we're continuously being battered from all sides as regards our skills as professionals'.

Concentration of finance and effort on short professional learning opportunities which predominantly focus upon institutionally defined needs may well, in the long term, result in cultural *isolation* and *parochialism.*

Personal Change, the Learning Community and Leadership

In a report on a two year research and development 'Improving Schools Project', involving thirty two schools, Connolly and James (1998) drew attention to the problematic nature of the change journey. They identified three broad phases of change: pre-acceleration (related to existing conditions), acceleration (characterized by rapid change) and post acceleration (when the school either returns to a 'non-acceleration' phase in which staff consolidate gains, continue to steadily improve, or 'decelerate', possibly losing previous gains). They drew attention particularly to the important part played by continuing professional development both within and between each phase, and found a relationship between successful CPD of different kinds, the quality of leadership and the prevailing learning culture of the school, underpinned by 'ownership' and 'motivation'. This created and sustained cultures which sought to involve staff through 'unlocking their potential' rather than 'bringing them up to standard' (p.278).

Models of change and cause and effect relationships which result from external intervention (CPD) into the learning lives of teachers are, then, problematic, partly because of unpredictable motivations and responses which will be affected by the individual learning histories of teachers and also, partly by the social dynamic (culture) in school:

> The school workplace is a physical setting, a formal organisation, an employer. It is also a social and psychological setting in which teachers construct a sense of practice, of professional efficacy, and of professional community. This aspect of the workplace – the nature of the professional community that exists there – appears more critical than any other factor to the character of teaching and learning for teachers and their students. (McLaughlin, 1993, p.99)

A school's culture is 'moulded by the unique and shared experiences of participants, which are influenced by their class, race and neighbourhood as well as their school's history and its leadership ...' (Finnan and Levin, 2000, p.89-90). Although various researchers have attempted to provide classifications or 'ideal types' (Nias et al., 1989; Rosenholtz, 1989; Hargreaves, A., 1994; Stoll and Fink, 1996; Hargreaves, D., 1995), each school's culture is unique and never static – hence Schein's (1985) dictum that the creation and management of cultures is possibly the only thing of real importance that leaders do. It is, therefore, useful to remember that dialogue needs to be continuous – a part of informal and formal cultures of CPD and it:

> should be understood as the capability to create active trust through an appreciation of the integrity of the other. Trust is a means of ordering social relations across time and space. It sustains that 'necessary silence' which allows individuals or groups to get on with their lives while still existing in a social relation with another or others. (Giddens, 1994, pp.115-116)

Learning communities with a commitment to improvement require ongoing individual as well as collective self examination through reflection on action, its context, and the values which inform. There will, at times, therefore, be a 'felt' tension between the purposes of development for individuals and organisations. Indeed, the challenge of true collegiality, a hallmark of learning communities, is:

> to foster a cohesive set of beliefs and interests while recognizing and growing from a plurality of ideas and perspectives. (Westheimer, 1998, pp.14-15)

It might be argued, then, that a school which does not support principles and practices of differentiation for teacher learning as well as for student learning is not a learning community for all. As de Lima suggests in his perceptive analysis of teacher collegiality as a lever for school change, 'conflict is not necessarily the enemy of effective and innovative group and organisational functioning in teaching: it can be its most valuable ally' (de Lima, 1999, p.25). In the past, individual and organisational need have been presented, unhelpfully, in an oppositional way. This is not surprising, given the widespread downturn in morale among teachers in England over the last two decades as worktime and workload have increased, and demands for systemic improvement in the name of raising standards of teaching and student achievement have been accompanied by short term instrumentalism in the provision of in-service training opportunities. Managerial cultures have focused upon measuring the results of teaching and identifying key characteristics of 'good' teachers so that teachers have either left the profession or remained with energy levels depleted as a result.

It is through a commitment to teacher growth through the design, development and application of models such as those cited that headteachers in schools may enhance both individual and organisational growth, encourage individual professional development planning and promote autonomy within cultures of interdependency and accountability.

Yet headteachers, like teachers and students and the learning communities of which they are a part, will be at different levels of maturity. In the current system of devolved management, the headteacher is crucial in setting the vision for a broad and balanced understanding of and approach to CPD, for:

> Managers know that people make the critical difference between success and failure. The effectiveness with which organisations manage, develop, motivate, involve and engage the willing contribution of the people who work in them is a key determinant of how well those organisations perform ... employee commitment and positive, 'psychological contact' between employer and employee are fundamental to improving performance.
>
> (Patterson et al., 1997, p.vii-viii)

A recent multiperspective empirical study of successful headteachers revealed that they placed a high priority on learning opportunities for staff as well as students (Day et al., 2000), and research from Australia provides additional evidence of the importance of the head's role in establishing positive learning conditions for teachers:

> To the extent that principals insist that professional growth be viewed as an ongoing, long-term process, teachers will feel a sense of security and personal identity that will contribute to their sense of professional worth. On the other hand, where principals fail to demonstrate leadership in these areas, the perceptions of teachers regarding professional development tend to be marked by a degree of futility and cynicism. (Crowther and Postle, 1991, p.96)

At the end of the day, however, it is individual teachers working within a culture which supports diversity within a broadly agreed values framework who will affect students' attitudes to learning, their motivation, self efficacy and, through these, their potential to achieve to the best of their ability. It would be foolish to disregard external influences and to over claim the 'value added' factor that schools can provide through particular models of culture which appear to indicate total consensus of values and practice. Nevertheless, unless teachers themselves are healthy, unless they are motivated, energetic, enthusiastic, have a sense of personal efficacy and are committed to care as well as achievement, it is unlikely that even those with the highest levels of subject and pedagogical knowledge will succeed. This is the flaw in the logic of David Hargreaves' proposition that 'to improve teachers, their professional development must be set within the context of institutional development' (Hargreaves, 1994, p.436). It oversimplifies the importance to teaching of teachers who are active agents within their own worlds, whose opportunities for success depend upon maintaining their agency as initiators of change and not merely 'sub-contractors' for others' change ideas.

Good Teaching, Rationality and Democracy

Good teaching has never been an entirely rational process, though it is only recently that the importance of emotions and emotional intelligence (Goleman, 1995) have been acknowledged in the management of teaching and learning. Emotional intelligence has been defined as:

- **Knowing one's emotions:** Self awareness is the keystone of emotional intelligence
- **Managing emotions:** Handling feelings so they are appropriate is an ability that builds on self-awareness
- **Recognizing emotions in others:** Empathy… is the fundamental 'people skill'
- **Handling relationships …** skill in managing emotions in others… social competence. These abilities underpin popularity, leadership and interpersonal effectiveness. (Goleman, 1995, pp.43-44)

Given that emotions are at the heart of the teacher learner interaction, and that teaching is essentially an interpersonal activity which relies as much on self knowledge as that of others, it is, perhaps, surprising that there has been so little emphasis placed upon the professional development of the teacher as person within the professional, despite overwhelming evidence that teachers must, as part of being competent technically be:

- knowledgeable, yet respectful of those who are ignorant
- kind and considerate, yet demanding and stern as the situation requires
- entirely free of prejudice and absolutely fair in their dealings with others
- responsive to individual students' needs, without neglecting the class as a whole
- able to maintain discipline and order, whilst allowing for spontaneity and caprice …
- optimistic and enthusiastic, even when harbouring private doubts and misgivings

- able to deal with the unexpected and sometimes even with the surly and abusive students without losing their composure and control
- able to smile and appear cheerful on days when they are not quite up to par and would rather be somewhere else.

(Jackson et al., 1993, p.233)

It is, then, a growing knowledge of self and the ability to manage the kinds of ambiguities listed above that provide the key to personal and professional growth and, thus, ultimately, to school improvement; though, even this is not without its complications in the shape of school leadership, culture (including student culture) and teachers' own life histories.

It should not be forgotten (as many of the systematically driven 'school improvement' programmes seem to have done) that 'the statistical evidence is that the best predictor of the performance of a community's schools, the best predictor of math scores and science scores, for example, is the social capital in that community, even better than class size' (Putnam, 2000).

The Role of the School

> … as other adults in children's lives have less time to spend with them and as neighbourhoods operate less as communities where people know and help one another, we as teachers have begun to more deliberately provide children with the experience of membership in a community – their school and classroom community – and more focused in helping them acquire the skills for maintaining community. (Dalton and Watson, 1997, p.5)

Various writers over the years have drawn attention to the role of the school in promoting the values of society. It is interesting that the elements identified in school improvement and effectiveness studies as being critical to successful school community are close to those espoused for participative democracies. For example, elements of a culture of inquiry have been identified by Lieberman and Grolnick (1997) as:

- norms of colleagueship, openness and trust (shared views and values)
- opportunities for time and disciplined inquiry (reflective dialogue)
- teacher learning of content in context (focus on student learning)
- reconstruction of leadership roles (distributed leadership)
- networks, collaborations and coalitions (deprivatisation of practice).

Essentially these authors are describing schools in which teachers are reflective and in which students 'learn to think for themselves and [are given] confidence to believe that they matter and that what they know and what they think matters' (Rudduck, 1999, p.11). In short, these cultures of inquiry promote what Lawrence Stenhouse termed 'emancipation':

> The essence of emancipation, as I conceive it, is the intellectual, moral and spiritual autonomy which we recognize when we eschew paternalism and the rule of authority and hold ourselves obliged to appeal to judgement. Emancipation rests not merely on the assertion of a right of the person to exercise intellectual, moral and spiritual judgement, but upon the passionate belief that the virtue of humanity is diminished in man when judgement is overruled by authority. (Stenhouse, 1979, p.163)

I am making here a link between what research tells us about effective schools which achieve the primary ingredients of a democracy which is working well ie. social trust, norms of reciprocity and networks of civic engagement (Putnam, 1993, p.180, cited in Osguthorpe, 1999) and the professional development of teachers. Arguably, teachers in this country are charged not only with delivering more economical, efficient and effective results, but must resist becoming only vehicles for the implementation of government policy (Popkewitz, 1996) and also prepare their students to take civic social responsibility. Judyth Sachs has written convincingly in the context of Australian school reform on the need for teachers to move to a new form of 'active' professionalism. Fundamental to this are five core values:

> **Learning:** as an individual and collective goal teachers should be seen to practise the value of learning, both with their colleagues and their students.
> **Participation:** in which teachers are supported in being active agents in their own professional worlds.
> **Collaboration:** an internal dialogic process through which people as individuals and groups change what it is they think and feel about something or someone; and external, through partnerships with key stakeholders and other interested groups.
> **Co-operation:** through professional dialogue by which teachers develop collective expertise and a common language for documenting and discussing practice and its outcomes.
> **Activism:** by standing up for the 'moral' purpose of teaching through, for example, engaging publicly with issues that relate directly or indirectly to education and schooling. It requires risk taking and fighting for ideals that

> enhance education. It requires also passion, determination and energy.
> (Sachs, 2000, pp.84-85)

Schools and classrooms are political places. They are part of rather than apart from society (Drucker, 1994). Engaging in 'active' professionalism enables teachers to exercise the ideal of a commitment to public service and altruism which matches the rhetoric of external policy directives whilst resisting its often 'coercive undertones' which seem to 'proscribe any variation from the one approved model' (Coombe, 1999, p.89). It reasserts the ethical responsibilities of teachers to their students and society at large:

> Ethics deals with what acts are morally right or wrong, what our obligations are, what the conditions are under which we are morally responsible for our acts, what moral rules or principles are justified, what traits or dispositions are morally good or bad, that is, virtues or vices, what things are desirable from a moral point of view. (Nias, 1989, p.3)

> Professional ethics are objectively regulated by system rules such as laws, formal guidelines and societal norms, and are subjectively bounded by personal values, beliefs and cultural background. (Liang et al., 1996, p.434)

It is the responsibility of those who initiate and implement policy to ensure that CPD is designed so that teachers' thinking and emotional well being as well as their practices are regularly revisited. Being active in their own development, which is about their intellectual health and their moral responsibilities and their broader roles as professionals in the classroom, school and community is the key to sustaining commitment and raising standards.

References

Argyris, C. and Schoen, D.A. (1976) *Theory in Practice: increasing professional effectiveness*. New York: Jossey-Bass.

Benner, P. (1984) *From Novice to Expert: Excellence and Power in Clinical Nursing Practice*. California: Addison Wesley Publishing Co.

Britzman, D.P. (1991) *Practice Makes Practice: A Critical Study of Learning to Teach*. Albany: State University Press.

Carr, W. and Kemmis, S. (1986) *Becoming Critical: education, knowledge and action research*. London: Falmer Press.

Clark, C.M. and Yinger, R.J. (1977) Research on teacher thinking. *Curriculum Inquiry* **7** (4), pp.279-305.

Cole, A.L. (1997) Impediments to reflective practice. *Teachers and Teaching: Theory and Practice* **3** (1), pp.7-27.

Connolly, U. and James, C. (1998) Managing the School Improvement Journey: the role of continuing professional development. *Journal of In-service Education* **24** (2), pp.271-282.

Coombe, K. (1999) Ethics and the Learning Community. In Retallick, J., Cocklin, B. and Coombe, K. (Eds.) *Learning Communities in Education*. London: Routledge.

Crowther, F. and Postle, G. (1991) *The Praxis of Professional Development: Setting Directions for Brisbane Catholic Education.* Brisbane: Brisbane Catholic Education Centre.

Dalton, J. and Watson, M. (1997) *Among Friends: Classrooms Where Caring and Learning Prevail.* Armadle, Australia: Eleanor Curtain Publishing.

Day, C. (1985) Professional Learning and Researcher Intervention: an action research perspective. *British Educational Research Journal* **11**, pp.133-151.

Day, C. (1991) Roles and Relationships in Qualitative Research. *Teaching and Teacher Education* **7**, pp.547-547.

Day, C. (1993) Reflection: a necessary but not sufficient condition for professional development. *British Educational Research Journal* **19**, pp.83-93.

Day, C. (1999) *Developing Teachers: the challenges of lifelong learning.* London: Falmer Press.

Day, C., Harris, A., Hadfield, M., Tolley, H., and Beresford, J. (2000) *Leading Schools in Times of Change*. Buckingham: Open University Press.

de Lima, J.A. (1999) *Teacher Collegiality as a Lever for School Change.* Paper presented to the 9th Biennial Conference of the International Study Association on Teachers and Teaching, Dublin, July 27-31.

Doyle, W. and Ponder, G. (1977) The practicality ethic and teacher decision Making. *Interchange* **8**, pp.1-12.

Drucker, P.F. (1994) *Post Capitalist Society.* Oxford: Butterworth-Heinemann.

Ebbutt, D. (1985) Educational Action Research: some general concerns and specific quibbles. In Burgess, R. (Ed.) *Issues in Educational Research.* Lewes: Falmer Press.

Fessler, R. and Christensen, J. (1992) *The Teacher Career Cycle: Understanding and Guiding the Professional Development of Teachers*. Boston: Allyn and Bacon.

Finnan, C. and Levin, H.M. (2000) Changing School Cultures. In Altrichter, H. and Elliott, J. (Eds.) *Images of Educational Change*. Buckingham: Open University Press.

Giddens, A. (1994) *Beyond Left and Right*. Cambridge: Polity Press.

Goleman, D. (1995) *Emotional Intelligence*. New York: Bantam Books.

Grimmett, P.P., MacKinnon, A.M., Erickson, G.L. and Riecken, T.J. (1990) Reflective Practice in Teacher Education. In Clift, R.T., Houston, R.W. and Pugach, M.C. (Eds.) *Encouraging Reflective Practice in Education: an analysis of issues and programs*. New York: Teachers College Press.

Hargreaves, A. (1994) *Changing Teachers, Changing Times: Teachers' Work and Culture in the Post Modern Age*. New York: Teachers College Press.

Hargreaves, A. (1997) Rethinking Educational Change: Going Deeper and Wider in the Quest for Success. In Hargreaves, A. (Ed.) *Rethinking Educational Change with Heart and Mind*, pp.1-26. Alexandra, Virginia: Association for Supervision and Curriculum Development.

Hargreaves, A. and Goodson, I. (1996) Teachers' Professional Lives: Aspirations and Actualities. In Goodson, I.F. and Hargreaves, A. (Eds.) *Teachers' Professional Lives*. London: Falmer Press.

Hargreaves, D. (1994) The New Professionalism: The synthesis of professional and institutional development. *Teaching and Teacher Education* **10** (4), pp.423-438.

Hargreaves, D.H. (1995) School culture, school effectiveness and school Improvement. *School Effectiveness and School Improvement* **6** (1), pp.23-46.

Harland, J. and Kinder, K. (1997) Teachers' continuing professional development: Framing a model of outcomes. *Journal of In-service Education* **23** (1), pp.71-84.

Hochschild, A.R. (1993) *The Managed Heart: Commercialization of Human Feeling*. Berkeley: University of California Press.

Jackson, P.W., Boostrom, R.E. and Hansen, D.T. (1993) *The Moral Life of Schools*. San Francisco: Jossey-Bass.

Johnston, R. and Badley, G. (1996) The Competent Reflective Practitioner. *Innovation and Learning in Education* **2**, pp.4-10.

Joyce, B. and Showers, B. (1988) *Student Achievement through Staff Development*. New York: Longman.

Leithwood, K. (1990) The principal's role in teacher development. In Joyce, B. (ed.) *Changing School through Staff Development*. Alexandria, Virginia: Association for Supervision and Curriculum Development.

Levin, B.B. (2001) *Reflections on Factors that Influence the Personal and Professional Lives of Teachers*. Paper presented to the American Educational Research Association, Seattle, April 10-14.

Liang, C., Schuen, T. and Neher, I. (1996) *The reality of corporate education: Proceedings of selected research and development presentations.* Presented at the 18th Convention for the Association for Educational Communication and Technology, Indianapolis.

Lieberman, A. and Grolnick, M. (1997) Networks, Reform and the Professional Development of Teachers. In Hargreaves, A. (Ed.) *Rethinking Educational Change with Heart and Mind.* Alexandra, Virginnia: ASCD.

Loughran, J.J. (1996) *Developing Reflective Practice: learning about teaching and learning through modelling*. London: Falmer Press.

McLaughlin, M.W. (1993) What matters most in teachers' workplace context? In Little, J.W. and McLaughlin, M.W. (Eds.) *Teachers' Work: Individuals, Colleagues and Contexts*. New York: Teachers College Press.

McMahon, A. (1999) Promoting Continual Professional Development for Teachers: An Achievable Target for School Leaders? In Bush,T., Bell, L., Bolam, R., Glatter, R. and Ribbens, P. (Eds.) *Educational Management: Redefining Theory, Policy and Practice*. London: Paul Chapman Ltd.

Mezirow, J. (1991) *Transformative Dimensions of Adult Learning*. San Francisco: Jossey Bass.

Nias, J., Southworth, G.W. and Yeomans, R. (1989) *Staff Relationships in the Primary School: A study of school culture*. London: Cassell.

OECD (1989) The condition of teaching: General report, Restricted Draft, Paris. Quoted in Sikes, P.J. (1992) Imposed change and the experienced teacher. In Fullan, M. and Hargreaves, A. (Eds.) *Teacher Development and Educational Change*. London: Falmer Press.

Osguthorpe, R.J. (1999) *The Role of Collaborative Reflection in Developing a Culture of Inquiry in a School-University Partnership: A U.S. Perspective.* Paper presented to the Annual Meeting of the American Educational Research Association, Montreal, April.

Patterson, M.G., West, M.A., Lawthom, R. and Nickell, S. (1997) *Impact of People Management Practices on Business Performance.* London: Institute of Personnel and Development.

Pedretti, E. (1990) Facilitating Action Research in Science, Technology and Society (STS) Education: an experience in reflective practice. *Educational Action Research* **4**, pp.307-327.

Peters, J.L. (1985) Research in Reflective Teaching: a form of laboratory teaching experience. *Journal of Research and Development in Education* **18** (3), pp.55-62.

Popkewitz, T. (1996) Rethinking Decentralization and State/Civil Society Distinctions: The State as a Problematic for Governing. *Journal of Educational Policy* **11** (1), pp.27-51.

Putnam, R. (2000) cited in Abbot, J. (2001) An Update on the Activities of the 21st Century Learning Initiative. *The Journal* May 2001. Stafford, UK: Network Educational Press Ltd.

Putnam, R.D. (1993) *Making Democracy Work: Civic traditions in modern Italy*. Princeton, New Jersey: Princeton University Press.

Rényi, J. (1998) Building learning into the teaching job. *Educational Leadership* **55** (5), pp.70-74.

Rosenholtz, S. (1989) *Teachers' Workplace: The Social Organisation of Schools*. New York: Longman.

Rudduck, J. (1999) Teacher Practice and the Student Voice. In Lang, M., Olson, J., Hanson, H. and Bunder, W. (Eds.) *Changing Schools, Changing Practices: Perspectives on Educational Reform and Teacher Professionalism*. Garant: Leuven/Apeldoorn.

Sachs, J. (2000) Rethinking Teacher Professionalism. In Day, C., Fernandez, A., Hauge, T.E, and Møller, J. (Eds.) *The Life and Work of Teachers: International Perspectives in Changing Times*. London: Falmer Press.

Sachs, J. and Logan, L. (1990) 'Control or development?' A Study of inservice education. *Journal of Curriculum Studies* **22** (5), pp.473-481.

Schein, E.H. (1985) *Organisational Culture and Leadership: A Dynamic View*. New York: Jossey-Bass.

Schoen, D.A. (1983) *The Reflective Practitioner*. New York: Basic Books.

Sergiovanni, T.J. (1996) Learning Community, Professional Community and the School as Centre of Inquiry. *Principal Matters*, April.

Sockett, H. (1993) *The Moral Base for Teacher Professionalism.* New York: Teachers College Press.

Stenhouse, L.A. (1979) Research as a basis for teaching. In Stenhouse, L.A. (1983) *Authority, Education and Emancipation*. London: Heinemann Books.

Stoll, L. and Fink, D. (1996) *Changing Our Schools: Linking School Effectiveness and School Improvement*. Buckingham: Open University Press.

Westheimer, J. (1998) *Among Schoolteachers: Community, Autonomy and Ideology in Teachers' Work*. New York: Teachers College Press.

Zeichner, K.M. and Liston, D.P. (1996) *Reflective Teaching: an introduction*. New Jersey: Lawrence Erlbaum Associates.

5 Career Dynamics in Further and Higher Education

JULIA CORKINDALE AND GILLIAN TROREY

Introduction

Further and Higher Education (FHE) institutions, like other organisations, each have a unique identity which is far more than the sum of their parts. Organisations are also made up of individuals, each with his or her own interests, values, attitudes and beliefs. Each has their own expectations and plans for their working and home lives. How far are FHE institutions aware of their staff's interests and expectations, particularly in respect of their professional development? Perhaps by identifying the individual professional development needs of academic staff and assessing how far these accord with the development needs of the institution, some useful comparisons may be made.

In the late 1990s, research was conducted in FHE institutions in England and Wales, approached from two perspectives:

- that of the *organisation* itself, as represented by relevant policy documentation and policy makers
- that of the *individual* member of staff.

The first study examined current organisational perspectives on professional development, and provided a benchmark for the rest of the research. It involved a content analysis of staff development policies collected from organisations in the two sectors, and was followed by a series of in-depth interviews with staff development managers in a range of further education (FE) colleges. In the second study, attitudes and perceptions of FE and higher education (HE) staff regarding their development needs and opportunities were collected by questionnaires and semi-structured interviews.

The Institution Versus the Individual

The results of this study suggest that teaching staff have noticed a change in the underlying epistemology of the FHE sector, from a generally pedagogic orientation towards a managerialist framework, largely based on theories of organisational behaviour. Like other public sector organisations, FHE institutions have been adopting practices formerly only used in business organisations, perhaps to signal their drive towards greater economy and efficiency; however, many of these practices are already considered to be outdated in the business world. There is an unease amongst many staff about the application of management theory and practices to education. For example, in talking about his own professional development, one FE college middle manager commented:

> [I favour] a situation where training [is] devised by teachers who've gone through a similar process of change rather than something that is bolted on and borrowed from, what I think is, quite an irrelevant field [management studies]. I don't want to manage in order to exploit. I want to manage to meet the needs of my students and my colleagues. I'm not just doing it to reduce costs.
>
> (FE college middle manager)

These findings are supported elsewhere in recent literature, notably in the work of Ralph (1995), Elliott (1996) and Robson and Bailey (1996). At one level, this has created a tension between senior management – the instigators of change – and the middle managers who are expected to implement these changes and to cultivate the kind of environment in which such change is accepted. In consequence, there is a likelihood of tension between middle managers and teaching staff, who perceive those managers as the instruments of change. The widespread unease among teaching staff emerged in the research interviews in a number of ways. The following members of staff, for example, were very conscious of how recent policy change had a direct bearing on the quality of the students' learning experiences outside of the academic curriculum:

> I feel that there are restrictions on my timetable brought about by the Funding Council wanting qualifications from the students. They [the students] really need a lot more on the personal, psychological and emotional side - one to one, and I feel that I have the skills but there are restrictions … there isn't the time for that … Under the old scheme, we had more flexibility but now it's about counting hours.
>
> (FE lecturer)

> ….the dialogue on teaching and learning is at the heart of everything we do.
> (Female HE senior lecturer)

In higher education, the competing pressures of teaching and research were always apparent. Two HE lecturers explained how the expectation that they would research and publish to contribute to the next Research Assessment Exercise meant that:

> Students were being neglected, not coming first. Staff felt that everything they stood for was being undermined. I agree we wanted people to do more research, but … our strength is to put students first, and this sense of purpose has been undermined. (Male HE middle manager)

> There was no recognition for good teaching. We felt pressurised to do research and publish. It was ignoring our core business – teaching. Students did not get enough support. (Female HE senior lecturer)

The findings of this study suggest that the priorities and focus of lecturing staff are primarily pedagogic; they are concerned with the immediate and broad educational needs of their students, not necessarily exclusively about academic qualifications. The managerialist approach, whilst purporting to be concerned with improving the quality of provision and widening participation, is widely perceived by teaching staff as concerned with cost-saving. This view is summed up quite effectively by two of the lecturers in the study who observed that:

> My immediate concerns are to do with meeting the needs of my students; in particular under-represented groups, such as mature students - widening the curriculum and making it more relevant to them. Although the college supports that, it doesn't earn them very much money. It's a luxury really. (FE lecturer)

> staff were genuinely trying to widen access and participation and by definition, working with students who needed more support, within the context of reduced time to provide that support. (Male HE senior lecturer)

In terms of the development of new courses and curricula, staff observed:

> Adopting new courses and new subjects … just isn't within the thinking of the departments, except of course when it's finance led. 'We need more students, we need more money' … it's only at that point … and that's all for the wrong reasons because the pressures are wrong. (FE lecturer)

> The curriculum revisions at the same time as everything else, although laudable – there seems to be a loading of everything at the same time.
>
> (Male HE senior lecturer)

A member of the FE senior management team concluded:

> I think FE is driven at the moment by the funding model. Inevitably, if each college is faced with the fact that its guaranteed funding for the following year is 90% of its present funding, there are changes which are forced upon everybody and that is going to continue unless there is a significant change in thinking about education or in government policy. (FE senior management)

The relationship between the changes in funding and the consequential focus on productivity and efficiency is a relatively simple one. However, it does not necessarily follow that the wholesale application of a managerialist or bureaucratic framework is the most effective way to achieve strategic objectives. Nor is it possible to consider a return to the fully collegial style of management that operated in many institutions pre-incorporation, when external pressures were less. Yet staff and students would reap the benefits of a more intelligent and considered implementation of policies that meet their needs, such as the model of educational management proposed by Davies and Morgan (1983), where initial negotiation results in agreed outcomes which are 'passed to the bureaucracy' for implementation. Establishing objectives appropriate and relevant to the needs of students should be the first step.

In the light of the findings of this study, together with more general predictions about demography, employment and the role of further and higher education over the next few years, consideration is given in the rest of this chapter to an alternative model of employment relationships; that of reciprocal contracting. Stemming from the principle of the psychological contract, it is suggested that reciprocal contracting would increase employee participation and distribute responsibility and decision-making more evenly between the various levels of an organisation, thus avoiding some of the 'patriarchal' elements evident in a managerial employer-employee framework.

Lecturers' Values: Institutional Agenda?

Since the Further and Higher Education Act of 1992, FHE institutions have been setting their own organisational agendas. Pressured from the outside by policy changes and market forces, all are now setting strategic objectives and seeking ways through which staff might meet - and be seen to be meeting - those objectives. Evidence from the interviews with staff development managers and staff themselves shows that this is generally perceived as a process driven from the top down. The apparent contradiction between pedagogic considerations, education policy and managerialist Human Resource Management (HRM) strategies may be difficult to reconcile. HRM presupposes a certain type of culture that is unlikely to work in all organisations, especially those concerned with education. Education is different from other kinds of organisational culture, being significantly different to the factory floor where HRM policies were first introduced. The principles of HRM are part of an ideology, like quality assurance, which is to do with organisational control and which does not sit comfortably with the pedagogic orientation of teachers. Whilst the individual lecturer's professional development needs are frequently driven by the needs of the students or the subject being taught, the organisation's needs are currently led by the external pressure to move from a service to a business orientation and by the system demands of incorporation.

However, any FE or HE lecturer undertaking a programme of initial or in-service teacher training or other professional development over the last decade will be familiar with and be able to apply the notion of reflective practice (Schoen, 1987). Reflection-in-action characterises the work of professionals and influences the decisions they make over the desired direction of their professional development. If FHE institutions are to benefit from a more teacher-centred epistemology that allows the individual more involvement in the creation and implementation of policy, the reflective practitioner model could provide a suitable framework. Elliott (1996) proposes this route, arguing that:

> The potential for lecturers to inform and influence policy, and the process by which lecturers make considered responses to political, cultural and technological change, and devise considered strategies to contain or exploit both intended or unintended consequences, are also key issues which are given prominence within a reflective practice model of teaching.
>
> (Elliot, 1996, p.109)

This view is supported by Griffiths and Tann (1991) who argue that:

> ... reflective teaching requires that public theories are translated into personal ones and vice versa, unless teachers are going to allow themselves to be turned into low-level operatives, content with carrying out their tasks more and more efficiently, while remaining blind to larger issues of the underlying purposes and results of schooling. (Griffiths and Tann, 1991, p.100)

These comments resonate with some of the observations made by lecturing staff during the interviews, where there clearly was a feeling that current policy is reconstructing lecturers as low-level operatives, or that they were not given the opportunity to reflect:

> To an extent I am [using my skills] but they could be better utilised, for instance on the management board for the department ... The departments here are in no way democratic. You've got a highly-skilled, highly-educated workforce. We're not bolt-tighteners on a production line, but that's often how we perceive the treatment that we get. (FE lecturer)

> What we were doing was sound, but we were not planning ahead. There was not the co-ordination and measure of reflection within that. I felt that that was where we were lacking – this sort of taking stock and then re-evaluating – do we want to go any further? Yes, no? How are we going to do it?
> (Male HE senior lecturer)

A recurring theme throughout the interviews was that lecturing staff often felt excluded from policy decisions to which they could usefully contribute. This is further reinforced by the trend towards the casualisation of lecturing staff and, in further education, the increasing use of NVQ D32 and D33 assessors who may not be teacher-trained. Elliott outlines the strengths of the reflective practice model:

> Reflective practice entails that the lecturer carries out his or her work towards ethical ends, which may characteristically be expressed by them altruistically. The work, no matter how varied, how menial in parts, is underpinned by a notion of educational worth. (Elliot, 1996, p.109)

Reflective practice has long been recognised as making a major contribution to professional development; Vulliamy and Webb (1992), studying teacher-researchers on a university course, concluded that:

> the in-depth reflection on practice, promoted on the course by case study and action research, often made a major contribution to participants' professional development and led to changes in policy and practice for which they were responsible. (Vulliamy and Webb, 1992, p.43)

It is not clear, in the institutions surveyed in this study, whether the underpinning principles of continuing professional development are currently rooted in the concept of reflective practice; this could provide a clear direction for development at all levels of the organisation.

Organisational Culture: individual needs

Contrary to some of the literature regarding resistance to change, (Squire, 1989; Faccenda, 1996), the current research demonstrated that, in practice, teaching staff seem to consider new initiatives on their individual merits, particularly in relation to their benefits in the classroom. The survey data showed considerable support for the introduction of some form of systematic professional development. On the other hand, there was widespread criticism of the increase in class sizes which was regarded as having a detrimental effect on the quality of educational provision. Resistance to change in further and higher education would appear to be by no means as universal or uniform as some researchers have suggested. This concurs with Elliott (1996) who concluded from his research that:

> lecturers actively evaluate new developments and changes on their merits. New initiatives are seldom pre-judged, but are addressed in relation to their perceived benefits for the students. (Elliott, 1996, p.111)

Another finding of this research which was supported by the findings of Elliott's study (op.cit.) is that lecturers' hostility to change is often directed at the process of implementation rather than the change itself. Time and again staff objected to what they saw as the management-led imposition of new initiatives, especially where they felt there was a lack of consultation and an inappropriate 'dictatorial' approach:

> We did not speak up or raise our concerns - we had the impression that we just had to do it. I didn't feel that I had the authority, for example, to make decisions about staffing [my course]. I felt I was losing control [of my course].
> (Female HE senior lecturer)

> We were able to articulate concerns and I know that some staff have. I don't necessarily believe that, having had the opportunity, that it [sic] was necessarily responded to. But at the end of the day there's always that difficulty with demonstrating leadership where you can seek advice or not, but you've got to make the decision. (Male HE senior lecturer)

For many, 'professionalism' involved a recognition of their expertise by colleagues and by senior management. When their advice was sought on professional issues, particularly by senior managers, teaching staff really appreciated that their input was valued and taken seriously. Staff frequently reported feeling undervalued; the interviews demonstrated that many had sophisticated and informed views on the changes currently sweeping FHE, which they rarely had the opportunity to voice. This is not only profoundly frustrating for the individual, but a loss for the organisation, which possesses a significant and under-utilised resource. The organisation would be much more powerful if staff and management were able to combine their considerable experience and expertise to implement and to challenge, where appropriate, policies imposed from outside the institution. Few other professions have the benefit of such a highly-educated and well-informed workforce coupled with the organisational and cultural diversity and subject expertise that the range of FHE teaching brings.

It is in the interests of students, individual members of staff and the organisation to explore the conditions under which new initiatives may thrive. While this may involve an informed examination of the initiatives themselves, it must also involve dialogue between all levels of the organisation, which is then considered and utilised in the implementation process. Lecturers need to see not only that their opinions are listened to, but that they are also acted upon. The views of teaching staff must influence and, crucially, be seen to influence policy. Elliott concludes that:

> Further study may need to assess how far policymakers may underestimate the extent to which their policies provoke resistance, especially if they fail to understand the degree to which lecturers resistance is circumscribed by their cultural and ideological assumptions and dispositions. Managers, too, may underplay these factors and may fail accurately to 'read' the real potential ... for changing practice and procedures in their colleges. (Elliot, 1996, p.111)

It was clear from the interviews that staff seek empowerment; many want to be involved in the decision-making which affects the quality of their students' education. They do not want to be 'reduced' to basic time-consuming administrative tasks which are part of a larger managerialist strategy in which they have no say. The current acquisition and retention of all key decisions by senior management carries with it messages of possessiveness and distrust which do nothing to engender an atmosphere of mutual professional respect. If such decision-making were to permeate throughout the organisation, if staff, within their course teams, were given more say in key areas such as staffing and resources, then many of the key decisions would be taken by the individuals closest to the heart of the operation - the students and the curriculum (West-Burnham, 1992). This is likely to require a further devolution of decisions relating to financial, staffing and curriculum matters. Not only would this tap into a largely under utilised resource of in-house expertise, it would also bring with it an ongoing professional development for all staff, especially in leadership and management. This would provide the true foundation for a 'learning organisation'. Learning, like professional development, must be learner-led. Whilst the terms, 'learning organisation' and 'lifelong learning' may currently be in vogue, there is a fundamental contradiction between the needs of the lecturer as learner and management-led policy change.

Any further study of organisational change in further and higher education would ideally need to examine more closely the motivations of the teaching staff. In return for long-term commitment and readiness to develop themselves, academics need to feel that they are working in an environment in which the value-systems tailor with their own. It is also clearly important, for most staff, to be treated as professionals; at one level this means being trusted to 'get on with the main job of teaching'; at another this means being consulted and involved more fully in the decisions which affect curriculum delivery.

The research touched on other individual needs. Organisations have paid little attention to the career aspirations of their staff. Yet the FHE sector is better placed than many to adopt more flexible career patterns and to be more receptive to the career development wishes of individuals. In the absence of better pay and working conditions and the attraction of better paid jobs in industry and business, FHE institutions could consider more carefully the working conditions that they can provide for their staff. They are uniquely placed to try a variety of career and professional development systems, such as mentoring, job sharing, job rotation, shadowing, sabbaticals and study leave and action research.

Career Dynamics

Staff Entitlement and Empowerment

Most FHE institutions have a staff development policy. Of those surveyed, many referred to a commitment to staff entitlement to training and development. While this may only be a semantic shift, the concept of 'entitlement' puts the focus on staff development as a right rather than as a privilege. Entitlements and charters may have been the 'flavour' of the last decade, but at least they are a step in the direction of acknowledging the rights of the individual at work, which have not been a major priority in recent times. It remains to be seen whether this signals a period of greater attention to the needs of the individual in the workplace. The specific references to staff entitlement varied from institution to institution, but frequently included some of the following points:

- providing access for all staff to a range of flexible developmental opportunities
- recognising that staff are the organisation's most important resource
- acknowledging that training and development are key aspects of enlivening and improving the work undertaken by individual members of staff
- asking staff to identify priority areas for development activities through team and college reviews and appraisal processes
- identifying and making known to all staff the priority developmental areas and how to access allocated resources
- promoting the training and development opportunities available to staff
- monitoring the take-up of activities and taking the necessary action to improve access
- ensuring that staff have, or acquire, qualifications appropriate to their roles within the college
- promoting equality of opportunity through all training and development activity
- evaluating the benefits to the individual, the team and the organisation of training and development.

The whole debate about the balance between individual and organisational needs is ultimately manifested in the dichotomy between 'staff' and 'professional' development. While staff development policies are beginning to acknowledge concepts like entitlement and empowerment, greater attention to these ideals could help place the emphasis on the individual. Over the last few years, institutions have had to put together mission statements and strategic plans, some for the first time. While legislation ensured that these were a priority, staff development and other policies slipped down the agenda. Inevitably, attention to personal development was non-existent. Now that they are in the position to have staff development and other policies derived from, and informed by, their strategic plans, organisations also have the opportunity to review what staff really wish, in development terms, for themselves and their students. For a considerable period of time, organisational change has been driven top-down; what is needed is the opportunity for individual needs to shape policy to some extent.

Reciprocal Contracting

A recurring message from the interview data was the need for staff to feel that their views and opinions were heard and considered. The following recommendations have been based on suggestions coming from staff during the course of interviews, examples of good practice taken from the staff development policies reviewed in this study and successful programmes described by staff development personnel during the research interviews.

Education may experience some benefits from the changes brought about by new management strategies, but the evidence from this study points towards the need for a new model of career and professional development, at the heart of which lies the principle of reciprocity and the recognition of the importance of tailoring individual and organisational needs. The findings suggest that many people are dissatisfied with the current status of professional and career development within FHE. Perhaps the first step in redefining 'professionalism' in the two sectors is to see it as entailing mutual trust and respect between the organisation and each member of staff, perhaps by allowing individuals greater freedom in identifying their own and their students' priorities. West-Burnham's (1992) and Elliott's (1996) work suggests that teachers or lecturers, being at the heart of the operation of the curriculum, are best placed in the organisation to understand their students' needs. Lecturers' professional and career development needs are generally grounded in pedagogic values; for most, their own professional development needs are wedded to the educational needs of their students or their subject.

Much of the research on the nature of the employment contract in organisations other than FHE (Herriot and Pemberton, 1995; Hirsh, 1995) has recognised the importance of the empowerment of the individual in the relationship with employers. This goes some way towards the tailoring of individuals' professional and career development needs to those of the organisation. This model of organisational career as a sequence of renegotiations over time has been described as 'psychological contracting' (Herriot, Manning and Kidd, 1997). The concept was first used by Argyris (1960) and was subsequently popularised by Levison, Price, Munden, Mandl and Solley (1962) and Schein (1978, 1980) A similar concept is proposed that:

> ... refers to the perceptions of mutual obligations to each other held by the two parties in the employment relationship, the organization and the employee. Such perceptions may be the result of formal contracts, or they may be implied by expectations which holds of the other and which are communicated in a multitude of subtle or not so subtle ways. (Herriot et al., 1997, p.151)

However, Herriot at al (op.cit.) point out that the term *psychological contracting* has, in recent times, been used to describe the concept in terms of the perceptions of the employee alone, for example by Rousseau (1990). In using the concept, then, we wish to return to the idea of the mutual obligation of employee and employer, with the label 'reciprocal contracting' to emphasise the need for equity in the relationship. This is the model that is being proposed for FHE, which would offer a way of addressing the differences in the perceptions of teaching staff and management which has been shown to affect staff motivation and morale.

This is not to suggest that members of staff are given carte blanche to dictate their exact terms and requirements, but that, in fully understanding their role in the organisation and the importance of their individual contribution to organisational goals, there is a possibility that the two sets of needs may become more closely aligned. Unless FHE institutions respond to changing demographics and work patterns, there are likely to be further difficulties recruiting, retaining and developing the kind of people who will add value to the organisation. FHE is unlikely to be in a position to offer the same kinds of salaries and incentives as private industry, nor do staff in education come into this arena for high financial rewards. However, FHE institutions are in a position to respect and respond to the needs of their staff in terms of their own professional development and desired working patterns, to the benefit of the individual and the organisation.

Both the organisation and the individuals within it are dynamic, evolving systems whose needs change because of the changing environment and changing internal factors deriving from, for example, contractual status, length of service, age, life experiences and family circumstances. The tailoring of individual and organisational requirements should therefore be an evolving, changing process that is regularly monitored and evaluated. FHE institutions are likely to be more effective and individuals more satisfied if there is a better understanding and more effective tailoring of organisational needs and those of individual staff in terms of professional development and career planning. This can only be achieved through consultation and discussion, with the creation of opportunities to reflect upon professional practice. Such discussions should not be limited to the confines of the professional development interview, although this could be an important starting point, but in time, should become part of the fabric of the institution.

Appraisal or Personal Development Review?

Evaluation of performance may be seen as essential for quality assurance procedures; indeed, it may become a necessity imposed by the requirements of external bodies. Appraisal is intended to improve both individual performance and organisational effectiveness (Middlewood, 1996). There is clearly a tension here between evaluation and development. If reciprocal contracting is to be based on the principles of egalitarian reciprocation, ideally it should be separate from processes of evaluative appraisal (Beer, 1986). It is important that the development of any appraisal or review strategy is based on the principles of reciprocal agreement between individual staff and the organisation. If it is devised and implemented only by senior management, it is likely to be perceived just as a management tool. *Appraisal* systems linked to the line management structure may not always encourage a sense of autonomy and professionalism. The language of appraisal systems ('appraiser/appraisee'; 'line manager/subordinate') extends and enshrines, in the terms of transactional analysis, a child-adult relationship which contradicts the concept of professionalism. Many of the concerns voiced over existing appraisal systems, for example, might be mitigated if the system was reconstructed as an opportunity for renegotiating and monitoring reciprocal contracts. Personal and professional development should not be used as a reward for effective individual performance, but recognised as mutually beneficial to both the individual and the organisation.

An effective professional development system, such as that of *personal* development review, could provide the necessary vehicle for such discussions. The effectiveness of the review process will depend heavily on the effectiveness of the individual manager or 'reviewer', who must be skilled in interpreting the organisation's strategic plan and in articulating the development needs of the organisation, whilst encouraging individuals to identify their own development needs that arise from these. At the same time, individual 'reviewees' are given the opportunity to describe their own specific requirements. Reciprocity arises when the 'reviewer' is able to support the individual in the identification of how these requirements would contribute to the development of the institution. In the instances where they are quite separate to those of the institution (Marklund, 1986) then it may still be possible for the reviewer to negotiate more limited support (in time or finances) in recognition of the importance of these needs to the individual.

Where discussion centres on individual development, it provides an invaluable forum for the individual to air his or her concerns, interests and wishes. While there is a need for such interviews to be linked into organisational strategy, many would advocate that the listener or 'reviewer' should be independent of line management. However, experience indicates that organisations which have used this approach have felt that in general, line managers have a better understanding of the individual's work role. However, the decision could rest with the individual as to whether they wish to discuss such issues in this context.

Individual Needs and Career Stages

If this process is to be effective, it will entail regular negotiating and renegotiating to ensure that the employment/development relationship remains acceptable to both. Institutions and individuals will need to ensure that reciprocal contracts are maintained and kept in mind during negotiations regarding workloads and roles within the organisation. In order to achieve this, staff managers specifically and all staff generally require a greater awareness of the importance of individual life patterns and how individual, career and family development interact over time, the nature of organisational career development and progression, and what Schein (1978) refers to as 'the reciprocal interaction of individual and organisation, the processes of organisational socialisation, and the process of individual innovation'. FHE institutions need to be more aware of the roles individuals play outside the organisation, such a parent, citizen, carer or researcher. During these times of increasing workloads, there is an even greater need for sensitive managers who at least attempt to plan teaching timetables to take account of these factors. The reward, in terms of staff motivation and effectiveness, is likely to more than repay the effort involved.

It is accepted that when a new member of staff joins an institution, attention needs to be given to the tailoring of their skills and specialisms to the needs of the organisation. This currently happens, to some extent, through the initial appointment interview, where potential members of staff have the opportunity to outline their career plans and professional interests, but priority could be given to the establishment of these once the individual is in post, in order to set up a mutually advantageous initial reciprocal contract. Undoubtedly, once in post, most competent staff shape their job and their role to make best use of their skills.

If the interview lays the foundation for this process, then induction is the first opportunity to realise some of the issues negotiated at interview. For most FHE institutions induction, like the perception of staff development generally, is something that is 'done to' individuals. Most documentation relating to induction programmes examined for the purpose of this study set out a clear one or two-day training course designed to acclimatise and orientate staff to the culture, systems and processes of the employing institution. This could provide an ideal opportunity for further discussion and negotiation on how the institution and the new member of staff can interact to make best use of existing skills and to develop others.

Educational institutions have a responsibility to help members of staff establish what they require in the way of professional and career development. There needs to be some formal opportunity for dialogue and feedback in order to establish, for each individual, what will lead to job satisfaction and self-fulfilment. Part of this strategy must be to focus on job and/or role planning in order to determine how key roles in the organisation will change as the organisation evolves and environmental changes take effect (Schein, 1986; Herriot, 1989). Individuals need to be kept informed of changes within the organisation in order to understand the need for flexibility in staffing matters.

While new academic staff and recently qualified lecturers are likely to have additional local support, teaching staff who have been in post for a while are more likely to experience dissatisfaction and a sense of neglect. While clearly it is important for the organisation to consider the particular dynamics of the early career, it is the following groups which may ultimately give cause for concern, as they perceive themselves as having a range of useful skills to offer, but are frustrated by lack of opportunity:

- non-promoted lecturing staff over the age of 35
- academic staff approaching retirement, particularly those below the level of senior management
- staff who have been teaching for 10 years or more
- staff involved in the transition from teaching to taking on administrative and managerial functions
- staff entering education at a later stage in career development, especially those with management experience in other areas.

Consideration of the needs of these groups is necessary to avoid the sense of neglect experienced by some staff, particularly in mid- and late-career. Regular monitoring will allow for individual planning and make provision for mutual discussion, support in managing change, and the negotiation of possible career developments or changes.

Mentoring can be one way in which staff can engage in mutual professional development. Definitions and models of mentoring vary considerably and the advantages or disadvantages experienced will depend largely on the model adopted. This study suggests that Clutterbuck's definition (2001) 'off-line help by one person to another in making significant transitions in knowledge, work or thinking' (p.3) is particularly applicable to staff in the FHE context. Extending mentoring schemes beyond the early career stage may be one way of encouraging productive professional relationships throughout career development. For more experienced members of staff in the later years of their career, who may not wish or have the opportunity to move into management, mentoring may enhance job satisfaction and provide an alternative career development route by creating a personal forum for the exchange and transmission of ideas (Clutterbuck, 2001). Schein (1978) describes 'the transition from maximum concern with [one's] own contribution to greater concern with being a mentor to others'.

Staff Support and Stress Management

Most FE colleges have long since recognised the importance of student support services, and following the lead of Higher Education, most have allocated resources to providing welfare and counselling facilities for students, some of which are also available to staff. Although the necessary expertise is now in place in many FHE institutions, few offer a particular service for staff or have undertaken studies of the psychosocial and emotional needs of employees. The perceived increase in stress levels among teaching staff, now well-documented (e.g. Kinman, 1996; 1998), suggests a greater need for occupational health advice and counselling support within the workplace. As a responsible employer, the college has a moral and legal obligation to attend to the health of its staff. Coupled with these recommendations is the need for greater organisational awareness of the problems of stress. Many organisations now recognise the importance of stress management, yet the emphasis is frequently placed on the individual managing his or her own stress by means of relaxation, time management and assertiveness techniques. The emphatic and repeated references during the research interviews, from academic staff at all levels, to increasing pressure and demands on time are reminders that stress is an organisational problem, which also requires organisational action (Earnshaw and Cooper, 1996). It is not enough to provide stress management courses as a means of 'staff development'; FHE institutions and universities must seek ways of mitigating the increasing administrative burden and utilise strategies for managing policy change which consult and communicate with staff. Communication and organisational culture are of particular importance; the following quote speaks eloquently for itself:

> If you look at those under stress, they haven't necessarily got the greatest teaching loads – it is a matter of perception – how they view their perceived role. A basic principle of management is to do with equity and when people think there is very little equity it physically manifests itself. Equity in workloads, in being involved in decision-making, in being able to cherry pick – resources, timetabling – they all relate to personal autonomy in one way. It is not necessarily the pressure of the job but the culture and climate.
>
> (Female HE senior lecturer)

Communication and organisational culture emerged from the interviews in this study as so important for staff morale that to ignore them could result in serious consequences for the future of staffing in both further and higher education.

Professional Tutor or Staff Development Officer?

The role of professional tutor, a widely held post in further education during the 1980s, seems largely to have disappeared post-incorporation. A number of college managers stated during the interviews that this post was a luxury they could no longer afford. Where job descriptions of this post did exist, these nearly always included a reference to the responsibility of the professional tutor for nurturing the career prospects of lecturing staff. For FHE institutions committed to improving professional development opportunities for their staff, the reinstatement of this or a similar role may prove a useful long-term investment.

Professional tutors have often been replaced by Staff Development Officers, a role that now also exists in many higher education institutions. There is considerable variation in the responsibilities attached to this role, and it has itself undergone considerable change over the last few years. More recently, the title 'officer' has frequently been replaced by that of 'manager' with all the attendant connotations. While staff development procedures are part of the overall strategic planning process of an organisation, they also must have their own processes and systems which identify the overall staff development needs arising from the strategic plan. It is important that staff developers are in direct contact with, or ideally are members of, the senior management team, yet in a position to represent individual staff in terms of their development needs. There is a danger, however, that their role is now largely seen as managing new administrative and functional processes.

Since the 1992 FHE Act, the strategic role of Staff Development Managers is generally concerned with interpreting the college's strategic plan in terms of human resource needs - whilst the functional role is concerned with the allocation and administration of the staff development budget. The post is usually less concerned with occupational counselling. A shift in emphasis would create the opportunity for this post to once again be more directly concerned with staff and professional development, from involvement in initial teacher education and continuing professional development through to individual staff support.

Flexible Teacher Training and Continuing Professional Development Programmes

In-service teacher training programmes such as the City and Guilds 730 in Further Education offer the opportunity for staff qualified in their own area of expertise to undertake teacher training once in post. Many Higher Education institutions also provide programmes of professional development in teaching and learning, often accredited by the Institute of Learning and Teaching. Some courses offer some degree of flexibility in terms of time and mode of study. The most recent version of the City and Guilds programme, the 7305, based on the principles of NVQ, allows for greater flexibility still, as in principle students can join and complete the programme at any time at their convenience. In practice, as is the case with NVQs across the curriculum, colleges are not always in a position to offer completely open access. The advantages and disadvantages of an NVQ approach versus more traditional courses are discussed extensively in Chapter 7, but participants do benefit from the chance to work together and engage in reflective practice as a group; complete freedom of access does not always allow for this. However, the right of the individual to study how and when she or he wishes and to tailor this around the other demands of a working life is an important consideration.

Increasingly, FHE institutions are recognising the advantage of linking staff and professional development programmes to accreditation schemes. A large number of FE colleges work in consortia or have franchise arrangements with local HE providers, who accredit staff training programmes. These vary in scope, but many aim to include continuing professional development within some kind of academic framework or credit scheme, with step off points at diploma, degree, masters and taught doctorate level. These programmes offer many obvious advantages for the individual and the organisation.

An extension of some of the principles of NVQ, some forms of accreditation provide individuals the opportunity to formally record some of the professional development work they have undertaken. In principle Accreditation of Prior Learning (APL) should provide individuals with recognition of professional development undertaken in the recent past. In practice, the compiling of evidence to this end can involve the individual in more work than simply signing up for a recognised course.

Conclusions

FHE institutions are becoming clearer about their goals and corporate objectives. The statutory requirement for strategic plans and mission statements has forced further and higher education institutions to examine their aims and priorities. Quality assurance procedures have helped to promote these aims throughout the organisation. Those organisations who have undertaken a commitment to Investors in People have to be able to demonstrate that:

> People can consistently explain the aims and objectives of the organisation at a level appropriate to their role. (IIP, www.iipuk.co.uk)

and that:

> People can explain how they contribute to achieving the organisation's aims and objectives. (op.cit.)

In terms of planning, FE colleges are required to show that:

- a written but flexible plan sets out the organisation's targets
- a written plan identifies the organisation's training and development needs and specifies what action will be taken to meet these needs
- training and development needs are regularly reviewed against goals and targets at the organisation, team and individual level
- a written plan identifies the resources that will be used to meet training and development needs
- responsibility for training and developing employees is clearly identified and understood throughout the organisation, starting at the top
- objectives are set for training and development actions at the organisation, team and individual level
- where appropriate, training and development objectives are linked to external Standards such as NVQs and units.

A similar framework is required for higher education.

All these structures are relatively new, having come into place since the Further and Higher Education Act of 1992. While undoubtedly many FHE institutions were clear about their aims and objectives prior to this period of change, the introduction of statutory frameworks has given this information a higher profile. What is apparent is the consistency of approach from one organisation to another, in both further and higher education establishments, driven by the principles of human resource management. The research reported in this chapter demonstrates that it is relatively easy to map out corporate objectives and to disseminate this information to staff members (although this did appear to be patchy), but it is much harder to guarantee the commitment of all staff to these goals. To assume that this is possible ignores the richness of cultural diversity within an organisation. What this research suggests is that FHE institutions must now step back and consider the people who make up the organisation; look at their skills, their strengths, their wishes, their interests, their life commitments, their career stages and plans - and tailor these with the needs of the institution. A more complex process than the existing systems, such an undertaking has the potential to create a more intelligent, dynamic organisation based on constructive collaboration and recognition of the existing wealth of professional expertise rather than managerial authoritarianism.

References

Beer, M. (1986) Performance appraisal. In Lorsch, J.W. (Ed.) *Handbook of Organizational Behaviour.* Englewood Cliffs, New Jersey: Prentice Hall.

Clutterbuck, D. (2001) *Everyone Needs a Mentor - Fostering Talent at Work.* Third Edition. London: CIPD.

Davies, J. L. and Morgan, A.W. (1983) Management of higher education in a period of contraction and uncertainty. In Boyd-Barrett, O., Bush, T., Goodey, J., McNay, I. and Preedy, M. (Eds.) *Approaches to Post-School Management.* London: Harper and Row.

Earnshaw, J. and Cooper, C. (1996) *Stress and Employer Liability.* London: IPD.

Elliott, G. (1996) *Crisis and Change in Vocational Education and Training*. London: Jessica Kingsley.

Faccenda, J. (1996) Human Resource Management - the case 'for' and 'against' in FE. *NASD Journal* **35**, pp.13-17.

Griffiths, M. and Tann, S. (1991) Ripples in the reflection. In Lomax, P. (ed.) *Managing Better Schools and FHE institutions: The Action Research Way.* Clevedon: Multilingual Matters.

Herriot, P. (1989) *Recruitment in the 90's*. London: IPM.

Herriot, P., Manning, W.E.G. and Kidd, J.M. (1997) The content of the psychological contract. *British Journal of Management* **8** (2), pp.151-162.

Herriot, P. and Pemberton, C. (1995) *New Deals: The Revolution in Managerial Careers*. Chichester: Wiley.

Hirsh, W. (1995) Unpublished paper given at Education, Training and Personnel Development Conference.

Investors in People (2001) www.iipuk.co.uk Accessed 19/10/01.

Kinman, G. (1996) *Occupational stress and health among lecturers working in further and higher education.* London: NATFHE.

Kinman, G. (1998) *Pressure points: a survey of the causes and consequences of occupational stress in UK academic and related staff.* London: Association of University Teachers.

Levison, H., Price, C.R., Munden, K.J., Mandl, H.J. and Solley, C.M. (1962) *Men, Management and Mental Health.* Cambridge Massachusetts: Harvard University Press.

Marklund, S. (1986) *Integration of School and the World of Work.* London: Dept. of International and Comparative Education.

Midwood, D. (1996) Managing Appraisal. In Bush, T. and Midwood, D. *Managing People in Education.* London: Paul Chapman.

Ralph, M. (1995) *Developing the College as a Learning Organisation.* Bristol: The FE Staff College.

Robson, J. and Bailey, B. (1996) Contextualizing professional development in the new sector. In Robson, J. (Ed.) *The Professional FE Teacher: Staff development and training in the corporate college.* Aldershot: Avebury.

Rousseau, D.M. (1990) New Hire Perceptions of their own and their Employers' obligations: A Study of Psychological Contracts. *Journal of Organisational Behaviour* **11** (5), pp.389-400.

Schein, E.H. (1978) *Career Dynamics: Matching individual and organizational needs.* Reading, Massachusetts: Addison Wesley.

Schein, E.H. (1980) *Organizational Psychology*. Englewood Cliffs New Jersey: Prentice Hall.

Schein, E.H. (1986) Culture as an environmental concept for careers. *Journal of Occupational Behaviour* **5**, pp.71-81.

Schoen, D. (1987) *Educating the Reflective Practitioner*. San Francisco: Jossey Bass.

Squire, W. (1989) The aetiology of a defective theory. In Riches, C. and Morgan, C. (Eds.) *Human Resource Management in Education*. Milton Keynes: Open University Press.

Vulliamy, G. and Webb, R. (1992) The influence of teacher research: process or product. *Educational Review* **44** (1), pp.41-51.

West-Burnham, J. (1992) *Managing Quality in Schools*. Harlow: Longman.

6 Educational Change and Teacher Development

CATHERINE SCOTT AND STEVE DINHAM

Introduction

Since the early 1990s we have carried out a number of research projects examining matters such as teacher induction, teacher resignation, the impact of teaching on teachers' partners, teacher and school executive satisfaction, teacher motivation and stress, successful teaching, teacher self-concept, middle management in schools and other related areas.

In the course of surveying and interviewing literally thousands of teachers in Australia, the USA, New Zealand, England and Malta, we have had many opportunities to access first hand accounts of how educational and societal change have influenced teachers and how they feel about teaching. A common thread running through much of this work has been how teachers have been placed in a paradoxical situation of rising societal expectations and widening responsibilities yet have experienced mounting criticism and declining status.

A lack of control over imposed change and 'change fatigue' has resulted in many teachers reacting by reassessing their workloads and their commitment to professional development. For many, decreased career satisfaction and increased stress can be attributed to such change (Dinham, 1992, 1997; Dinham & Scott, 2000). In this chapter we examine some of the causes and manifestations of teachers' changing commitment to their professional development in the context of social and educational change.

Negative Collaboration or 'Balkanisation'

Hargreaves (1994) has written on the phenomenon of 'balkanisation', a form of 'negative collaboration', whereby teachers and schools under pressure fragment and withdraw into sub-groups. Balkanisation can result from the sheer size of schools, where people only interact personally with a fraction of the teaching staff, but it can also result from external pressures associated with the kinds of educational restructuring and change common in most educational settings and systems over the past two decades. Balkanised groupings – such as high school faculties or other formal or informal units – can have dysfunctional consequences for the school as a whole, for student learning, for other teachers and groups within the school, and for those within the group itself. Such groupings are not to be confused with what could be termed 'healthy' forms of collaboration or co-operation which occur in every school on an on-going basis.

Balkanised groups exhibit many of the characteristics and outcomes of what Janis (1971, reprinted in Kolb, 1991) identified as 'group-think', a term with its antecedents in George Orwell's 'newspeak' in his novel *1984*. Janis writes of perceived 'invulnerability', 'inherent morality', 'stereotypes', 'pressure', 'self-censorship', 'unanimity' and 'mindguards' being present and active within groups subject to group-think (pp.259-269). Hargreaves (1994) meanwhile, notes 'low permeability', 'high permanence', 'personal identification' and 'political complexion' as being characteristic of balkanised teacher cultures (pp.213-215).

In short, balkanised groups tend to be made up of individuals who strongly identify with the 'cause'; they 'police' their members and present a common face to what they perceive to be as opposing groups. Their operation is political in that they pursue resources, power and influence within their host organisation. Frequently, there is a discrepancy between the goals and methods of the group and its members, those of other groups and those espoused for the organisation as a whole.

Our research findings support the existence of such balkanised teacher cultures and identify the role that 'group-think' plays in forming and maintaining such groups. One English teacher remarked on her experience of a balkanised school:

> There seems to be little ability to communicate between departments and there seems to be competition between individual staff and departments. Competition in the sense of students, financial allocation, staff competencies, results.

Why is balkanisation such a concern? Preston (2001), in her discussion of the nature of teacher professionalism, has provided valuable insights on the matter. Teacher professionalism is, Preston maintains, not a matter of individual expertise. Instead it is a collective phenomenon, composed in part of the interactions between teachers and other members of the education community. She notes, and her words are worth quoting at length:

> Effective teaching is inherently *collective and strategic.* These characteristics are features of teaching far more than many other professions. Teachers' work is not primarily the aggregation of discrete one-to-one relationships between professional and client. In a classroom teachers are relating to a group of students, and while individualising their teaching much of the time, the complex inter-relationships between all the students in the class and between the students and the teacher is something the teacher needs to constantly manage. In addition, the education of particular students is dependent on the inter-relationships between the work of many teachers over many years. Some of those teachers have a direct teaching relationship with the students, while others play a part in curriculum development and creating the structure, culture and climate of schools and the system as a whole. These inter-relationships indicate the collective nature of teaching. That the education of students through schooling occurs over a period of time, and that the pattern and sequence of inter-relationships between the work of different teachers in part determines the nature and quality of learning, indicates the strategic nature of effective teaching ... There is more to teachers' professional practice, such as the professional education of other teachers, and research and scholarship to develop the knowledge base of teaching - informing their own and other's practice. Effective teaching is *democratic* because effective learning requires respectful and willing collaboration between teachers and students ... and in the early years especially, between teachers and parents.
>
> (Preston, 2001, pp.15-16)

However, balkanised groups, by definition, are not characterised by 'respectful and willing collaboration', but are a form of negative coalescence. Clearly, balkanisation and the 'group-think' which frequently accompanies it presents a real challenge to teacher professionalism, and effective teaching. Where the phenomenon is present to any extent, teachers' individual and collective professional development are at risk.

However as Hargreaves (1994) has pointed out, collegiality cannot be 'contrived' or forced. He believes that what could be termed 'authentic' collegiality is characterised by relationships between teachers which are:

- Spontaneous
- Voluntary
- Development-orientated
- Pervasive across time
- Unpredictable

On the other hand, 'contrived collegiality', where school leaders attempt to force teachers into collaborative working relationships is characterised by relationships which are:

- Administratively regulated
- Compulsory
- Implementation-orientated
- Fixed in time and space
- Predictable

It is quite likely that attempts to force teachers into collaborative relationships for the perceived good of the school will actually hasten and reinforce balkanisation, particularly when the collaboration is focused on 'extra' work on committees or teams over and above 'regular' classroom teaching duties.

The 'Retreating' Phenomenon

In addition to the withdrawal of teachers into groups, we have identified from our research a concept related to balkanisation and group-think we call 'retreating', a phenomenon affecting individual teachers rather than groups.

In our various studies, teacher after teacher, particularly those with more experience, have spoken of progressively 'shedding' or giving up the extra-curricular responsibilities they once performed with enthusiasm, activities that formerly connected them with other teachers, students and in many cases parents and community members (Dinham, 1992; Dinham & Scott, 1996). This has been recognised by employers and governments which, in some cases, have attempted to mandate what were formerly voluntary commitments on the part of teachers. In Ontario, for example, it is interesting and somewhat alarming to note that the government has attempted via the contentious 'Bill 74' to:

> declare volunteerism [in extracurricular activities] to be compulsory. In classic newspeak fashion, Bill 74 purges the word 'extracurricular' from Ontario's educational lexicon and substitutes 'co-instructional' ... a significant part of teachers' work would now be legislated rather than negotiated or chosen.
>
> (Robertson, 2001, p.559)

This represents an extreme attempt to overcome the problems caused by retreating, in this case largely due to teachers' reactions to attempts to increase their workloads and to reduce educational funding.

Teachers who coached sports, took debating teams, contributed to whole-school committee work, led bands and orchestras and contributed to musicals and plays have related how the pressures of coping with educational change and increases in school responsibilities such as new curricula, standardised testing, more detailed and demanding assessment and reporting, social welfare roles and rising administrative requirements have caused them to reassess their overall workload. In effect, they have said they are 'retreating' or reverting to a narrower range of responsibilities, usually centred in their classrooms and more characteristic of beginning teachers. In doing this, many have actually withdrawn from their formal or informal groups, both balkanised and otherwise.

School principals have noted how it has become harder and harder to find teachers who are willing to volunteer for 'out of class' roles. Increasingly it is necessary to offer teachers inducements such as time allowances to take on 'extras' – financial compensation is usually out of the question – and this can cause its own problems through large numbers of teachers being on reduced teaching loads. Teachers' goodwill, sense of duty and appeals for the common good of the school are no longer sufficient to ensure this involvement.

A real concern flowing from this situation is that it is the 'extras' which make schools so rewarding for teachers and students, as well as enhancing the overall quality and effectiveness of the school, not to mention its reputation in the community. Many if not all teachers can tell stories of how a previously 'difficult to reach' student 'came around' as a result of a less academic, more informal student-teacher relationship established through sport, the arts or some other activity. This then enabled both teacher and student to see each other in a different, more positive light which carried over to the classroom.

For the school, teacher and student involvement in extra-curricular activity is the 'cream' which adds significantly to school climate, culture and reputation. One quote from an English classroom teacher sums it up nicely:

> I love my job and am passionate about giving pupils a variety of experiences in my area of the curriculum. I feel very supported by my Head Teacher and the members of my Faculty. However, I am very tired and often I completely run out of energy, and will often go home and go straight to bed. I am getting

> more disinterested in running extra-curricular activities as I do these every lunchtime and even after school - exhausting! As a teacher of Music and Head of Performing Arts, with all members participating in extra-curricular work, I don't see how I can change this unless I get promotion and my responsibilities change.

Another related sentiment expressed by teachers was that retreating to the classroom was not enough and that, after years of giving and striving, exhaustion and demoralisation had reached the stage where the only solution was to leave teaching altogether:

> I really don't want to carry on teaching or as a Head Teacher until retirement age. I feel I've put so much into the job that I won't have the stamina or commitment to last another ten years - anyway there are many other things I would like to put my energies into.

Some of our research participants gave telling thumb nail sketches of their colleagues who remained in teaching but wished they had not, often because they are 'too old' to change careers, but too young to retire:

> Almost all those over 50 have taken early retirement, but no new teachers have been appointed. The establishment is run by 40-somethings who wish they had been 50 and could have retired as well!

> I feel concerned about the many negative comments from colleagues. I'm fed up, can't wait to get out, I've had enough of this.

Retreating is not only confined to schools – we have also witnessed the phenomenon in universities, where staff are finding it increasingly difficult to cope with additional responsibilities and pressures; key positions on committees and in degree co-ordination and student support are harder to fill.

The issue of retreating is partly related to the ageing of the teaching population in many 'advanced' countries. In the past, particularly the post-World War II 'baby boom' and the 'shadow boom' era of the 1970s when the children of the 'baby boomers' entered schools, there was a younger teacher profile and a better balance of young and experienced teachers in schools.

However, an ageing population generally and an ageing teaching service in many countries has restricted opportunities for younger teachers to enter schools. Thus, whereas in the past older teachers would have been in a position to 'pass the baton' to younger teachers who could have taken over the school orchestra or debating team, this is less likely to occur. One English classroom teacher observed about this effect:

> An aged and demoralised work force, many of which might have retired, is hardly likely to deliver new ideas and initiatives well.

A key aspect of retreating with particular relevance to the present discussion is that of some teachers' and school executives' declining commitment to professional development, an issue that will be taken up later in this chapter.

Time in School

Unlike the standard results of research into occupational satisfaction that reveal increased satisfaction with longer tenure in the job – people who stay in an occupation become more efficacious, receive recognition and in some cases promotion, whilst those who don't enjoy the job often leave – our results in the International Teacher 2000 Project have found no association between overall time in teaching and occupational contentment.

However, a finding that has been replicated across the four Anglophone samples is a negative association between time in the current school and satisfaction, that is, there was a tendency for teachers who had been in their current school for longer periods to be less satisfied. There are number of possible and related reasons for this phenomenon, including that the slowing of growth in systems had made mobility more difficult, leading to the sensation of being 'trapped' in one's situation, a problem compounded by the ageing of the teaching force. As one English teacher observed of her own experience:

> I feel stressed out, trapped in a post and a school I don't want to be in, yet because of my age, being unable to get a job elsewhere.

For some older teachers the decision or necessity to leave their current school was occasion for forced retirement because of 'ageist' attitudes to older staff. Knowing this potential fate undoubtedly kept many dissatisfied experienced teachers in unsatisfactory circumstances:

> I love my job and my students, but I feel desperately sorry that I can't do more useful things with them. I'm 50; I'm on basic pay - I've chosen not to pursue promotion. I'm re-locating because of my husband's job - he's already re-located.

> I know I will not be able to continue my teaching career because I'm too old. I was only able to get a post six years ago because I re-located to my home town. Staff still remembered me from my first job there, 1967-75 (including 1972-74 to have children). It's great to be back 'home' - I'm teaching my first pupils' children. What will happen next year? Scrap heap! What a waste!

Another aspect of the situation is the lack of opportunity for the renewing and refreshing aspects of change, again commented on by some of our participants:

> If teaching is your career it is a long time to be doing the same sort of thing (35+ years). Career breaks, sabbatical courses don't exist or are not encouraged.

Where such changes had been experienced, some teachers commented on their revitalising effect and the boost to professional development:

> Ironically this year I feel better and my Faculty is also pulling together better because I have been appointed on a two term secondment as an Adviser with the County. This gives me an opportunity to develop but also releases opportunities for people within the Faculty.

Unfortunately, the two phenomena of too long in the one school and declining commitment to professional development often go hand in hand and are mutually reinforcing. Many teachers interviewed in our research offered the view that a transfer or even resignation would be beneficial to both themselves and their students, but there were compelling reasons not to proceed with either.

As well as financial constraints and personal concerns to do with disrupting family life, a frequently cited reason for not moving was the view that the teacher would have to re-establish his or her 'discipline' and 'reputation' in a new school. This seems a real fear for some older teachers, as it would place them once more in the circumstances of being a beginning teacher, unknown by students and staff and having to start over. These same people often spoke of no longer being interested in promotion, advancement or professional development, resigned to staying in their same school and situation for the duration. The disturbing thing is that teachers as young as 35 were making such statements.

Teachers not actually affected by the phenomenon of too long at the same school also remarked on the demoralisation attendant upon the devaluing of older and more experienced teachers, and the negative effect this has on the possibility of sharing the fruits of experience, to the benefit of both new and older staff:

> [We need] money being put into education and special needs, *more* teachers, not less, *smaller* classes not larger, better resources, schools repaired, morale of teachers raised, more older teachers given value - we need *experience* in the teaching profession as well as young and innovative ideas. Balance is necessary.

> Experience is not 'valued'; she/he is older and must be losing their ability to do the job better (too much is asked).

Generally the feeling of being trapped – 'cannot or dare not move' – contributes to the phenomenon of retreating described above, both because the resulting demoralisation reduces commitment to professional development and because being denied the opportunity to experience the challenge of moving to a new setting further cuts off potential sources of professional renewal.

Further Views on Professional Development

When highly 'successful' teachers were interviewed as part of a study attempting to explore links between teaching methodologies and student success in the context of a final secondary external examination (Ayres et al., 2000), the matter of how these teachers had acquired their professional expertise and how they share this with others, was examined.

A key finding of the study was that these teachers had – either on their own or with a mentor or other colleagues – reflected on and identified their professional strengths and weaknesses. They had then formulated – either formally or informally – a personal professional development plan to meet these needs, and had taken steps to put this plan into action. However, in planning to meet these needs, these successful teachers gave low priority to formal employer-led professional development, whether in-service, higher degrees or other programs. A sample of secondary heads of department in another study (Dinham et al., 2000) had similar views.

Generally, educational employers and systems are perceived by teachers to be providing various training packages which are often generic in nature, covering areas such as leadership, school management, child protection and other mandatory legislation or requirements. However, teachers and school managers in both studies noted above showed a clear preference for professional development which was focussed on their subject discipline and area of teaching and tailored to meet their needs. That provided by employers was frequently concerned with current priorities, which were more to do with systems, school administration and policy rather than actual teaching practice. Further, rather than being seen as engaging with other professionals, system-based professional development was seen to be 'training' through packages and instruction.

The climate of imposed educational change, reform and restructuring since the 1980s has been perceived by teachers to be about anything but teaching. Increased school responsibilities, social expectations, and changes to assessment, testing and reporting have been seen to detract from teaching. Teachers – in part due to the retreating phenomenon noted above – have turned away from system-led and employer-led professional development which is not seen to have ready relevance and application in the classroom and is not geared to teachers' needs (Ayres et al., 2000; Dinham et al., 2000).

The pendulum is now swinging with 'quality teaching' becoming a major focus in the educational systems of many countries, but the question arises as to whether 'change fatigue' will result in reluctance on the part of teachers to increase or even maintain their current involvement with professional development, even if the focus is more on teaching.

A further key question is whether the 'average' teacher is so disposed to 'taking charge' of his or her professional development, as was the case with the 'successful' teachers mentioned above. If teachers have to find the time – and money – to fund their professional development at a time when they feel overloaded, undervalued and underpaid, there is a very real chance that they will continue to 'retreat' from professional development, as they have from extra curricular involvement.

The Problem of De-Professionalisation

Teachers from all the countries surveyed under the Teacher 2000 Project (Dinham & Scott, 2000) commented favourably on aspects of teaching work that allowed for both the utilisation of personal qualities such as flexibility, creativity and the ability to respond well to challenge, and the opportunity to continue to grow and develop as an individual:

> The scope for being creative, improvising and exploring different ways to teach/meet students' needs. That every day is different - bringing new surprises/challenges. The classroom is a very vibrant place to be.
> (New Zealand classroom teacher, aged 30)

> I like teaching because it allows me to continue to learn and grow in many ways. (USA classroom teacher, aged 58)

> The adventure of learning - both pupils and teacher.
> (UK specialist teacher, aged 52)

However, teachers from all the countries surveyed saw the nature and pace of educational change threatening teacher professionalism and its associated commitment to professional growth and development. Erosion of professionalism has at least two aspects:

- Lowering of the status of and respect for the profession, symbolised for many teachers by the relatively low pay the work is awarded.
- Erosion of the scope for exercising professional judgement, independence and competence and of the time to do 'real teaching'.

The lack of trust in the professionalism of teachers and anxiety about the use and potential misuse of national educational standards have led to a policing mentality among administrators, a tendency noted across many domains in the widespread move towards the adopting of financial auditing models of 'quality assurance' (Scott & Dinham, 2000). The consequence has been a proclivity to standardise and document as many aspects of the work of teachers and schools as possible, lest quality be compromised by leaving too much to the judgement of practitioners.

The introduction of many more reporting and documenting requirements, as well as the standardisation of many aspects of teaching, contribute both to the much noted increase in overall work load and to the erosion of the sorts of pleasures of the job described above, i.e. flexibility, challenge, creativity, working with and for people and genuine collaboration. These two facets of the erosion of professionalism, increased work and decreased respect, were summed up by one New Zealand teacher as 'constant demands and negative comments'.

Accompanying the erosion of professionalism for many or most teachers is the increasing intrusion and interference by those – education administrators, politicians, the press, school governors – who know 'naff all' about teaching, to quote an English head teacher. The politicisation of education in recent decades is well documented. What follows are some final comments from respondents to our Teacher 2000 survey in Australia, England and New Zealand:

> Teachers gain little respect ... I feel more like a slave than an educator.
> (Australian classroom teacher)

> Erosion of professionalism - we are completely emasculated by the National Curriculum/OFSTED/targets. (UK head of dept)

> Schools become the 'meat in the sandwich' during elections. Politicians use Education as a political football. Those in power beat their chests about 'reforms' they have achieved and those wanting power assault us with what they will do to make teachers work more efficiently and produce improved student outcomes. To listen to their drivel on the TV and radio an ordinary person would think that teachers totally lack intelligence and the professional will to direct their own activities towards improved outcomes for the students.
> (Australian classroom teacher)

> Teachers are not allowed to be professionals - every move has to be documented and ready to be presented as 'evidence', therefore they are being treated like students/trainees who have to justify their decisions (and decision making) however banal. (New Zealand classroom teacher)

Conclusion

The net effects of the negative pressures on teachers and schools have been, for many teachers, to suppress the opportunity and the incentive to devote time and attention to personal professional development. The increase in workload has taken away time and energy for reflection on practice and to talk with and learn from one's colleagues. It seems the harder teachers work, the less they are appreciated, and it is difficult to blame some teachers for retreating and becoming cynical and defensive.

However whilst understandable, a defensive mentality is ultimately self-defeating. If many of the present generation of teachers have become embittered or simply worn out and ground down by social and educational change - only around 50% of teachers in our international samples rate themselves as satisfied with teaching to any degree and most say they are now less satisfied than when they began (Dinham & Scott, 2000) - present arrangements for professional development are unlikely to remedy this situation. Either we adopt radically new approaches to the professional support and opportunities we offer practicing teachers, or failing this, we may need to concentrate on the next generation of teachers and school leaders if so many of our present teachers are saying 'I want to be alone'.

References

Ayres, P., Dinham, S. and Sawyer, W. (2000) Successful Senior Secondary Teaching. *Quality Teaching Series* **1** (September), pp.1-20 Australian College of Education.

Dinham, S. (1992) *Human Perspectives on the Resignation of Teachers From the New South Wales Department of School Education: Towards a Model of Teacher Persistence*. Doctor of Philosophy thesis, Armidale: University of New England.

Dinham, S., Brennan, K., Collier, J., Deece, A. and Mulford, D. (2000) The Secondary Head of Department: Key Link in the Quality Teaching and Learning Chain. *Quality Teaching Series* **2** (September), pp.1-35 Australian College of Education.

Dinham, S. (1997) Teaching and Teachers' Families. *Australian Educational Researcher*, AARE **24** (2), pp.59-88.

Dinham, S. and Scott, C. (1996) *The Teacher 2000 Project: A Study of Teacher Satisfaction, Motivation and Health*. Penrith: University of Western Sydney, Nepean.

Dinham, S. and Scott, C. (2000) Moving Into The Third, Outer Domain Of Teacher Satisfaction. *Journal of Educational Administration* **38** (4), pp.379-396.

Hargreaves, A. (1994) *Changing Teachers, Changing Times*. London: Cassell.

Janis, I.L. (1971). Group Think. *Psychology Today*, (November), reprinted in Kolb, D.A., Rubin, I.M. and Osland, J.S. (1991) *The Organizational Behavior Reader* (5th Edition). Englewood Cliffs, New Jersey: Prentice Hall.

Preston, B. (2001) *Myths and Realities: Teaching Futures*. Paper presented to Australian Teacher Credit Unions Annual Conference. Crown Plaza, Coogee Beach, New South Wales, 8th January.

Robertson, H.J. (2001) The Teacher Indentured Servitude Act. *Phi Delta Kappan* March, pp.559-560.

Scott, C, and Dinham, S. (2000) Auditing the Auditors. *Campus Review* **10** (35), p.12.

7 Professionals or Prisoners? The Competency-Based Approach to Professional Development

ROS OLLIN

Introduction

The post-compulsory sector of education and training has experienced many changes over the last three decades, which have resulted in different demands on the staff involved, together with changes to the function and purposes of staff development. This chapter considers the effects of some of these changes, in particular the effect of increased accountability and control and the introduction of competence-based occupational standards on staff development processes. Reference is also made to parallel developments in other sectors, in particular higher education (HE) and the health service. These developments have taken place against a background of wider debates on the processes of teaching and learning and shifting political perceptions on the purpose and scope of education. Of relevance also is the continuing debate on the notion of professionalism and how it impacts on the role of the teacher. The term staff development is used as a generic descriptor for policies and actions which relate to the development of employees. Other terms, for example professional development, are considered in their own right as part of a consideration of how changing terminology reflects different perceptions and approaches in this area.

Further Education in the 1970s and 1980s

In the 1970s staff development in the Further Education (FE) sector was perceived as an *ad hoc* affair with little direction or common agreement of what needed to be accomplished (Harding and Scott, 1980). FE teachers were, in general, vocational specialists, without a teaching qualification, operating within a fairly static environment where opportunities for advancement existed if sufficient time had been served. The students they taught were mainly in employment and attending college on part-time day-release. This situation had a number of implications for the teaching environment. In general, students were relatively highly motivated as learning was linked closely to employment requirements. Employers supported their trainees through giving them time to attend and had varying degrees of contact, usually informal, with individual college staff. A wide variety of different vocational qualifications were available, representing fairly narrow specialisms, but with significant areas of duplication between awards (Jessup, 1990). These qualifications were developed by awarding bodies such as City and Guilds and followed a traditional format with assessment being conducted through formal tests and written examinations.

Staff development tended to be concentrated in two areas - initial teacher training (ITT) and attendance at specific short courses, usually related to developments in the vocational area, each based more on individual rather than defined organisational needs. The James report (DES, 1972) supported this emphasis, in which staff development was related to identifying the professional needs of individual teachers and devising programmes to meet these needs. Although the Department for Education and Science (DES) Oxford conference in 1976 offered a more integrated approach, defining staff development as 'an ongoing process designed to maximise human resources in order to achieve the objectives of an organisation', the idea appeared more rhetoric than reality, with many educational establishments lacking clear organisational objectives.

At the end of the 1970s the social, political and educational climate began to change, with a resulting impact on the role of FE and the work of the FE teacher. The Ruskin College speech by James Callaghan in 1976 clearly articulated the need for a close partnership between educators and employers and an education system which would prepare young people for employment. Government policy in education and training over the next two decades would be driven by the need to produce the skilled workforce required to improve industrial performance in competition with overseas markets. This perspective crystallised with the advent of a new Tory government, under Margaret Thatcher, prepared to develop strong policies to propel a new vocationalism and market orientation into the education and training sector (Dale, 1985). There were severe skills shortages amongst the existing workforce, young people were leaving school without any qualifications and there was a lack of qualifications among the population at large. There was widespread growth in unemployment, due partly to the collapse of the manufacturing base, coupled with signs of social unrest, manifested for example in the youth riots of 1981. This combination of factors indicated the need for sweeping reform in vocational education and training, a reform that had to take into account not just the updating of skills of the existing workforce but the development of policies and initiatives which would address the qualifications shortfall and the growing numbers of the unemployed.

In the early 1980s the protagonists of FE staff development at national level were the Department of Education and Science, informing local authority action, and the Manpower Services Commission (MSC), created in 1981 and linked to the Department of Employment (DoE). The MSC was created for the purpose of transforming education and training, with FE being given a central role in the proposed transformation. This was to have substantial implications for the future development of FE teachers. Instead of the relatively stable and comfortable environment of the 1970s, FE staff were now faced with new types of programme initiated, and funded, by the MSC. These included the Youth Opportunities Programme, Youth Training Scheme and the Certificate of Pre-Vocational Education. These programmes were aimed mainly at a new type of student, who was unemployed or had not yet entered employment. The students were often unmotivated, sometimes disaffected, requiring a broader approach to teaching and learning encompassing social and life skills as well as narrow occupational skills (Broomhead and Coles, 1988). The challenge to teachers also encompassed the need to teach a far wider range of students, with many more mature adults attending courses and a greater provision for students with physical or learning disabilities. In a very short space of time, FE staff development was required to prepare and train staff to use different teaching and learning methods in order to motivate and engage the new types of student and to engage in creative processes of curriculum development, producing courses which would conform to MSC guidelines. As a result of these demands, subject staff, previously confined to their own subject disciplines, were required to work on a cross-college basis with colleagues from other disciplines (Chesson and Silverleaf, 1983). The increase in the number of part-time staff employed to deliver parts of these courses created an additional issue for staff development, which has continued to the present day.

Despite such wide ranging changes, initial teacher training for FE was not a government priority in the 1980s. The DES conference report on staff development estimated that about 45% of FE teachers had some kind of teaching qualification (DES, 1986a), but in this, as in subsequent attempts to quantify qualified teaching staff in FE (Martinez, 1994; FEFC, 1999), accurate data proved hard to elicit. However, there was little government commitment to explore the introduction of qualified teacher status for FE, and although Local Education Authorities (LEAs) did allocate funding for ITT, it was left to individual authorities to decide the appropriate balance between this and other types of staff development. With pressure from the DES and MSC to address immediate, short term demands, this decade saw a priority shift away from ITT to curriculum-led staff development. It also saw the creation of an embryonic framework of accountability for FE staff development activity linked, as perhaps might be expected, to funding requirements. LEAs, the main dispensaries for FE staff development funding, had been allocating funding often apparently on a fairly random basis, with the overall picture being of insufficient and inadequate provision (Foden, 1979). In 1986, DES circular 6/86 (DES, 1986b) introduced the Local Authority Grants Training Scheme which required LEAs to declare their in-service education and training policy across school and FE sectors, indicating priorities in the allocation of expenditure. Furthermore the MSC, with 5% of its budget allocated for staff development, required a cohesive planning, monitoring and evaluation system (MSC, 1989). This process of integration into a planning and monitoring framework was to be an increasingly defining characteristic of staff development in the 1990s.

The 1980s saw major changes in society at large with external pressures leading to a re-conceptualisation of how learning opportunities might be offered. The governmental impetus to increase skills and qualification levels was taking place within a political context where consumerist ideology and a belief in the efficacy of market forces prevailed (Ainley and Corney, 1990). It was also taking place within a social context where large-scale working communities such as the mining and the steel industries were being disbanded and employment for life was no longer the norm. As a result, individuals might expect to move between employment, unemployment and, where appropriate, a formal learning situation, during their adult lives. As it would not be possible, nor feasible, to attract everyone into formal education environments, another way needed to be found to increase qualification levels and to provide a framework for development. In the 1980s, and into the 1990s, government policy began to promote the view that learning takes place in a variety of different contexts, throughout the period of an individual's life. The concept of *lifelong learning* itself has received much critical attention (Coffield, 1999; Field and Leicester, 2000), however it is significant that learning is seen here as a continuum, occurring in formal and non-formal learning contexts and that the resulting individual achievements could be legitimised through some process of accreditation.

This viewpoint in one sense could be seen to represent a humanistic view of adult growth and development, using attributes of models of adult learning contemporary to that period (e.g. Knowles, 1984), experiential learning (Kolb, 1984) and *learner-centred learning* (Rogers, 1983), where an individual's continuing potential to learn and progress is acknowledged. Alternatively, it could also be seen as the construct of a society where ideas of 'community' have atrophied and social functioning is 'atomised' in the process of transition from a modernist to a post-modernist society (Morrison, 1998). The main characteristics of this society centre around an increased emphasis on difference and individuality, played out within a culture of consumerism and overt bureacratic control (Jameson, 1991, cited in Morrison, op.cit.). It could be argued that approaches to FE staff development from the 1980s onwards, as in the education sector as a whole, might encapsulate aspects of both these positions - the promotion of individual choice and responsibility for achievement, fixed within an externally-imposed framework, which delineates the nature of the choices which can be made.

A New Qualifications Framework

The term 'framework', suggesting both structure, cohesion and boundaries, is a term that reoccurs in the discourse of successive governments seeking to impose overarching systems onto different aspects of educational life. A key example of this was the establishment of the National Council for Vocational Qualifications (NCVQ) in 1986 with the task of rationalising the plethora of existing qualifications and providing a common framework which would offer a means of national comparability and transfer between different individual learning experiences. NCVQ was also responsible for the development and accreditation of national occupational standards, which would provide a benchmark for performance and achievement across all occupational sectors and form the basis of unitised National Vocational Qualifications (NVQs). NVQs, and later, General National Qualifications (GNVQs) were to form a large part of the work of FE, led by the requirement to meet government targets for increasing skills and qualification levels. The use of national standards and performance measurement, characteristic of the business environment, was to feature more strongly over the next decade in the approach to staff development. A significant feature here was the greater involvement of employers both in standard setting and in the delivery of staff development. In the case of ITT, where the FE college was the employer, this meant much greater college involvement in teaching on ITT courses which trained their own staff. However, the emphasis on short programmes of skills development for staff, prevalent at this time, concentrated more on specific types of curriculum development, for example the design and delivery of open learning materials.

In the 1980s the growth of student-centred learning and the introduction of modularised, flexible curricula were accompanied by new systems of assessment and accreditation. Although systems using continuous assessment against criteria were already in use, as in the Technical Education Council and Business Education Council qualifications introduced in the late 1970s, these ideas had been taken further. Systems of assessment which involved a continuous monitoring of performance with a focus on an individual's capacity to actually 'do the job' gained increased prominence in the latter part of the decade. The competency-based approach, prompted by NCVQ and articulated in practice through national occupational standards and NVQs, had been a source of controversy and debate within the field of education and training from its inception. However, many components of this approach have had a significant effect on staff development from the 1980s onwards, both in terms of development needs (FEU, 1986) and in terms of the methodology used. In particular, the use of national standards for teachers and trainers, to provide a framework for development and benchmarks for performance, has been a recurring theme in government policy since this time.

The idea that accreditation can occur based on experience, but without a formal course of study has other implications if linked to the use of standards. As they provide a means by which individual learning and achievement can be profiled against pre-determined competences, individual progression through different job roles increases the number and variety of competences which can be achieved. The idea of evidence being accumulated and recorded over a period of time links the competency initiative with concepts further developed in the 1990s such as *lifelong learning* and *continuing professional development* (CPD). The production of a portfolio of evidence, compiled by the individual showing how defined standards have been achieved, has been used as evidence of CPD for various professional bodies, for example in the United Kingdom Central Council for Nursing, Midwifery and Health Visiting (UKCC) Post-Registration Education and Practice file required to maintain membership of the professional body, and in the requirements for individual membership of the Institute for Learning and Teaching for Higher Education (ILT). In addition, the use of a competency-based approach which encourages the use of systematic needs analysis leading to action planning and monitoring of progress has increasingly been used to identify organisational as well as individual needs. This relates closely to the market-oriented business ethos being promoted within FE - an ethos based on organisational theory which emphasises goal-setting, planning, monitoring and evaluation in the pursuit of the elusive chimera of quality.

Quality Assurance Processes

In the 1980s the term *quality* became part of the discourse of government policy. Although industrial quality control systems such as BS5750 were used to a certain extent within the education sector, it was the philosophy of Total Quality Management (TQM) that became popular from the 1980s onwards. TQM is based on a service model that contains a number of key ideas: all employees are suppliers of services to customers, both internal and external; organisations are characterised by a shared vision led at the highest level of management; and systematic strategic and operational management is closely linked to target-setting and measurement of performance. The use of needs analysis to target staff development requirements, providing the first point in a systematic planning cycle, is congruent with the TQM philosophy and signalled an attempt to introduce a more integrated approach to the process of staff development. However in the 1980s, the means for obtaining the necessary information at local level was not without its problems. LEAs, in control of funding for staff development in colleges, had to preserve a distinction between meeting government priorities and addressing local needs. Although national priorities were identified and would drive funding for certain development initiatives, the mechanisms used by LEAs to assess FE staff development needs at local level were often inadequate in terms of providing the necessary information (DES, 1986a). It has also been suggested that different local authorities had different priorities which could be based on the preferences of a particular senior officer rather than any robust policy development (Stevens, 1988).

However there were certain consistent elements in national and local approaches to staff development activities in the 1980s. One was a reluctance to invest in long-term benefits for staff, an apparent lack of commitment to supporting a cohesive provision of professional training. In contrast, there was government, LEA and college employer support for more instrumental forms of staff development, in particular attendance on short skills-related courses which could produce more immediate results (DES, 1986b). This is not to say that there were not good examples of short course provision, such as those provided by LEAs at local teacher centres, the Further Education Unit (FEU) and the Further Education Staff College at Coombe Lodge, Bristol. These had the advantage of offering a relatively neutral forum where staff from different colleges could discuss and share ideas. One negative result of college incorporation in 1993 was the loss of these facilities for inter-college synergy and the resultant lack of opportunity for the growth of informal learning communities involving colleagues from different organisations.

Staff Development Post-Incorporation

The role of the LEAs in staff development was to further decrease following the 1988 Education Reform Act, which required extensive delegation of responsibility from LEAs to college governing bodies. The creation of Training and Enterprise Councils (TECs) in 1989 produced a different source of income and control for colleges at a local level and made the links between the FE college and the world of business far closer. This relationship was consolidated through the 1992 Further and Higher Education Act, which incorporated FE colleges and Higher Education Institutions into self governing bodies which included representatives from employers as governors. Colleges were to be run as competitive businesses, with business plans and the imperative to generate income. As the move towards local management of colleges occurred, so the relationship between staff development and line management increased. More financial accountability, a modularised curriculum which provided more flexibility but with a commensurate growth in support and guidance services, an increased use of student-centred resource-based-learning and developments in new technology - all these placed yet more demand on the skills of FE teachers. Staff development in the late 1980s had to address the need to train staff to fit a multiplicity of roles within an ever more complex teacher profile, whilst broadening its remit to include college support staff. By the time of incorporation in April 1993, colleges, like any other business organisation, were entirely responsible for the appraisal and training of their own staff, and the monitoring of staff performance became a feature of more tightly controlled, organisationally focused staff development.

This approach was compatible with monitoring structures at government level. The Further Education Funding Council (FEFC), the funding body established in 1993 to monitor performance of the FE sector, imposed a far tighter structure of financial accountability onto colleges. Within this framework, efficient management and deployment of staff were key factors. Curriculum audits which included staff skills were undertaken by some colleges, and other indications of the increased emphasis on quality control and quality assurance began to emerge. Ideas of 'efficiency' (the relationship of inputs to outcomes) and 'effectiveness' (the relationship of objectives to outcomes), coupled with performance indicators, had gained prominence in the mid-1980s in both FE and in HE (Audit Commission, 1985; FEU, 1989). FEFC's demand for value for money and a reduction in unit costs, together with the role of the TECs in agreeing college strategic plans meant that a tighter and more accountable operating framework was required of college organisation.

Within the organisational context of incorporation, a culture of performance management began to assume prominence, with the performance of individual staff under increasing documented scrutiny. One method of providing information to plan and monitor staff development was the use of appraisal systems. By 1987 the idea of appraisal, which had been on the agenda since 1973 (ACFHE/APC, 1973) was under serious discussion as a means of identifying staff development needs both at individual and at organisational level. College managers were being placed under increasing pressure to improve the performance of the college in meeting government priorities, with the veiled threat of increased intervention if they failed to do so. As Collings (1986) observes:

> [The] DES … makes it very clear that if educational institutions are not prepared to accept responsibility for evaluating and reporting what they are doing, others will do it for them. (Collings, 1986, p.19)

Anxieties about the purpose and processes of appraisal were reported at the time (Grindrod, 1987) and the tensions between government pressure on

FE, college management policies and individual staff fears and aspirations become apparent. Certainly, by the early 1990s most colleges had established a system of staff appraisal which linked into the strategic planning cycle at organisational, and where the organisational structure permitted, at departmental level. Appraisal and staff development were increasingly linked to a line management function which led to concerns about the extent to which appraisal was used supportively and developmentally as opposed to having a more direct 'policing' function (Grindrod op.cit.). This changing culture provoked strong criticism from some quarters, for example equating the new FE with Foucault's 'panopticon', the prison symbolising disciplinary power which functions through observation and surveillance, capturing the performance of individuals in an array of documents (Foucault, 1979, cited in Usher and Edwards, 1994). Certainly the increased bureaucracy that began to emerge in order to record auditable performance has been a feature of FE college management since the 1980s. However in spite of strong criticism of the culture of managerialism in FE, a paradox has been suggested - that increased accountability could have a democratising effect on the context and conditions under which professionals operate within the sector, in that these could be open to scrutiny and hence to debate (Avis, 1996). Robson (1998) to some extent supports this view, seeing areas of communality between managers and teachers which may benefit the profession as a whole.

The business-oriented culture, operating within a TQM model, had its effect on staff development within the college as college managers increasingly favoured a Human Resource Management (HRM) function which identifies staff as an organisation's major asset:

> HRM emphasises that employees are the primary resource for gaining sustainable competitive advantage, that human resource activites must be integrated with the corportate strategy, and that human resource specialists help organisational controllers to meet both efficiency and equity objectives.
>
> (Bratton and Gold, 1994, p.5)

In a number of instances, colleges created a separate Human Resource Unit, into which staff development and personnel functions were subsumed. In some cases, human resource managers were appointed from a business rather than an educational background. It has been suggested that this caused problems for college management and for teaching staff, as a result of the tension between the different cultures of business and education

(Elliott, 1996). Other tensions arose between the micro-cultures of different vocational specialisms within the college environment. An ageing population of teachers who began working in the 1970s under a regime of greater professional freedom were being placed in an enterprise culture which appeared to promote different values and priorities (Hall, 1990; Gray, 1991, cited in Faccenda, 1996). The introduction of new, more demanding contracts created an atmosphere of mistrust and anxiety, which was reinforced by large scale staff redundancies. This had a negative effect on the motivation to undertake the staff development necessary to meet rapidly changing demands, especially as this was seen to be directed purely to the fulfilment of organisational requirements; an approach which has been criticised elsewhere (Eraut, 1994; Castling, 1996; Huddlestone and Unwin, 1997).

National Standards for Training and Development

The Investors in People (IIP) award, introduced by the government in 1991, established a national 'ideal' organisational model of employee development in industry, business and settings such as education and health. The award was based on four major principles which explicitly linked individual development to the achievement of the employing organisation's objectives. The four principles were, in brief:

- a commitment by senior management to develop all staff
- identified targets for training and development
- action planning to train and develop staff throughout their employment
- sytems of monitoring and evaluating the impact of training and development on the organisation.

IIP is one example of how the government at this time was trying to promote the importance of cohesive staff development systems in all sectors of employment (Morrison, 1998). Despite management and financial responsibility being devolved to organisational level, the government was also trying to ensure a centralised control of standards and quality. The standards were nationally applied and the control of the award was through the local government-funded TEC which appointed the external assessors who would inspect participating institutions. It has been argued that the use of national occupational standards was a method by which central control could be exercised over disparate institutions. For example, as Kedney and Parkes suggest:

> Wherever we look we find centralisation occurring alongside deregulation; privatisation occurring alongside central government intervention alongside specific funding and short term schemes. (Kedney and Parkes, 1988, p.76)

Certainly, for FE, government policy on the introduction of national standards was to have a sizeable impact on the formation of staff development methodology within the sector. Of particular impact was the establishment of the Training and Development Lead Body (TDLB) in 1991, given the task of providing a series of nationally determined benchmarks in training and development to be used by employers and individual trainers. These national standards for Training and Development were intended to be used across all occupational areas, the idea being that the processes involved were generic and essentially independent of context. The first standards, published in 1991 were, predictably, closely allied with government policy, defining the key purpose of training and development as 'the development of human potential to enable individuals and organisations to meet their objectives'. The FEU reacted positively to the standards, suggesting that:

> national standards could provide a recognisable and nationally consistent means of describing the professionalism of staff, within job/person specifications and for the purpose of performance reviews, career planning and programmes of continuing professional development. (FEU, 1992, p.1)

These two quotes are significant, the first through the explicit linkage of individuals, organisations and objectives, the second through the reintroduction of a national perspective on the qualifications of the FE workforce and the strengthening of the debate on professionalism in FE.

This first draft of the standards was poorly received. On an operational level of detail, criticism focused on tortuously-expressed criteria, which used over-complicated and bureaucratic language to express relatively simple ideas and which even skilled practitioners found difficult to disentangle (Reid, Barrington, Kenney, 1992; Carroll, 1994). Objections at the philosophical level reflected wider concerns about competence-based approaches and focused on the positivistic and minimalist approach to the complex and subtle processes involved in teaching and learning which, it was argued, de-professionalised and de-skilled this area of work (Ashworth and Saxton, 1990; Chown and Last, 1993; Hyland, 1994). A recurring debate on different notions of professionalism and professional knowledge was to be a continuing feature over the next decade (Apple, 1993; Eraut, 1994; Robson, 1996) and paradoxically, it was at this time that the Department of Health and Social Security was actually raising the academic standards for nurse education, suggesting that good research-based practice should be informing the work of the nursing professional, rather than the development of practical skills without a robust and informed knowledge base (DHSS, 1991). The negative reception given by the post sixteen education sector to the TDLB standards and the NVQs formed from them was one of the reasons for a substantial review and revision in 1993.

The re-elected Conservative government used a range of approaches in their attempt to gain acceptance for the TDLB standards and the use of NVQs in the training and development of FE staff. One method was to engage the support of the FEU to promote the use of these standards through a series of conferences, workshops and a resulting publication *Standards in Action* (FEU, 1993). This attempted to show how the standards could be used by FE employers for organisational development, linking them closely to the HRM function, to provide benchmarks to be used in internal staff skill audits and also to the increasingly popular concept of the *learning organisation* (Pedlar et al., 1991). It is perhaps interesting to note that this is a different emphasis from the later standards for FE teachers, produced by the Further Education National Training Organisation (FENTO) which focus more on the national need to have a qualified teaching workforce in this sector.

Apart from the persuasive approach which sought to explain the organisational benefits of the standards, the government also introduced a compulsory component into its acceptance strategy. This was done by requiring that all those involved in the assessment of NVQs and the broader, more educational GNVQs, both core business for FE, achieve NVQ units in assessment from the Training and Development standards. Apart from attempting to impose national control over the quality of NVQs in general, this also suggested a strategy based on an incremental approach leading to gradual acceptance of the standards within the FE context. A survey of FE staff development priorities undertaken at this time (Martinez, 1994) indicates that the TDLB assessor awards (known often by their unit titles of D32 and D33) were second in priority only to management development in the colleges surveyed, and that there was a significant impetus for staff to become qualified. A later report by the FEFC placed assessor award training as the highest priority in the colleges inspected (FEFC, 1999). As staff went through the same kind of evidence gathering process and accreditation of 'performance on the job' as the students (or 'candidates') they were assessing, this also marked a particular experiential method of staff development which would, in theory, help staff understand and accept the different approach required by NVQs. The general unpopularity of these assessor awards may actually have had the opposite effect, with staff unenthusiastic and, in many cases, antagonistic to the experience.

The government pressure on the introduction of the TDLB standards introduced the threat for Higher Education Institutions offering Initial Teacher Training that colleges would use the NVQs to train their own staff without HE involvement. Attempts to ally existing programmes with TDLB standards were made by many higher education institutions offering the Certificate in Education and Postgraduate Certificate in Education. Some went wholeheartedly down the competence-based route and others developed systems of dual accreditation to meet, in particular, the demand for assessor units from the FE staff on their programmes. At this time City and Guilds also introduced a purely competence-based programme the 7306, based entirely on NVQ units in Training and Development, with the idea that this would eventually replace their popular basic teaching qualification, the 7307. Concerns were expressed about the direction being taken, with criticisms of the use of NVQs in professional development, a policy perceived as driven by ideology rather than research. Concerns identified included a potential loss of professional autonomy, an increase in centralised control and the limitations of development, being product and outcome-related rather than a process of growth and critical engagement (Childs, 1997; Bathmaker, 1999).

Another trend which emerges here, which relates to individual as opposed to organisational development is the notion of flexibility and potential for credit accumulation. This reflects what may be seen as the prevailing model of an individual career path - initial training, followed by the uptake of different learning opportunities as the occupational role expands or alters in response to external requirements (Jessup, 1990). The idea of continuing professional development had been in existence for a considerable amount of time and the use of NVQs or Credit Accumulation and Transfer Schemes by higher education institutions was seen as a means of accrediting in-house training and relevant professional experience. However CPD was now being linked into a framework of pre-defined standards, to be achieved at different stages in an individual's career. This was a pattern which was to recur generally in government policy towards teacher development in the 1990s, for example in the national standards for teachers defined in 1998 by the Teacher Training Agency, which identified competences required at different levels of the profession. Interestingly, as far back as 1974 doubts were expressed about the advisability of over-prescriptive routes for the professional development of teachers which would 'make inroads into the concept of teacher freedom and the right of professionals to choose the courses they wish to attend' (Cave, 1974, cited in FEU, 1992a, p.29).

Mapping of Roles in the FE Sector

The lack of enthusiasm for adoption of the TDLB standards as a vehicle for the development of FE staff led the government to explore means of gathering more information about the sector to determine whether FE required its own lead body. In 1995, the Further Education Development Association (FEDA), created by a merger of FEU and the Further Eduction Staff College, managed a project which undertook a major occupational map of the sector (DfEE, 1995). The mapping identified a number of trends including an increasing number of part-time staff and a wide range of support staff roles throughout the sector. It suggested that just under 50% of FE staff in England and Wales were qualified as teachers (and 67% in Scotland). It identified various types of CPD being undertaken, including assessor awards, specialist awards for basic skills and language teaching, a continued rise in management development and a variety of higher education awards. It also identified the increasingly competitive environment and the growth in customer entitlement. The mapping attempted to detail the number, nature and distribution of all occupations within the FE sector and attempted to provide a description of all roles and functions undertaken.

Following the results of the mapping, the National Training Organisation for Further Education (FENTO) was established. The national standards for FE (generally known as the FENTO standards) were developed through a process of consultations with key players; attitudes from some staff developers were more positive than with the TDLB standards (Martinez and Seymour, 1998). A particular point in their favour was that the FENTO standards did contain some reference to reflective practice and to underpinning values in professional practice, both missing from the TDLB standards. However there remained strong concerns from some quarters about the prevailing model being used i.e. a model which, although not exactly an NVQ, had to fit into the existing NVQ framework. Just as with TDLB, there were objections for operational reasons, such as the difficulty of teachers being able to achieve such a very large number of standards. More fundamentally, criticisms of this model related to epistemological concerns and the philosophical constraints of behaviourist models of teaching and learning (Petty, 1998) and the limitations of instrumental credentialism as opposed to universal transformation (Fevre, Rees and Gorard, 1999). There were also challenges by organisational theorists to the pervasive ethos of TQM, where commonality and prescribed 'vision' replace the fuzziness, divergence and contradictions necessary for growth and change (Pascale, 1990; Fullan, 1999).

Parallel Development in Other Sectors

In the mid 1990s the context for FE staff development continued to alter in the light of changes in government policy that resulted in a shift towards a more integrated framework for the education sector as a whole. This was intended to create a relatively seamless process of transition between the environments of school, college and university which previously had been relatively discrete in their scope and operation. In 1996 the government merged the Schools Curriculum and Assessment Authority (SCAA) and NCVQ to create a national body, the Qualifications and Curriculum Authority (QCA) overseeing academic and vocational qualifications for all but the university sector. The aim of this initiative was to develop more points of convergence between academic and vocational routes - a trend further continued with the more recent introduction of Curriculum 2000 in both schools and FE. These changes were influenced by reviews of the National Curriculum (Dearing, 1994) and of 16-19 qualifications (Dearing, 1996).

With the new curricula placing similar demands on staff from both sectors, staff development for schools and FE was showing substantial convergence. In a situation where the same qualifications were being taught and assessed, an increasing anomaly was the legal requirement for school teachers to have qualified teacher status, without any commensurate requirement that FE teachers should possess a professional teaching qualification. A general awareness of the need to prioritise improvements in the quality of teaching was revealed in various government documents. The Fryer Report on lifelong learning (Fryer, 1997) proposed the introduction of nationally recognised initial teacher training for FE, and the Kennedy report on widening participation (Kennedy, 1997) also identified the need for highly effective teachers. FEFC inspection policies on college self assessment also called for FE staff to be appropriately qualified and to be given opportunities for professional development. Major weaknesses in pedagogy were identified in the FEFC report of 1998/9; this report also promoted the use of national standards in the inspection process seing them as a means of improving the performance of individual teachers, by offering 'a way of addressing the persistent weaknesses identified through inspection' (FEFC, 1999, p.13).

The FENTO standards were launched in 1999 with the requirement that all providers of initial teacher training, both higher education institutions and awarding bodies such as City and Guilds, must incorporate these standards into their programmes; all programmes must be endorsed by FENTO or they will not be recognised by the new Department for Education and Skills (DfES). This parallels the control over school teacher training, where higher education programmes must provide evidence that the Teacher Training Agency (TTA) teacher competences are met in the HE programmes; provision must also be endorsed by the TTA. The English National Board for Nursing, Midwifery and Health Visiting (ENB) has the same function in relation to programmes related to nurse tutor education in England, which must meet standards developed through the UKCC (UKCC, 2000). From September 2001, there is a statutory requirement for full-time, fractional and part-time teachers new to FE to achieve a qualification meeting the FENTO standards, within a given timescale. The DfES will also fund existing unqualified staff to achieve these qualifications through matched funding from the FE Standards Fund, managed by the Learning and Skills Councils (LSCs), which at the time of writing are administering funding to promote and support FE staff development at national and local level. In keeping with current trends of accountability, performance measurement is integral to the operation of the LSCs themselves, being identified by external inspection grades and feedback from stakeholders and announced through the publication of league tables.

Staff Development for HE in FE

At this point, however, it is important to consider that the FENTO standards are not the only externally devised benchmark which currently drives FE staff development. Another influence, prompted by national policy on widening participation, has been the growth of HE provision in FE. By 1995, the Higher Education Funding Council had begun consultations on the direct funding of HE courses through FE colleges, which were seen as cheaper and offering local opportunities. With the introduction of tuition fees, which impacted on the financial capacity of students to study away from home, the role of FE in providing HE level courses has grown significantly. An issue here for FE staff has been the need to provide students studying HE courses in colleges with a comparable experience to those studying at a university with teaching informed by research. Subsequent government-backed initiatives such as the Higher Education Funding Council for England (HEFCE) funding to promote teaching and learning appropriate to HE and the FEDA (later Learning and Skills Development Agency) research network promoting a research culture in FE (Smithson, 2000) are currently attempting to address this issue. A major problem here, currently unresolved, is how FE staff, teaching on high class contact hours and over a wide range of levels, can find adequate time or support to develop their professional subject expertise to a standard expected of a teacher in a university. However, the current promotion of Foundation Degrees, offered in FE with the opportunity for students to complete a final year at University is an example of where FE and HE are working together on joint curriculum developments and where staff development can occur through a mutual understanding of different delivery and accreditation systems. Although debates on similar issues in teacher professionalism are occurring in HE as in FE (Light and Cox, 2001; Nicholls, 2001), there are many broad cultural differences between the two sectors, manifested, for example, in the differing systems of external quality assurance (Underwood and Connell, 2000). FE colleges offering HE programmes will have to accommodate both systems - subject review by the Quality Assurance Agency (QAA) as well as monitoring by the FE-related inspectorate. At the same time increased comparability between external quality assurance of schools and FE is almost certain to occur as the schools inspectorate, the Office for Standards of Teaching in Education (OFSTED), takes over from FEFC in inspecting FE provision. Staff development for beleaguered college staff may well have to focus on ensuring that the needs of all these external systems are met.

Convergence in aspects of curriculum development and inspection systems highlights some consistencies in government policies across the educational sector as a whole. Apart from curriculum convergence, this is also evident in the area of professional teacher accreditation for FE and HE. At the time when the FENTO standards were being developed, the Dearing report on HE (NCIHE, 1997) proposed the creation of the Institute for Learning and Teaching in Higher Education (ILT) to act as the professional body for teachers in HE. Unlike the large number of FENTO standards, membership of ILT is contingent on the ability to demonstrate achievement of a small number of broad-based standards. Following Dearing there is also a strong recommendation that all new staff teaching at a university should seek accreditation through a qualification which enables them to meet these standards. The effect of this on staff development in FE has, as a result, become even more confusing, with staff teaching in FE required to meet FENTO standards, staff teaching HE also expected to meet ILT standards, and, at present little integration between the two bodies. However, the approach to teacher accreditation in HE suggests a strategy based more on 'winning hearts and minds' both of individuals and institutions, than the more coercive nature of expectations for FE.

Conclusion

So to summarise, what is the current picture of staff development in FE? The FENTO workforce consultation (FENTO, 2001) identifies the current picture in the FE sector: with 12% of course managers and 28% of part-time staff having no form of teaching qualification. The age profile of the largest cohort of lecturers is in the 40 to 49 range, although redundancy and replacement in new skill areas is seeing an influx of younger staff into the sector. The main subject skills gaps reflected in the report are business development, research skills, information and learning technology and working with the disaffected; a significant growth in HE level work is also identified. There are now compulsory national standards for FE teachers, with QTS a strong possibility. There are externally imposed inspection systems with identified performance indicators operating within the competitive environment of published league tables. Staff development is linked closely to organisational needs and objectives, although evaluation of how this helps to meet objectives is still weak (Martinez, 1999). Continuing professional development may involve the achievement of further national standards, either FENTO or in another occupational area such as management. It may include accreditation for curriculum-led developments, probably by a body approved by QCA or QAA, or attendance on a formal programme of study usually at HE level. These HE programmes will themselves be subject to the QAA subject benchmarks and level descriptors. Evidence of CPD is likely to become a professional requirement and a professional body for FE, on a par with the General Teaching Council for school teachers or ILT for HE staff, is being considered.

It could be argued that many of the changes that have occurred in the last decade have finally improved the public perception of FE teachers, in that government funding is clearly supporting staff development for this sector in an unprecedented manner. There are also clearer expectations of what a teacher in FE should be able to achieve and a clearer public understanding of what the work entails. By making teaching qualifications a requirement to practice, it could also be said that the government has finally legitimised the professional status of the FE teacher and the importance of high quality teaching in a sector which has often been seen as the pedagogical poor relation of other educational sectors.

However, an alternative viewpoint to this optimistic vision may also be expressed, with criticism at both operational and philosophical levels. At an operational level, there has been a significant lack of consultation about how the standards from different educational sectors relate to each other. In other words, rationalisation through creating a sector specific framework for staff development has not been matched by rationalisation of the areas of overlap between sectors. As increased convergence of teaching and curriculum activity occurs, teaching staff may be forced to accommodate different sectoral requirements, adding to an already stressful and burdensome bureaucracy.

At a more philosophical level, the 'professional' status now accorded the FE teacher through prescribed standards and a framework for continuing professional development may represent a debased view of the notion of professionalism, where teaching professionals act in accordance with state requirements and under state control - a framework turned into prison bars - instead of engaging at a profound level with the synergy of personal and professional goals and values and with the subtleties of richer and more complex communities of practice.

References

ACFHE/APC (1973) *Report on Staff development in FE.* Association of Colleges of Further and Higher Education/Association of Principals of Colleges.

Ainley, P. and Corney, M. (1990) *Training for the Future: The Rise and Fall of the MSC.* London: Cassell.

Apple, M. (1993) *Official Knowledge: Democratic Education in a Conservative Age.* London: Routledge.

Ashworth, P.D. and Saxton, J. (1990) On 'Competence'. *Journal of Further and Higher Education* **14** (2), pp.3-25.

Audit Commission (1985) *Obtaining Better Value from Further Education.* London: HMSO.

Avis, J. (1996) The Enemy Within: Quality and Managerialism in Education. In Avis, J. et al. (Eds.) *Knowledge and Nationhood*, pp.105-120. London: Cassell.

Bathmaker, A.M. (1999) Managing messes and coping with uncertainty: Reviewing training for teachers in post-compulsory education and training. *Journal of Further and Higher Education* **23** (2), pp.185-195.

Bratton, J. and Gold, J. (1994) *Human Resource Development: Theory and Practice.* London: Macmillan.

Broomhead, S. and Coles, B. (1988) Youth Unemployment and the Growth of 'New Further Education'. In Coles, B. (Ed) *Young Careers: The Search for Jobs and the New Vocationalism* pp.164-180. Milton Keynes: Open University Press.

Carroll, S. (1994) National Standards for FE: An Update. *National Association for Staff Development Journal* **30**, pp.5-10.

Castling, A. (1996) The role of the staff development practitioner in the FE college. In Robson, J. (Ed.) *The Professional FE Teacher.* Aldershot: Avebury.

Chesson, J. and Silverleaf, J. (1983) *Inside Staff Development.* Windsor: NFER Nelson.

Childs, B. (1997) National Vocational Qualifications and the Professions: a long overdue debate. *National Association for Staff Development Journal* **36**, pp.13-22.

Chown, A. and Last, J. (1993) Can The NCVQ Model Be Used for Teacher Training? *Journal of Further and Higher Education* **17** (2), pp.15-26.

Coffield, F. (1999) *Breaking the Consensus: Lifelong Learning as Social Control.* Inaugural Lecture, University of Newcastle, Department of Education.

Collings, C. (1986) Appraisal Policy and Practice: Facing the Issues. *National Association for Staff Development Journal* **15,** pp.19-22.

Dale, R. (1985) Introduction. In Dale, R. (Ed) *Education, Training and Employment: Towards a New Vocationalism?* pp.1-7. Oxford: Pergamon Press.

Dearing, R. (1994) *Review of National Curriculum and its Assessment: Final Report.* London: Schools Curriculum and Assessment Authority.

Dearing, R. (1996) *Review of 16-19 Qualifications: Summary Report.* London: Schools Curriculum and Assessment Authority.

DES (1972) *Teacher Education and Training.* (James Report). London: HMSO.

DES (1986a) *The Way Ahead in Staff Development: Conference Report.* Bristol: Further Education Staff College.

DES (1986b) *Local Education Authorities Training Grants Scheme.* Circular 6/86. London: Department for Education and Science.

DfEE (1995) *Mapping the FE Sector.* London: Department for Education and Employment.

DfEE (1998) *Teaching: High Status, High Standards.* Circular 4/98 London: Department for Education and Employment.

DHSS (1991) *A Strategy for Nursing, Midwifery and Health Visiting in Northern Ireland.* Belfast: Department for Health and Social Security.

Elliott, G. (1996) Educational Management and The Crisis of Reform in Further Education. *Journal of Vocational Education and Training* **48** (1), pp.5-23.

Eraut, M. (1994) *Developing Professional Knowledge and Competence.* London: Falmer Press.

Faccenda, J. (1996) Human Resource Management: The Case 'For' and 'Against' in FE. *National Association for Staff Development Journal* **35**, pp.13-17.

FEFC (1999) *Professional Development in Further Education: National Report from the Inspectorate 1998/99.* Coventry: Further Education Funding Council.

FENTO (2001) *Further Education Sector: Workforce Development Plan: Consultation Version.* London: Further Education National Training Organisation.

FEU (1986) *Investing in Change: an appraisal of staff development needs for the delivery of modernised occupational training.* London: Further Education Unit.

FEU (1989) *Towards an Educational Audit.* London: Further Education Unit.

FEU (1992a) *Teaching Skills.* London: Further Education Unit.

FEU (1992b) *TDLB Standards in FE.* London: Further Education Unit.

FEU (1993) *Standards in Action.* London: Further Education Unit.

Fevre, R., Rees, G. and Gorard, S. (1999) Some Sociological Alternatives to Human Capital Theory and Their Implications for Post-Compulsory Education and Training. *Journal of Education and Work* **12** (2), pp.117-139.

Field, J. and Leicester, M. (2000) Introduction: Lifelong Learning or Permanent Schooling? In Field, J. and Leicester, M. (Eds.) *Lifelong Learning: Education Across the Lifespan*, pp.16-19. London: Routledge/Falmer.

Foden, F. (1979) Making Staff Development Work. *National Association for Staff Development Journal* **2**, p.1.

Foucault, M. (1979) *Discipline and Punish: The Birth of the Prison.* Harmondsworth: Penguin.

Fryer, R. H. (1997) *Learning for the Twenty-First Century.* First Report of the National Advisory Group for Continuing Education and Lifelong Learning. Sheffield: NAGCELL.

Fullan, M. (1999) *Change Forces: The Sequel.* London: Falmer Press.

Gray, L. (1991) *Managing Colleges in a Changing World.* Bristol: Further Education Staff College.

Grindrod, B. (1987) Appraisal - The FE Way. *National Association for Staff Development Journal* **17**, pp.3-9.

Hall, V. (1990) *Maintained Further Education in the United Kingdom.* Bristol: Further Education Staff College.

Harding, P. and Scott, G. (1980) Staff Development in Colleges of Further Education: some organisational considerations. *National Association for Staff Development Journal* **4**, pp.8-13.

Huddlestone, P. and Unwin, L. (1997) *Teaching and Learning in Further Education: diversity and change.* London: Routledge.

Hyland, T. (1994) *Competence, Education and NVQs: dissenting perspectives.* London: Cassell.

Jameson, F. (1991) *Postmodernism or the Cultural Logic of Late Capitalism.* London: Verso.

Jessup, G. (1990) NVQs: Implications for FE. In Bees, M. and Swords, M. (Eds.) *NVQs and Further Education.* London: Kogan Page.

Kedney, R. and Parkes. D. (1988) (Eds.) *Planning the FE Curriculum.* London: Further Education Unit.

Kennedy, H. (1997) *Learning Works: Widening Participation in Further Education.* Coventry: Further Education Funding Council.

Knowles, M. (1984) *The Adult Learner: A Neglected Species*. Houston: Gulf Publishing.

Kolb, D.A. (1984) *Experiential Learning: Experience as a Source of Learning and Development.* New Jersey: Prentice-Hall.

Light, G. and Cox, R. (2001) *Learning and Teaching in Higher Education: The Reflective Professional.* London: Paul Chapman.

Martinez, P. (1994) Staff development in the FE Sector. *National Association for Staff Development Journal* **31**, pp.3-9.

Martinez, P. (1999) *Staff Development in Transition*. London: FEDA.

Martinez, P. and Seymour, J. (1998) Editorial. *National Association for Staff Development Journal* **3**, p.3.

Morrison, K. (1998) *Management Theories for Educational Change.* London: Paul Chapman/Sage.

MSC (1989) *Work-Related Further Education Development Fund: Guidance for Local Authority Applicants.* Sheffield: Manpower Services Commission.

National Committee for Inquiry into Higher Education (NCIHE) (1997) *Higher Education for a Learning Society* (The Dearing Report). London: HMSO.

Nicholls, G. (2001) *Professional Development in Higher Education: new dimensions and directions.* London: Kogan Page.

Pascale, R. (1990) *Managing on the Edge.* London: Penguin.

Pedlar, M., Burgoyne, J. and Boydell, T. (1991) *The Learning Organisation: a strategy for sustainable development.* London: McGraw-Hill.

Petty, G. (1998) Standards or Striving? *National Association for Staff Development Journal* **39**, pp.18-21.

Reid, M., Barrington, H. and Kenney, J. (1992) *Training Interventions: Managing Employee Development.* Melksham: Cromwell Press.

Robson, J. (1996). *The Professional FE Teacher.* Aldeshot: Avebury.

Robson, J. (1998) A Profession in Crisis: Status, Culture and Identity in the Further Education College. *Journal of Vocational Education and Training* **50** (4), pp.585-607.

Rogers, C. (1983) *Freedom to Learn for the 80's*. Columbus: Charles E. Merrill.

Smithson, T. (2000) Development of a Research Culture. *FEDA College Research* **3** (13), pp.19-20.

Stevens, D (1988) Policy Statements in the Management of Staff Development for FE Teachers. *National Association for Staff Development Journal* **19**, pp. 7-12.

UKCC (2000) *Standards for the Preparation of Teachers of Midwifery, Nursing and Health Visiting*. London: United Kingdom Central Council for Midwifery, Nursing and Health Visiting.

Underwood, S. and Connell, P. (2000) *Through the Looking Glass - FE Colleges, HE Inspection Systems.* London: FEDA.

Usher, R. and Edwards, R. (1994) *Examining the Case: Competences and Management in Postmodernism and Education.* London: Routledge.

8 School Needs, Teachers' Personal Needs and the Set Agenda: Conflict and Challenges

STEVE BELBIN AND HELEN SWIFT

Introduction

Within educational establishments there has always been the need to keep abreast of change, subject knowledge and the most effective ways of teaching. All schools have a delegated training budget that increases year upon year. The name changes (GEST, Standards Fund, School Improvement Grant), and the fences that are placed around it to prevent schools from either (depending on your point of view) raiding it or re-cycling it grow ever higher. Equally, the number of people who are intended to benefit from it increases. One thing is certain; under the current Government, the training grant will continue to increase as schools are funded directly. But the demands on the grant will match this growth as the flood of new initiatives continues.

Within this funding, schools have to identify their needs and priorities and spend the money wisely. Deciding whether the priorities should be those of the whole school or reflect the needs of the individual teacher can create internal tensions. How do you decide whether Mr. Chips, recently identified by OFSTED as needing help with his classroom organisation, should have priority over Miss Gofar, who is an aspiring teacher urgently wishing to go on a management course? At the same time, all staff need training in Information and Communications Technology, and there is not the money to do all three.

This is an interesting dilemma within school management that is certain to grow in importance over the next few years particularly as Performance Management is implemented. The two key issues that this chapter will be attempting to address are (a) how schools are influenced when identifying training needs, and (b) how schools balance these influences in view of the role that the government is taking in setting the educational agenda for schools. These will be discussed with special reference to primary schools.

Training for Staff

On that rare occasion when you wish to go to the bank early, you are bound to be delayed by a polite notice informing you that the branch is closed until 9.30 for staff training. Training for employees in any walk of life is an accepted and expected part of any job, and teachers are no different.

Within the school where one of the authors is Head, we have noticed a swing away from continual criticism about training. From interviews and surveys conducted as part of our annual review, we believe that the majority of parents would agree that teachers need to be trained and are sympathetic to the huge changes the teaching profession has had to absorb in recent years. Most accept the need for teachers to be absent for the occasional day-course. Long-term courses that require a colleague to be out of class several times a week remain unpopular because of the perceived disruption to their child's education.

Training for staff takes several forms. It might include courses run by the Local Education Authority (LEA) or another provider such as a college or university. Training may be in-house, perhaps involving a senior member of staff, during school time, or in twilight meetings or on the training days that each school has.

Training for teaching staff has moved on considerably over the last 15 years or so. The establishment of Training Days by Kenneth Baker when he was Secretary of State for Education was a structural change that has made a significant difference. From having very amateurish and haphazard origins, schools now run their own training days, thereby developing their own training materials, methods and expertise. This growth in expertise is echoed elsewhere. The effective LEA will also provide a comprehensive programme of training opportunities that can be used to support all members of the teaching establishment. Most institutions of Higher Education now offer courses of study which lead to higher degrees, such as Master's programmes or Educational doctorates.

All recent governments have given credence to a particular view of school effectiveness which influences professional development:

> School effectiveness is directly tied into the National Curriculum since the effectiveness is predominately judged in accordance with criteria derived from

> it, mediated through league tables and the performance indicators of OFSTED inspection reports. Concomitantly teacher education, professional development and quality teaching are to be interpreted vis-à-vis such 'effectivity'.
>
> (Hexhall and Mahoney, 1998, p.131)

The current Government recognises the importance of effective training for all teachers, from the Newly Qualified Teacher (NQT) stage through to support for teachers in leadership roles. It has proved its commitment by funding the necessary training for its new initiatives, by supporting NQTs through the Standards Fund budget and by setting up the new College of Headship (at a cost of £10 million). Part of the General Teaching Council's role will be to promote professional development. The Department for Education and Skills (DfES) has launched a raft of funding streams to support teachers with professional development. These range from Best Practice Research Scholarships which allow teachers to bid for money to undertake a small action research project in schools, early professional development which aims to support teachers in the second and third years of their careers, and is currently being piloted, to International Professional Development which gives teachers and other professionals opportunities to undertake short study visits or exchanges to learn from excellent practice in other countries.

There is a wealth of training opportunities for schools to choose from. A significant proportion of the mail every school receives each week concerns training. Competition between providers is intense. The annual budget for training has risen dramatically, amounting to, for example, £20,000 for large primary schools. Of course it needs no brilliant observer of primary education to note that the list of identified training needs (i.e. what you can spend the money on) has grown considerably, even though, at the same time, generic professional targets have become very explicit.

Most teachers will need help with some aspect of their teaching at some stage of their career. LEA and other providers have always promoted basic courses on aspects of teaching, such as classroom management, or subject knowledge, and there are always members of staff who need further development in these areas. Before the school effectiveness agenda was adopted by central government, training needs were likely to be individually based. After the Education Reform Act there was suddenly a more proactive involvement of the Government in staff development, which has added a third dimension to aspects of training. This involvement is becoming more direct as the recent Literacy and Numeracy initiatives and the introduction of Performance Management demonstrate. There is obvious potential here for conflict between the different training dimensions. At what point should the needs that have been identified by a school become secondary to those imposed from the Government? The skill lies in the effective management of the staff development budget, in order that it may achieve its function in a cost-effective manner. This major responsibility makes the careful identification of training needs vital for all schools.

Perhaps the crucial factor in the new decision-making process is the link between the headteacher making autonomous decisions and the strong sense of accountability. With the extending of central funding into schools and more delegation of responsibility, the role of the head teacher is extending to allow them the autonomy to manage and appropriate resources to meet the School Development Plan targets and priorities. Blandford (2000) believes that:

> the best heads have leadership skills comparable to those of the best leaders in any other sector, including business. (Blandford, 2000, p.117)

Blandford goes on to describe the key expectations of the government regarding the head teacher role:

> It believes that every school needs a leader to create a sense of purpose and direction, to set high expectations of staff and pupils, focus on improving teaching and learning, monitor performance and motivate the staff to give of their best. (ibid.)

Training Needs: the road to school effectiveness

Morley et al. (1999) believe that:

> School effectiveness depicts a transition from a monopolistic to a competitive mode of production in education. Rather than a flexible system suggested by the 'notion' of the 'free market', schools and other public service organisations are to be run like rationally structured machines. (Morley et al., 1999, p.63)

They go on to suggest that the profession is allowing the body politic to decide the priorities that a school should have for its training needs. In the actual experience of most heads, deciding the priorities is a very difficult balancing process that depends on the situation within the individual school. They state that the new emphases in place in schools are:

> classroom action research, classroom observation, team teaching, demonstration of good classroom practice, staff conferencing on individual pupils, monitoring pupils' work and analysis of pupil outcome data.
>
> (Morley et al., 1999, p.90)

So far three main categories of training need have been identified: individual, school and government-led. Every school is different, with so many variables, which may give an almost three-dimensional nature to problem solving. Let us imagine that a given school has identified several major priorities for the forthcoming year:

Figure 8.1 Balancing school development priorities

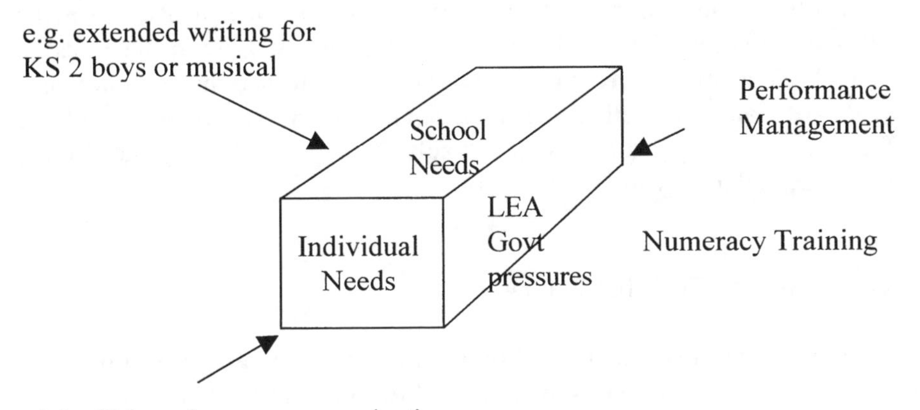

The school management has to place these training needs in some form of priority. They have to decide which are whole-school issues and which are relevant to individual members of staff only. If there are constraints on available time and finances, there is room for conflict to arise. Where the desires of individual members of staff are necessarily put on hold, the conflict may be long lasting and potentially damaging. There will be some issues that have a greater influence, and which face all schools:

- when the last inspection was; its success or otherwise, key issues for action
- the outcomes of Performance Management
- the age and experience of the staff
- the strengths and weaknesses in the curriculum provided
- the aspirations of individual staff
- the philosophy of the leadership and the ethos they are trying to develop.

The list is not exhaustive and at this point the reader will probably note other training needs that have been missed, or wish to place the above in a different order. This is exactly the point. Each school is pretty much unique. While training needs may be the same or similar in some areas, in others there will be marked differences. Furthermore, each school is at a different stage on the road to school effectiveness. The judgement of the senior managers will depend on their interpretation of what constitutes school effectiveness, and what they feel the school needs to do to make itself more effective. The quality of these decisions will in turn be assessed by OFSTED or other accredited assessors. They will use their opinion as a part determinant of whether the management of the school is considered effective. Increasingly the agenda is likely to be prescribed by outside the school, particularly by the government.

Identification of Training Priorities

It is obvious that, even with a training budget that has grown significantly in recent years, there remains the potential for disagreement within a school about how it should be distributed. Everard and Morris (1996) consider that schools should:

> recognise that there are different kinds of priority, and the different categories have to be treated differently. The critical distinction is between what is urgent and what is important. (Everard and Morris, 1996, p.112)

It is essential that primary schools have some form of rational policy for determining which areas should receive a higher priority than others. Recent years have seen primary schools develop a strategic plan that maps out their direction over the next few years. Known as the School

Development (or Management) Plan, it refers to its curriculum, staffing, budget and building needs. Staff training needs should reflect these priorities.

To avoid the School Development Plan gathering dust in colleagues' in-trays, all of these connected with the school, both teaching and non-teaching staff, should be involved in setting these priorities. This process has benefits for all. The staff will feel that they are being listened to and that their views are being taken into account, and as a consequence are more likely to have shared ownership of the outcomes, as well as being better able to set their own development needs into the context of the whole school. The senior management team are more likely to gather a true 'warts and all' picture of the current situation in the school. The outcomes may not be those anticipated or welcomed by senior management, but should nevertheless be addressed. There are several management tools available to facilitate this process, such as the self-evaluation materials from OFSTED, which have been found effective by some schools.

It is argued that involvement in school evaluation and review should be extended to Governors, parents and children. Having gathered these additional opinions, school managers would need to balance these against (or alongside) the development needs already identified from the school strategic plan, individual development needs from performance reviews, and of course any new initiatives introduced by the Government. It is at this stage that the management of a school really earn those extra responsibility points they have negotiated with the Governing Body!

Handling the demands on the training budget and effective utilisation of the time available requires some guiding principles, which should be open and transparent for all to see. It is considered that there are three main principles, set out here in order or priority:

- the needs of the school
- the needs of the individual
- requirements from Government (only in third place because everyone knows we have to do it anyway).

Ultimately, the Standards Fund budget is given to each school to give the children the opportunity to achieve the highest possible levels of attainment. All staff must have the necessary skills to enable them to do this. Laudable sentiments perhaps, but this should be the very essence of every school's aims or mission statement. The first guiding principle should be the needs of the whole school. If a school has just had a poor OFSTED report, perhaps containing criticisms of teaching methods or standards of attainment, the training budget should be prioritised to support these. If a whole-school need to develop Information and Communication Technology capability has been an identified, then the fund should support this. It is only when these major issues are judged, by the school and outside agencies, to be satisfactory or above, that attention (and the staff development budget) can turn to more individual needs.

The recent implementation of Performance Management can be interpreted as reinforcing this view. The target-setting process includes a meeting where the individual teacher's objectives and training needs are set 'within the context of the school's priorities' (DfEE, 2000).

At this point it seems appropriate to consider two practical examples, based loosely on experience as headteacher. Both are large primary schools situated in the heart of a northern city. The examples demonstrate the range of training needs and are broken down into a profile of the school, staff and individual training needs.

Example 1: Bridgewater North

Profile: Popular, with a queue of parents wishing to send their children there, it had a static, well-established staff. A poor OFSTED report came as a shock to many of the major stakeholders. Teaching and standards of attainment were judged unsatisfactory in nearly all subjects; classroom management was criticised, as was the management of the school. As a result, the school roll started to fall.

Staff training needs: In these circumstances, the temptation is to attempt to do everything at once. This should be avoided, despite the likely pressure from the LEA, Governors and particularly parents. In many ways it is a case of starting with the basics: planning, teaching and assessment. The Action Plan the school is required to submit needs to outline, step-by-step, a programme of training that attempts to resolve the criticisms. Although the current emphasis on Literacy and Numeracy may appear to be an unnecessary distraction, this can actually help the process as the framework they contain can provide a blueprint for other subjects, which may provide support and a structure for colleagues. All LEAs have appointed personnel who can help with development needs related to planning, teaching and assessment.

Individual training needs: It is after this first cycle of whole school training that account can be taken of individual needs. While direct involvement of the senior management team is required for improving school performance, at some stage there is a need to develop the skills of those who are leading in subject areas. Colleagues need to take charge of and responsibility for their own subjects, and this is likely to require an element of training. It is only through the sharing of responsibility 'outwards' and 'downwards' that a school can develop a shared, collective responsibility for children's attainment and achievement.

Example 2: Northwater Bridge

Profile: Sited just a few miles away, this school was not quite so popular, although the number on roll remained quite high. The staff at this school were justifiably proud of their achievement, and the progress the school had made over a number of years. There was a regular turnover of staff. After a reasonably successful inspection, standards were felt to be in-line or above national norms. There was one key issue to address, arising from the inspection, that involved the whole staff. Other development issues were connected to national initiatives such as computer provision and standards of attainment.

Staff training needs: The School Action Plan has as its main priority the need to raise standards of attainment among children (and staff) in Information and Communications Technology. It is also recognised that other whole school issues remain, such as Literacy and Numeracy, but the staff development needs here are more individualised. The training budget is therefore used to support newly appointed curriculum co-ordinators, and to develop teachers who have aspirations for leadership.

Individual training needs: A need to develop individual staff, in foundation subjects such as music and art, has been identified. Thus staff development provision is able to move away from the concentration on whole school issues that has been necessary for the last few years.

These two case studies show that schools can have differing development opportunities and needs at different times. In these examples, it was decided that the whole-school issues, addressing school effectiveness, pupil achievement and attainment should be given first priority. Once these areas are secured, then the move can be made to equip colleagues to take responsibility for their own subjects or managerial roles. Thus schools go through cycles in their training needs. Regardless of whether there is a regular turnover of staff, it is always necessary to revisit a number of areas connected to teaching, both related to subjects and also to aspects such as teaching styles and behaviour management. This 'traditional' cycle has become modified by the government-led drive to raise standards, and so it is to this issue that we now turn.

Raising Standards

The drive to raise standards in schools has created an interesting challenge. Every school (and indeed every LEA) has been given targets to achieve in the core subjects. Fielding (1999) argues that:

> At its best then, target setting is potentially and pre-eminently a means of helping us actually achieve what we aspire to, holding us to account to ourselves and others, and doing so in a way that is entirely consistent with democratic values; it democratises achievement in the sense that it makes achievement possible for all and visible to all. (Fielding, 1999, p.279)

All those connected to primary education will agree with the principle of enabling each child to reach the highest possible levels of attainment. This concentration on core subjects, however has resulted in a potential neglect of other subjects. It has had an impact on subject training programmes as well as the amount of time devoted to the various subjects in the classroom. In terms of time allocation, staff training must respond to the new initiatives flowing from the Department for Education and Skills, but not lose sight of the other aspects. This balance is difficult to maintain, and is further compounded by the introduction of performance indicators. Gray and Wilcox (1995) argue that:

> The case for the introduction of performance indicators flows from the model of the school that is implicit in government education policy. This seeks to

> describe schools in terms that refer directly to their 'performance' or 'effectiveness'.
> (Gray and Wilcox, 1995, p.70)

The inevitable consequence of this process is to make the government's agenda stronger and a balanced view of training needs more difficult to achieve.

Skill or Professional Development?

The emphasis on core subjects, the drive to raise standards and the Literacy and Numeracy strategies have had a major impact on how schools spend their training budget. The materials from the recent Hay McBer research (DfEE, 2000), which have shaped the Leadership Programme for Serving Heads Model for Organisational Effectiveness, offers a way forward. The research suggests that the most successful heads make a difference by using a wide range of professional skills and abilities to create learning environments which foster pupil progress:

> Outstanding teachers create an excellent classroom climate and achieve superior pupil progress largely by displaying more professional characteristics at higher levels of sophistication within a very structured learning environment.
> (DfEE, 2000, section 1.1.9)

The challenge for current school managers and others involved in professional development is to guide the professional and personal development of all staff towards such a sophisticated understanding of effective learning environments.

For effective leadership, Hay McBer list a number of skills, characteristics and attributes that headteachers should ideally possess. They place the greatest emphasis on 'attributes', but suggest that the most successful heads will exhibit the majority of characteristics in each category. In guiding the development of future leaders, one way forward is to concentrate on the development of these competencies and characteristics. There may well be a considerable difference between the knowledge and understanding considered to be desirable and the skills, competencies and characteristics currently being demonstrated by heads.

Similarly, training on more generic issues of teaching could focus on the same characteristics and competencies of successful teachers. Such skills could and should be transferable between subjects. Such issues as assessment, differentiation and classroom management could be approached through perhaps one subject, at the same time stressing the inter-relationship with other subjects and aspects of teaching.

A New Influence: the needs of all school staff

Recent years have seen an increase in the total number of employees in most schools, taking each establishment beyond the notion of one class, one teacher. These include teaching assistants (either for specific children or groups of youngsters), maintenance and secretarial staff. Even the smallest schools have more assistants in than ever before. When the first training budgets were delegated to schools, only the most enlightened leaders saw the need to include all members of staff, not just the teachers, in the training and development process. The main restriction then was the limited budget and the lack of any relevant courses provided by the LEAs or other trainers. The need to provide training for these valuable members of staff is a matter of urgency, particularly as their job requirements have grown markedly. No longer do we require non-teaching assistants to just sharpen pencils and tidy the art corner. Now each has a detailed job description that involves them working with groups of children on aspects of literacy and numeracy, following plans developed by the teaching staff. In this age of national and school targets, these involve all classes, and therefore all staff.

Conclusion

Gray and Wilcox (1995) argue that:

> the national and international press towards 'raising achievement' is something that can engage the professional commitment of teachers. It is potentially a powerful enough rallying cry to allow schools to review their routine ways of going about things.
>
> (Gray and Wilcox, 1995, p.258)

However, there appears to be no firm model that can be applied to all schools. A school is a complex institution that is continually developing, shaping up to meet the new challenges and opportunities that are presented each year. The guiding principle for school management must be to provide strong leadership within a climate of democracy. There is a need to develop all individuals to their full potential, to help those with aspirations for leadership as well as those whose future remains in the classroom. There is a need to help those who are confident in identifying their own development needs and coming forward for In-Service Education and Training (INSET) opportunities, as well as those who must be encouraged to do so. In this chapter, the case has been made for priority to be given to the school's needs, where the institutional picture takes precedence. The acceptance of this by all staff depends on how successful the management has been in involving all those involved in the school in the decision-making processes.

References

Blandford, S. (2000) *Managing Professional Development in Schools*. London: Routledge.

DfEE (2000) *Research into Teacher Effectiveness: A Model of Teacher Effectiveness*. Report by Hay McBer to the Department for Education and Employment. London: DfEE.

Everard, K.B. and Morris, G. (1996) *Effective School Management* (3rd Ed). London: Paul Chapman Publishing.

Fielding, M. (1999) Target Setting, Policy Pathology and Student Perspectives: learning to labour in new times. *Cambridge Journal of Education* **29** (2), pp.277-287.

Gray, J. and Wilcox, B. (1995) *Good School, Bad School: Evaluating performance and encouraging improvement.* Buckingham: Open University Press.

Harris, A., Bennett, N. and Preedy, M. (1997) *Introduction: organizational effectiveness and improvement.* In Harris, A., Bennett, N. and Preedy, M. (Eds.) *Organizational effectiveness and improvement in education.* Buckingham: Open University Press.

Hexhall, I. and Mahoney, P. (1998) Effective Teachers for Effective Schools. In Slee, R., Weiner, G., with Tomlinson, S. (Eds.) *School Effectiveness for Whom? Challenges to the School Effectiveness and Improvement Movements.* London: Falmer Press.

Morley, L. and Rassool, N. (1999) *School Effectiveness - Fracturing the Discourse.* London: Falmer Press.

9 Complexity, Creativity and Personal Development in Headship

ADRIAN RAYNOR

Introduction

> Every few hundred years throughout Western history a sharp transformation has occurred. In a matter of decades, society altogether rearranges itself - its worldview; its basic values; its social and political structure; its arts, its key institutions. Fifty years later, a new world exists ... Our age is such a period of transformation. (Drucker, 1992, p.95)

Drucker's perception of a paradigm shift is shown in the rise of the 'knowledge industries' and the realisation by governments that survival in world competition depends on producing an educated workforce, with a consequent emphasis on developing schools and learning. Contingent upon this perception is the need to develop teachers and heads, the leadership qualities of the latter being seen as central to school effectiveness (e.g. Mortimore et al., 1988; DfEE, 1997). Consequently, management learning for heads has developed strongly, and is about to become a compulsory requirement for aspiring heads. In this chapter I consider the balance between institutionally-driven development and personal development of heads and staff, drawing largely on my research into headship, using interviews and case studies over a three year period to 1998 (Raynor, 2000).

Institutional and Personal Learning

By institutional development I refer to that based on the perceived needs of the organisation, typically involving initiatives designed to develop the organisation as a whole, and generally based on top-down decisions about what those needs are. It relies, then, on intervention at an organisational level, through organisation-wide initiatives to which individuals conform. A second manifestation derives from this, and involves the training of individuals in those skills and techniques seen, at institutional level, as necessary for pursuing its aims.

Personal development differs from this in two respects. First, it may involve development of more fundamental abilities that are not specific techniques identified for the purpose of working practice within the organisation, but which would be useful to the individual in a variety of situations. Such generalised skills are sometimes referred to as meta-abilities. Butcher et al. (1997) identify four such meta-abilities: cognitive skills, self-knowledge, emotional resilience and personal drive. They believe that personal development in such meta-abilities is a fundamental basis for organisational development, and demonstrates the difference between training and development, the later demanding increasing self-knowledge and improvement of meta-abilities. Such development, then, encourages versatile, thinking professionals. However, even though this is personal development, it is clearly aligned with organisational development.

A second approach is one that follows the interests of the individual, where the learning involved has no apparent direct bearing on the work to be performed. At first sight, such development would seem irrelevant to organisational needs, but the consequent width of expertise and experience can increase the capacity for change in the organisation, since the individual acquires the ability to see things in a fresh light, using different metaphors to frame experience. I will argue later that the heterogeneity of thinking that this can produce is an important factor in developing creative schools. The two types of development, institutional and personal, can be seen to form a continuum, rather than being mutually exclusive.

The institutional approach to development as described above has been a feature of the education system in England over a number of years, where concepts of 'best practice' have been generalised into approaches to teaching - seen, for example, in the centrally determined numeracy and literacy strategies and, more subtly, in the inspection criteria for judging good teaching (OFSTED, 1995). Indeed, the degree to which the OFSTED model has become standard practice is shown in the statement that school self-evaluation 'should be based on the OFSTED model' (OFSTED, 1998). The approach is also seen in management training for headteachers, where a set of institutionally approved management techniques and standards underpins the training of aspiring, new and practising heads (DfEE, 1999). Although many underlying skills are recognised in the standards for the National Professional Qualification for Headteachers (NPQH), they are not specifically developed, though expected to be used. Whilst *in theory* aspiring heads could seek alternative training in management, the fact that the NPQH qualification is to become mandatory for headship effectively restricts those options. The result is a tendency towards a standardised practice of headship.

Institutional development is also apparent in the performance management systems that schools are required to operate from September 2000. These are based on the setting of annual and professional development objectives for heads and teachers. Although these include reference to the teacher's career aspirations, it is stressed that 'objectives must always relate to the situation in the school' ... and 'Headteachers and team leaders will need to decide how individual objectives relate to school-level planning' (DfEE, 2000, p.14).

In bureaucratic organisations, a greater emphasis on institutional development may be appropriate, whilst in learning organisations (Senge, 1990), personal and institutional developments may become synonymous phenomena, where the learning capacity of the organisation is enhanced by the personal development of its people. Thus neither is intrinsically right or wrong, but dependent on context, and the maintenance of an appropriate balance between the two. If all development in schools is at the whim of individuals, it will be difficult to align with organisational needs; if it is too top-down, it will be too controlling and will inhibit creative responses at individual and group levels.

Three factors, then, can be seen to affect the balance between institutional and personal learning:

- The nature of the organisation and the degree of autonomy expected of individuals within it.
- The need for creativity within the organisation.
- The complexity individuals face in their work.

Clearly these factors are interrelated, but for simplicity I will consider each separately as it applies to schools.

The Organisational Nature of Schools

A central issue, then, is the way the school is, or should be, perceived as an organisation. Should it, for example, be seen as a mechanistic organisation, in which:

> The new and revolutionary doctrine of scientific management states in no uncertain terms that the management, the supervisory staff, has the largest share of the work in the determination of the proper methods. The burden of finding the best methods is too large and too complicated to be laid on the shoulders of the teachers. (Bobbitt, 1913, p.53; quoted in Bottery, 1992)

Or should schools be more like the 'knowledge' or 'high tech' industries that the new world paradigm is producing? An experienced manager in one such company writes:

> There are two key principles that high-tech organisations understand at a visceral level. The first is that ... an organisation has to match the rate of change in its environment ... The second key principle is to recognise that people are the key asset of any organisation. Why? Because people are the adaptive element of organisations. Learning and innovation come only from human cognition ... The critical management task is to enable employees to most effectively use these capabilities to learn and adapt for the benefit of the corporation. (Maxfield, 1998)

The first view sees schools on a factory model. The second sees schools as entities that must change, develop and co-evolve with the changing environment, driven by the creativity of staff. The parallel between this exposition of 'scientific' management and current processes in education suggests that, at least unconsciously, policy-makers regard schools largely within the factory model. Glatter (1999) notes the rise in technical-rational processes in education, typified by the approach to performance management currently being demanded of schools, and the tight control on educational practice being exercised by the centre. He points out the detrimental effect of such tight control on creativity, which, it is suggested, is only being encouraged in educational action zones that are given more freedom. Tye (2000) explores the effects of 'deep structures' in education, reflecting a conventional wisdom based on taken for granted assumptions about the nature of schools. This world view she believes to be predominantly behaviouristic and mechanistic, the unconscious effects of developments in science and technology, producing a cult of efficiency where the school is seen as a factory, and containing deeply ingrained assumptions of social Darwinism. Her analysis supports that of Gunter (1997), suggesting that the policy context is driven by a mindset based on Newtonian science which has become an unconscious part of people's thinking, informing their 'common sense' understanding of how the world works.

My own study supports this view, but also shows that the approach has had its successes. Heads referred to the 'measured' outputs of the system, in terms of test and examination results, that have publicly demonstrated the successes of government policy. Additionally, they found policy changes to be successful in several ways. For example, they could now ensure a good balance in the curriculum, a factor particularly noted in primary schools. Teachers now had developed a wider skill base, and attention to assessment and monitoring had risen, with vastly increasing availability of data about pupil performance. Heads felt that consequently the professionalism of teachers had increased.

However, they also noted other, perhaps unintended consequences of the policy context. Heads now felt they had no voice in curriculum matters, and teachers felt unable to produce a curriculum suitable for their particular pupils, realising that 'one size' did not fit all. The degree of professional judgement that could be applied to the curriculum was therefore drastically lessened. The forces deriving from external accountability also produced counter tendencies, effectively narrowing the curriculum to concentrate on test subjects. Some heads reported the tendency to 'teach to the tests' as a necessity that conflicted with their ideals.

Perhaps the most serious concern was the reduction of creativity in the curriculum, both at school and individual teacher level. It was interesting that the majority of the heads interviewed and observed professed a vision for the school, but only one expounded any educational philosophy at length, most professing to be concerned with improving pupils' learning, but without any observation of what such learning should entail. There had been a tendency towards standardisation in teaching. As one local inspector put it:

> I think what we have seen is a moving up of standards in the poor schools. What I haven't seen is any school come forward and rush out to the LEA and say 'You must come to see this experiment' - because everything's about guarantees.
>
> (LEA inspector)

A management trainer had found that many heads felt teachers had become 'so kind of hide-bound by the national curriculum that they've forgotten what the whole purpose of teaching is about - that they're behaving like automata' who are 'not thinking of the deeper questions about young people's learning'. The result is that such heads, whilst wishing on the one hand to keep the rigour of the national curriculum, also feel they must get teachers back to thinking what they are really about in teaching children. Other central initiatives such as the literacy and numeracy hours have attracted a similar mixture of positive and negative comments in the Times Educational Supplement.

Some heads saw the effects of accountability as adding further to the decline in creativity in teachers as they tried to align themselves with what were seen to be acceptable standards - for example, what OFSTED would expect. Similarly, inspectors perceived a move towards dependence and docility amongst teachers:

> One of the things I've noticed about working with teachers over the years ... is that long ago teachers used to be very stroppy people to work with. They'd be challenging you at every step along the way ... Now they're easy. You almost could say anything - oh, right - tell us what to do. And I think that's been one of the bad side effects of what's been happening to teachers. And some heads - not all by any means - because for some it suits them well that the teachers are fairly compliant again. But for some heads it seems that's what got lost is this, this real kind of in depth professional challenge ... to each other.
>
> (LEA inspector)

This passage underlines the feeling of de-skilling that teachers are feeling, and the resultant lack of commitment to personal ideas and ideals. Although some heads might welcome this, since it reduces the complexity in their own job, for others it reduces the creative base of the school.

I am not suggesting that there is no use for the mechanistic orientation to school organisation. Schools need an element of balance and stability that such an orientation can bring. Looked at as dissipative systems which, according to complexity theory, maintain global stability whilst undergoing change, we can see that schools need to maintain stability as well as change. The balance between top-down imposed systems and bottom-up organic systems depends on the current state of the system itself. In 1988, the fragmentation of the system and the lack of accountability of schools could be said to have required powerful direct and central action. The situation now is clearly different. Heads, staff and schools are far more accountable and professional in their approach, and schools are more effective and efficient.

However, in complex systems you can never do just one thing. Whatever you do will impact on other, often distant, factors within the system (O'Connor and McDermott, 1997). Senge has graphically described the 'Limits to Growth' system archetype, where the very solution to one problem produces other problems that accumulate over time and eventually limit growth. Heads were already noting such potentially delimiting factors, seeing tendencies towards lower morale (also impacting on recruitment), fear, reduced creativity and dependency. These unintended consequences of policy will eventually limit growth in the education system, once 'the low hanging fruit' have been picked (Senge, 1990).

The argument is not so much about *which* process, mechanistic or organic, is correct as about *when* it is correct. What is of concern is the power of the system to attain internal coherence with the complex external requirements demanded of it, a power that can be regarded as the school's strategic fitness level.

For example, one head in a secondary school, faced with external pressures of being in special measures, threatened with closure and with a staff unsure of its competence to do what was required, turned to very directive methods, with the staff's backing, even though her favoured approach was to 'sow seeds and watch them grow'.

This, however, is a special case scenario, achievable over the short term. A sustainable high strategic fitness level, capable of continuous co-evolution with the environment involves the ability to continually self-organise in the most appropriate way.

Table 9.1 School strategic fitness levels

	Failing School	*Adaptive School*	*Creative School*
Coherence	Incoherent	Coherent	Coherent
Self-organisation	Dysfunctional Inappropriate	Functional Unconscious	Functional Conscious
Co-evolution	Not adapting to environment	Reacts to environment	Co-evolves with environment
Leadership needed	Direct	Motivational	Indirect
Sustainability	Short term	Medium term	Long term

Table 9.1 models developing strategic fitness levels according to various configurations of coherence, co-evolution with the changing environment, leadership style and sustainability. The model proposes that levels of self-

organisation and co-evolution define the strategic fitness of schools. Schools in the left column rely upon direct leadership and control, whilst those in the right column have developed a high level of empowerment and distributed leadership. No longer relying on one person for strategic development, this school has the competence to self-organise through the activities of all its members in a conscious way, acting on its environment as well as reacting to it. Most English schools currently fall into the central column as they react to constant initiatives from the centre.

At the level of the education system itself, greater strategic fitness may now be achieved by moving from a generally mechanistic to a more creative base, encouraging grass root innovation and co-evolution through the system. At individual school level, the balance will need to be judged according to the current situation within it.

The Need for Creativity

The idea that there is a tendency towards reduced creativity will be hotly contested by some, who see teachers working very had, developing and planning programmes of study. Further, school improvement strategies have been gaining pace at both individual school and national level. The key question is what kind of learning this represents, and whether at a time of such social change, it is the most appropriate and the most sustainable. The concept of double and single loop learning (Argyris and Schön, 1978) can be used to consider this question.

A number of different models of single and double loop learning have developed from Argyris and Schön's model (Morgan, 1997; Stacey, 1996; Sweiringa and Wierdsma, 1992). Figure 9.2 is based on Stacey (1996). In Figure 9.2, single loop learning (A) can be seen as a negative feedback system maintaining stability with the environment. Changes in the environment are detected, and corrective action is determined based upon the operating norms in current use. These are the often unconscious, implicit mental models based on past experience of how the system and its environment work. In this learning, these 'rules' are not questioned, with the result that this learning consists of more of the same, only better. It is about improving, but within the current rules (Swieringa and Wierdsma, 1992).

Double-loop learning is more complex, and theoretically comes into play when corrective single-loop learning is no longer effective. Here there

Figure 9.2 Double-loop learning

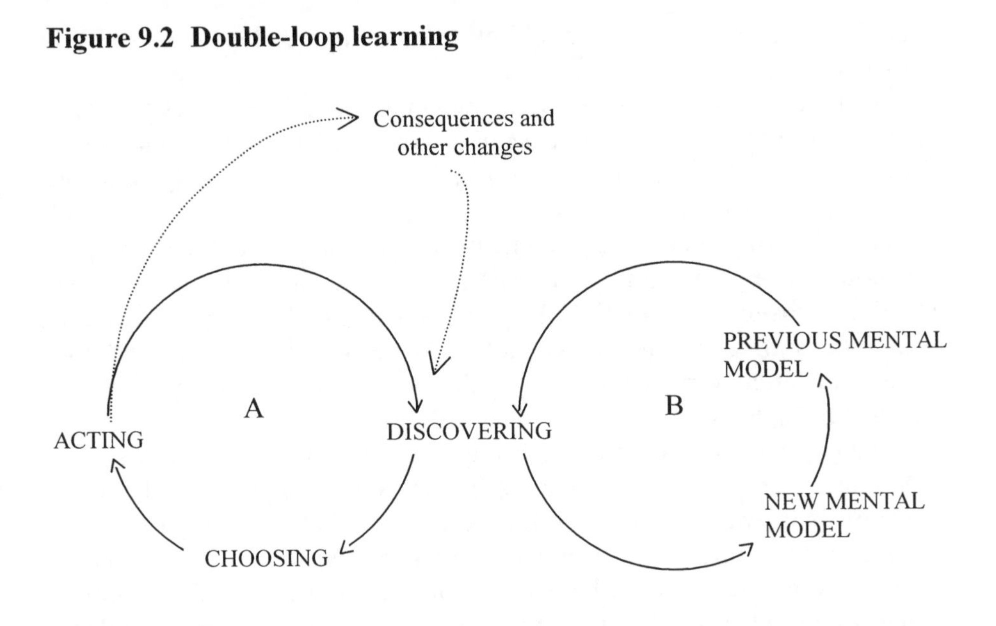

(Based on Stacey, 1996)

is a second feedback loop (B) which questions the underlying assumptions that have been producing actions, and may lead to a change in the mental model being used. This new mental model then replaces or modifies the existing one. It is the development of a new way of looking at the world by questioning underlying assumptions. This complex learning is essential, claims Stacey (1996), for innovation and creativity. This is what Hargreaves (1998) means when he suggests that although government emphasis on tried and tested methods is welcome, longer-term effectiveness will depend on teachers' ability to create new knowledge. Looked at from this perspective, it seems clear that the vast majority of learning by government and schools as they improve is single-loop: that is, more of the same, only better. As one head said, 'What do we do after we've done all the tricks?'.

As the limits of single loop learning are reached, double loop learning becomes important. Complexity theory shows us that in complex systems, creativity occurs most readily at the edge of chaos, far from equilibrium. In organisations, this state involves the micro-political interactions of autonomous agents (Stacey, 1996), from which double loop learning, new mental models and new configurations self-organise. It is the degree of ability to continuously self-organise that indicates an organisation's strategic fitness level, that is its ability to adapt *and* to lead events (Kelly and Allison, 1998).

Such interactions, with their dialectical underpinning, are less likely to happen where all agents share the same mental models. Only when there is diversity of thinking can innovative behaviour, in the form of spontaneous self-organisation, occur.

The kind of personal development that will facilitate such processes will not arise by institutional learning that trains individuals in current techniques, useful though they may be. To attain diversity in thinking, heads and staff need first to be able to reflect and question, and then develop different ways of looking at the world, different mental models, different metaphors.

There are three ways in which the creativity of teachers needs to be encouraged. The first is in their ability to respond appropriately to the needs of their own students. Central prescriptions cannot take into account the nuances of context that teachers experience. The second is in the nature of classroom interaction, where much of the teacher's skill is intuitive rather than deliberate. Atkinson and Claxton (2000) stress the complexity and dynamic interactions involved in teaching a lesson, where the context is constantly changing. This infers an ability to react quickly to changing patterns of events in the classroom. The balance between intuitive processes, reflection, implicit theories and more objective theories (Atkinson, 2000) is too large an issue to explore here, but it is clear that in practice, teachers must respond to the classroom environment and dynamics in fast, real-time sequences of plan, execute and review, constantly modifying plans as they go.

The suppression of these two modes of creativity in the classroom is becoming more apparent. In one survey, nearly two-thirds of those who left teaching wanted a job with more initiative and creativity, factors that were more important than pay (Times Educational Supplement, 2000). Reid et al., (1999) were critical of 'recipe' teachers and teaching as represented in the literacy and numeracy hours. Although the recipes may be props for less competent teachers, they say that teaching is too complex for such recipes, and that all teachers need to become problem-solvers and thinkers. Jenkins (1999) found science teachers demoralised by the national curriculum, which was too inflexible to allow them to meet the needs of their pupils. Even the notion that they could decide *how* to teach was being steadily eroded by the promotion of 'best practice'.

Addressing the needs of student teachers, John (2000) questions the dominant method of lesson planning 'which is increasingly supported by external effectiveness criteria', suggesting that intuition needs to be given a more formative role:

> ruminating in the bath, mulling over ideas in the car, thinking about lessons in bed are perhaps as powerful as those tightly scripted plans with their narrow objectives and endless evaluations. (John, 2000, p.103)

The third need for encouraging creativity is to enable the creation and dispersal of curriculum by co-evolution through the system. Complexity theory suggests two reasons why this is important. First, if an organisation is to match the complexity of its external environment, it must itself contain requisite complexity to match that environment, and second, that when a single component (say a head, or a government) controls a collective behaviour, the system cannot be more complex than the individual behaviour of that component (McKelvey, 1999). This means that the creative behaviour of the system is reduced, and thus its ability to respond to its external environment. Promoting complexity promotes creativity, and is a key aspect of the head's role, which I will now consider.

The Complexity of Headship

Schools are open systems, and therefore a constant relationship does not exist between variables. In open systems, outcomes are generally co-determined by effects of other mechanisms (Manicas and Secord, 1983). Thus simple linear cause and effect rarely occurs. Instead, heads have to operate in a system where patterns of events are the result of complex causal configurations, of which the head is part. Such configurations self-organise, and cannot be controlled, only influenced (Morgan, 1997). Thus headteachers, like other managers, rarely deal with discrete, single events but rather with interconnected events. Such configurations often mean that management problems and decisions are not clearly bounded, but exist in the 'swamp', where 'messy, confusing problems exist' (Schön, 1983).

Because of such factors, it was evident that 'causes' in the form of, say, headteacher intervention, could produce different effects according to the current state of this configuration space (Raynor, 2000). For example, one newly-appointed head tried to influence events in her new school using consultative and participative approaches that had operated in her previous school, but the approach produced, not the positive results she anticipated, but negative ones. The configuration space in the school, following years of directive headship, was not conducive to such an approach. Thus the same kind of 'causal' input, or 'best practice' produced opposite effects because of the different configuration space to which it was applied.

However, the configuration space is also dynamic as factors co-evolve over time, changing the nature of the particular school in the process. If such change is to be functional, then the head's approach also needs to co-evolve with the other factors. If this does not happen, then problems arise. One secondary school had made great strides under a head who was directive. Behaviour, results and subscription to the school had risen dramatically as a result of the head's clear focus and determination. However, after five years of such progress, this was a new organisation ready to move forward in new ways. This he recognised, but was unable to change his own style. He recognised that staff came to seek his opinion and judgement on many matters they should have decided for themselves:

> I do too much. I interfere too much. I don't let people get on with it. But that's me. I cannot change that … (Secondary head)

A senior manager in the school recognised that a new creativity was needed:

> … we've gone as far as we can mechanistically. I think we need to re-introduce creativity. I think there's a need to allow teachers more scope to be able to do things their way, and I think that would bring increased GCSE results. The school's now ripe for the next phase of development. We will never go any further with that style of leadership. That's the limit. We can't go any further because all we're doing is reproducing the same ideas we had five years ago. Teachers stop listening then. (Senior teacher)

Dealing with configurations of events is central to the work of a head, guiding them towards an overall coherence that produces effective education. The skill contains what Glatter (1997) has referred to as 'juggling', but is deeper than this word would suggest: rather than keeping the various factors within a configuration spinning like so many plates, the head must adjust all factors in relation to each other to shape the configuration itself, even as it changes, to produce alignment and coherence.

Many of the heads recognised their place in this configuration, expressing the need for 'flexible leadership', for 'knowing when to lead from the front, the middle and the back', for leadership which fits the people and the situation:

> You can't say 'I lead from the front', and when you hear that, that's when people are making desperate mistakes. Some people are very proud of it. They're aggressive, they're abrasive, and they say 'I'll take anybody on, a parent, the press', so they plough on with that rigid style in despair ... (Head)

This head is not saying that leading from the front is wrong. It is only wrong when this becomes a rigid model, unable to be modified according to circumstances. At root, there is a false perception. They may be 'proud' of their style because they think it is respected, but the reference to abrasiveness also shows the importance of understanding the self and the projection of self.

Another head worried that he allowed staff too much freedom. After a meeting with the school's special educational needs co-ordinator, he worried all the following evening that he was not being directive enough. The discussion was as if between equals. They had known each other for a long time, but he was concerned. Here he thinks out the ramifications:

> I felt a tension with the meeting although it was very friendly. It's sort of me looking over my shoulder. Should I be more directive, more up front? (She) seems to treat me as an equal, and here's a tension. You can sometimes see people coming in with both feet - very directive - and often regret it. Also some staff would prefer it - it's a lot easier. But there's more than one way to influence, which is a build up of little things. I felt that there definitely was a sense of shared leadership there. (Head P)

The tension in the meeting was because of contradictory mental models he held of his role relationship with the special needs co-ordinator. Whereas he knew her well and trusted her implicitly, suggesting it was right to talk person-to-person informally, there was also the suspicion that the role relationship would suffer, with unforeseen consequences, perhaps that she would start to take advantage. Here again is a reference to the directive head, who is characterised as being thoughtless, but who is at least clear. He also has the idea that some staff would prefer this. These would be staff who themselves were perhaps uni-dimensional, liked to know where they stood, and were unable to adapt to differing styles of leadership, which they would regard as inconsistency. He is looking over his shoulder, then, with an eye to what other staff will think, and how they will react, if this role relationship falters. Finally, he resolves the issue in his own mind, accepts the need for multi-dimensionality in leadership, and recognises shared leadership as appropriate.

Although one perhaps has to know oneself, one also has to be prepared to adopt other strategies. Heads must understand themselves and their actions in the context of others:

> I mean it's thinking time as well which I'm not used to. Sitting down, just thinking. Thinking about how I'm going to approach matters that will be acceptable to everybody on the staff, who are very, you know, got very different personalities ... (thinking about) strategies and approaches, like a chess game ...
>
> (Head E)

Understanding and enacting the role, then, involves a degree of cognitive flexibility and complexity, but these cannot operate unless perceptions are right to begin with.

Resolving or living with paradox is a key ingredient of cognitively complex thinking, and of headship:

> that is the nature of the job, in that there are groups who are interested in what's going on in schools and their wishes are different, and that's where the problems really lie. For example, where you've got competing groups all wanting you to move in different ways ... Governors are one, parents another, and staff another.
>
> (Head A)

His way of dealing with such ambiguity was by coming to his own decisions, and then following them, even though this would upset some people. He was 'not a great compromiser'. A head cannot, he says, be continually 'trying to hedge, fudge, trying to agree with everybody - it can't be done'. This would only create a problem for the future rather than taking a difficult decision now. He sees ambiguous or paradoxical situations, then, from a point of view of 'either/or', or adversarial thinking, and compromise as the only alternative.

The head's multiple roles are often paradoxical and complex. Here one head considers how the new context had been partly responsible for a more 'hard-edged' approach:

> it would have been better if it had been owned by us, if we'd made those changes ourselves rather than have them imposed upon us. I honestly do regret that at the time that I for instance took up headship, I wasn't more like that then, because I think you can be both things. You can be both a friend and a mentor and a colleague - because you can be that thing called a critical friend. (Head Q)

As opposed to Head A's adversarial thinking, this involves, 'both-and' thinking. This is not easy, and 'you don't half have to learn some skills on judging it right, don't you, because if you get it wrong it can be pretty damn devastating' (Head Q).

Heads need to think in a wide and interrelated way about many issues, often unexpected. Exclusion of a pupil, for example, carries with it implications for:

> staff relations, relations between staff and head, between staff and governors, head and governors, the parents, the community. It's just a giant thing, and you think you're resolving something simple and technical ... (it is when) it bursts into flames all around you that you realise that you can't just resolve it with a neat technical solution. (LEA inspector)

This infers the ability to think holistically, which was a recurring theme throughout the interviews, and is a subset of cognitive complexity, where heads need to be able to process a wide range of information simultaneously. Several staff attested to one head's ability to do this:

> He has everything in his mind and can shift gear from one subject to another without problem. He has an amazing memory. (Head of maths)

The second deputy concurred: he was 'on the ball instantly' seeing all the ramifications of an issue or problem at once. To another senior teacher, this was the ability to think quickly 'on his feet'. A key feature of such multiple processing is width of attention. According to staff, he knew 'what's going on right cross the board' (Deputy head). This means he 'holds a lot of information' and 'has his finger on the button' (Faculty head), and could evaluate 'huge and diverse areas' (maths teacher).

Parikh et al., (1994) have shown how much managers rely on intuition, and the heads in this study were no exception:

> All I can say is that if you were me you could understand why I was doing it, but there's something inside which says the right thing to do is this, and in that

> sense that particular action isn't analysable. You've certainly drawn on past experience, but you've also drawn on what you are, what your character is, what your personality is, and it's fantastically complex. How do you explain to somebody why I decided to do that? In that particular situation, something decided the best way is to do that. (Head A)

Here another head considers his intuitive grasp of people, singly and in groups, where the key is:

> ... gut instincts about how to deal with people, and social dynamics, and knowing who's who and what's what ... understanding how people think and do things ... (Head)

His 'dealing with people' means developing an intuitive understanding of the shadow organisation, the informal relationships and power nexuses in the school, as well as deliberately seeking an understanding of people's mindsets. This shows in the way he respects others' mental models. He fully realises they construct their own reality through such models. This was the foundation of the great political acumen and 'nous' he demonstrated.

Three things become clear in this analysis. The first is that there is no one best way of headship. Rather, headship must be requisite for the current configuration and then co-evolve with the organisation as it develops, at the same time shaping and being shaped. The second is that handling complexity is central to the head's role, and shaping multiple forces, fitting chance events into a wider picture and seizing opportunities as they occur demand cognitive abilities that go beyond rational techniques, procedures and deterministic planning:

> I find strategic planning very difficult. The reason is I would like to think that it was actually possible to start at position A and finish up at position B ... you plan along a certain line, and you are deflected from that by forces which are out of your control ... you are not always in charge. There are other forces at work, like the external agencies, like unforeseen circumstances, like a member of staff being away ill suddenly, or having to go home in the middle of a day, or long-term absence suddenly thrust upon you. You're forced along a certain path by the funding, or lack of it, the things that are governed by that. You are pulled away from the kinds of plans you have set up by changes in direction from the LEA - sudden changes of direction, sudden inexplicable changes of direction sometimes. So there are external forces at work which make that very hard. There are also internal things at work, you know, things in your own mind, which make you say 'That was right last term, that plan, but this term, I

think the school has changed. We have to move in a different direction.

(Head D)

Thirdly, this blend of forces means that each school is unique. Cilliers (1998) points out that there is no overarching theory of complexity that allows the ignoring of contingency: if something is complex, it cannot be adequately described by means of a simple theory. The specific complex system will be irreducible. This means that competencies may sometimes be generally applicable, but they cannot replace the deeper cognitive abilities used to understand the particular dynamic system.

The Need for Personal Development

The analysis to this point shows the unique qualities of each school and that handling the complex interplay of factors is central to headship. It also shows the need for the school to be a creative organisation if it is to attain the higher levels of strategic fitness. Because of these twin factors of shifting configurations and self-organising creativity, technical solutions are insufficient. While competences based on the specific tasks of headship will continue to be needed, the development of foundational meta-abilities and diversity in thinking, to be found in personal development, are needed for processing complex information and increasing creativity.

I have pursued two main arguments in this chapter. The first relates to the head's handling of complex processes. I have suggested that the head needs to maintain a constant though changing coherence in the configuration arising from the task to be accomplished, the internal environment of the school, the external environment and the leadership function if optimum outcomes are to be continually attained. The nature of leadership, ranging from direct and autocratic, to entirely distributed throughout the school, will depend crucially on its appropriateness to the current configuration, whilst at the same time changing it. The whole causal configuration is constantly developing and the head's actions over time will be part of those changes, an influence with potential to change the configuration. This is a complex process in which techniques take second place to wisdom, perception and judgement. Elements of the configuration, such as the head's own role, their relationship to the whole context, the people in the organisation and the external context, all add paradox, ambiguity and the need for interrelated thinking. Cognition is an important element in the successful management of these factors.

Experienced heads and inspectors agreed that a key leadership skill is to be able to hold in mind both the overview of the organisation, with a wide attention span, and the detail of it at the same time. This represents an aspect of cognitive complexity, the blending of two areas 'which often do not go together' (Head G), and demonstrates the processes of differentiation and integration (Streufert and Swezey, 1986). It is 'the ability to take multiple and integrated perspectives' and 'recognise and hold conflicting concepts in mind' and is seen as an essential ability for reading the environment, understanding one's own impact on others, managing complex roles and relationships, seeing things from others' points of view and managing diverse information flows (Butcher et al., 1997).

These areas of cognition go beyond the kind of technical-rational approaches currently being stressed (Glatter, 1999). Indeed, Nørretranders (1998) has pointed out that the bandwidth of consciousness is about 16 bits per second, and that processing information solely by conscious/rational means actually involves a reduction in bandwidth. More information is actually processed non-consciously. However, even non-conscious information processing may rely on 'framing' through schemas or cognitive maps (Bolman and Deal, 1993), metaphors (Morgan, 1997), mindscapes (Maruyama, 1994) or logic bubbles (DeBono, 1996). Here again, new ways of seeing and interpreting the world are of the essence.

My second argument has been that the strategic fitness level of schools, and consequently their capacity for development, depends upon the configuration of essential factors within them. Schools generally show much different configurations than they did in 1988, with leadership, staff competence, and professionalism all of a different order. However, top-down policies and intense accountability are constricting creativity at individual and school level, effectively depriving the whole system of a wide creative base. To attain the higher levels of strategic fitness, schools will need to increase their capacity to innovate in two ways. The first relies on the creative acts of individuals, which then amass support in a Darwinian manner. For Stacey (1996) this occurs through political interaction in the informal shadow system of the organisation.

There are two important points about these processes. The first is that the creative thoughts of individuals occur through seeing things in a new way, that is, through new metaphors and new mental models. This implies a width of experience, so that apparently disparate ideas are brought together. Perhaps this is what virtuoso violinist Oscar Shumsky meant when he attributed his success to his wide interests, saying that thinking about what a painter visualises had a great effect on his violin playing (Daily Telegraph, 2000).

Secondly, if Darwinism is to relate to the transmission of new ideas, Lewontin (2000) reminds us that the 'variations' on which Darwin's scheme of evolution depends arise from causes *internal* to the organism, and *not* as responses to the external environment. It is rather by chance that a mutation enables survival in that environment, and therefore spreads throughout the species. Thus, rather than, or in addition to, the current idea of strategic management attempting to align the organisation with the environment, Darwinian selection suggests the opposite. The organisation would produce changes internally, and some of these would be selected by the environment. This is the basis of co-evolution - aligning with the environment, yet through internal creativity contributing to that environment.

A second route to innovation lies through the interactions of individuals in groups. Here heterogeneity of thinking needs to be combined with homogeneity of values and purposes. Some have seen a parallel between this process and jazz playing, where all players align with an underlying structure (the harmonic sequence) whilst improvising and relating to each other's ideas (Bell, 1998; Hall, 2000).

It is the head's role to develop the school's strategic fitness level. This means understanding the school's current configuration space, leaving room for the self-organising activities of individuals and groups appropriate to that configuration, and perceiving points of leverage in the system which can be 'nudged' in broad directions (Morgan, 1997). These needs confirm the importance of personal development, rooted especially in ways of thinking.

As Marsick (1994) notes, in the knowledge companies where the need to innovate is paramount, managers must learn to shift their managerial frames of reference or mental models. This involves learning new ways of thinking, rather than the kind of behaviour changes that have been the focus of management training programmes. Grey and French (1996) see 'educative' development as an alternative to the managerialism fostered by a utilitarian concept of management, and they stress analysis over techniques. Encouraging such thinking can also lead to a questioning of the way utilitarian approaches are concerned only with means rather than ends (French and Grey, 1996), surely a point which Freire (1972) would have supported, and which would cause heads to think beyond their concern for helping pupils to learn, to debating what they actually need to learn.

The importance given above to different ways of seeing, cognitive complexity and intuition, is indicative of the question posed by some of how far rationality can be applied to management, and how far the competencies approach to development actually relates to what managers have to do. It is in relation to these concerns that Anthony (1986) has described 'real' and 'official' theory. According to official theory, managers act rationally, and this idea is shown in conventional management education through topics such as leadership, coordination, motivation and so on. Real theory on the other hand stresses the social and political nature of management work, which is complex and messy, involves ambiguous roles and 'playing it by ear' - far from rational processes.

I have argued in this chapter that while technical and competence-based development is still required for headteachers, personal development has been under-represented. Whilst this may include a number of meta-abilities, I have suggested that the development of cognition and self-knowledge are fundamental to handling complexity, to engaging with the world in new and different ways, and to increasing the strategic fitness levels of schools.

Finally, it is important once again to be reminded that schools exist in a context which powerfully affects what is possible and not possible. It was suggested that the policy context reflects a Newtonian-positivistic paradigm, and the present forms of accountability and centrally-determined teaching prescriptions constitute a command and control model. These suppress the co-evolution of schools. Given more microscopic freedom and flexible forms of accountability, new forms of leadership could evolve and schools could self-organise and be more creative. They would co-evolve with each other and the external context, and a powerful evolutionary source of school improvement would be released.

References

Anthony, P. (1986) *The Foundation of Management*. London: Tavistock.

Argyris, C. and Schön, D. (1978) *Organizational Learning: a Theory of Action Perspective*. Reading, Massachusetts: Addison Wesley.

Atkinson, T. (2000) Learning to teach: intuitive skills and reasoned objectivity. In Atkinson, T. and Claxton, G. *The Intuitive Practitioner*. Buckingham: Open University Press.

Atkinson, T. and Claxton, G. (2000) *The Intuitive Practitioner*, Buckingham: Open University Press.

Bell, L. (1998) From Symphony to Jazz: the concept of strategy in education. *School Leadership and Management* **18** (4), pp.449-460.

Bobbitt, F. (1913) quoted in Bottery, M. (1992) *The Ethics of Educational management*. London: Cassell.

Bolman, L. and Deal, T.E. (1993) Everyday Epistemology in School Leadership: Patterns and Prospects. In Hallinger, P., Leithwood, K. and Murphy, J. (Eds) *Cognitive Perspectives on Educational Leadership*. New York: Teacher's College Press.

Butcher, D., Harvey, P. and Atkinson, S. (1997) *Developing Businesses through Developing Individuals*. Cranfield: Cranfield School of Management.

Cilliers, P. (1998) *Complexity and Postmodernism*. London: Routledge.

Daily Telegraph (2000) Obituary for Oscar Shumsky. 9 August.

DeBono, E. (1996) *Textbook of Wisdom*. London: Viking.

DfEE (1997) *Excellence in Schools*. London: Department for Education and Employment.

DfEE (1999) *NPQH: Handbook for Trainers, Tutor Mentors and Assessors*. London: Department for Education and Employment.

DfEE (2000) *Performance Management in Schools: Performance management framework*. London: Department for Education and Employment.

Drucker, P.F. (1992) The New Society of Organizations. *Harvard Business Review* **70** (5), pp.95-104.

Freire, P. (1972) *Pedagogy of the Oppressed*. London: Penguin.

French, R. and Grey, C. (1996) *Rethinking Management Education*. London: Sage.

Glatter, R. (1997) Context and Capability in Educational Management. *Educational Management and Administration BEMAS* **25** (2), pp.181-192.

Glatter, R. (1999) From Struggling to Juggling: towards a Redefinition of the field of Educational Leadership and Management. *Educational Management and Administration* **27** (3), pp.253-265.

Grey, C. and French, R. (1996) Rethinking Management Education: an introduction. In French, R. and Grey, C. *Rethinking Management Education*. London: Sage.

Gunter, H. (1997) *Rethinking Education: the consequences of Jurassic management*. London: Cassell.

Hall, V. (2000) *Management Teams in Education: An Unequal Music?* Paper presented to the BEMAS Conference, 22-24 September, Bristol.

Hargreaves, D. (1998) *Creative Professionalism: The Role of Teachers in the Knowledge Society*. London: Demos.

Jenkins, E. (1999) Report at the Association for Science Education Conference.

John, P. (2000) Awareness and intuition: how student teachers read their own lessons. In Atkinson, T. and Claxton, G. *The Intuitive Practitioner*. Buckingham: Open University Press.

Kelly, S. and Allison, M.A. (1998) *The Complexity Advantage: how the science of complexity can help your business achieve peak performance*. New York: McGraw-Hill.

Lewontin, R. (2000) *It ain't necessarily so*. London: Granta.

Manicas, P.T. and Secord, P.F. (1983) Implications for Psychology of the New Philosophy of Science. *American Psychologist* **38** (4), pp.399-413.

Marsick, V. (1994) Trends in Managerial Reinvention: Creating a Learning Map. *Management Learning* **25** (1), pp.11-33.

Maruyama, M. (1994) *Mindscapes in Management*. Aldershot: Dartmouth.

Maxfield, R.R. (1998) Complexity and Organization Management. In Alberts, D.S. and Czerwinski, T.J. *Complexity, Global Politics and National Security*. Washington, DC: National Defense University. Read online: www.ndu.edu/inss/books/complexity/index.html.

McKelvey, B. (1999) The Gurus Speak: Complexity and Organizations. *Emergence* **1** (1).

Morgan, G. (1997) *Images of Organization*. (2nd ed) London: Sage.

Mortimore, P., Sammons, P., Stoll, L., Lewis, D. and Ecob, R. (1988) *School Matters: the Junior Years*. Wells, Somerset: Open Books.

National Advisory Committee on Creative and Cultural Education (1999) *All our Futures: creativity, culture and education*. London: DfEE.

Nørretranders, T. (1998) *The User Illusion: Cutting Consciousness down to Size*. London: Allen Lane, Penguin Press.

O'Connor, J. and McDermott, I. (1997) *The Art of Systems Thinking*. London: Harper Collins.

OFSTED (1995) *Framework for the Inspection of Schools*. London: OFSTED.

OFSTED (1998) *School Evaluation Matters*. London: OFSTED.

Parikh, J., Neubauer, F. and Lank, A.G. (1994) *Intuition: the New Frontier of Management*. London: Blackwell.

Raynor, A. (2000) *A Study of complexity, Cognition and Competence in Headship*. Unpublished PhD dissertation, University of Huddersfield, England.

Reid, I., Thornton, M. and Bricheno, P. (1999) *The Apple Project.* Paper presented at the BERA conference.

Schön, D.A. (1983) *The Reflective Practitioner*. New York: Basic Books.

Senge, P. (1990) *The Fifth Discipline: the Art and Practice of the Learning Organization*. New York: Doubleday.

Stacey, R.D. (1996) *Strategic Management and Organisational Dynamics*, (2nd edn.) London: Pitman.

Streufert, S. and Swezey, R.W. (1986) *Organizations and Complexity*. New York: Academic Press.

Swieringa, J. and Wierdsma, A. (1992) *Becoming a Learning Organization: Beyond the Learning Curve*. Wokingham, England: Addison Wesley.

Times Educational Supplement (2000) Report on University of North London's Teacher Retention and Supply Project, 21 January.

Tye, B.B. (2000) *Hard Truths: uncovering the Deep Structure of Schooling*. New York: Teachers' College Press.

10 The Impact of Information on Individuals and Organisations

CEDRIC CULLINGFORD AND HELEN SWIFT

Introduction

Those concerned with the improvement of educational institutions need as much information about their institution as possible, in order to present an accurate picture of relative performance. Judgements can only be made, whether about the appraisal of individuals, or more general outcomes such as comparative rates of staff absence, if there is an expressed basis for them. There are, of course, tensions that surround any information, since information can be misused as easily as it can be used constructively. Information is never neutral. Information is less useful when it is limited to what is easily measured rather than that which provides worthwhile data. League tables are one example of the use of information that can cause much distress, yet information about pupil performance is often a useful starting point for the recognition of a teacher's performance. The relationship between accountability and information gathering is taken for granted, but this is because it is the starting point for continuing professional development (SCAA, 1997a). Individuals cannot be held accountable without clear measurement, nor can improvement be seen to be taking place unless clear comparisons between 'before' and 'after' can be made.

The information that is available to schools is immense and complicated. Most of it is internal, but there is also a plethora of facts imposed from outside. Every pupil's Standard Attainment Targets (SATs) results are just the start: classes and subjects can be compared to each other, and every school can be compared to others. In an age fascinated by performance indicators, there are powerful databases which can compare a wide range of factors, from the 'percentage of child protection cases which should have been reviewed that were reviewed' to 'the percentage of eligible four year olds in validated provision'. To the government's mandatory indicators, local authorities add their own. The data that has been collected all over the country is enormous. How it is used is another matter.

However much one questions the quality of some of the information, there is no doubting its potential usefulness. In order to develop staff, head teachers need to know about their rates of success in terms of the results of their pupils and the improvements that have been made over time. SATs and examination results are a starting point. Headteachers can also learn about the functioning of their schools. They are aware of the number of pupils statemented and the proportion playing truant or excluded. They know how much their school costs to run, and the number of staff absences. All these can provide useful insights into the successes and difficulties of their own schools. It is also interesting for them, and could be valuable, to compare their own performance with those of other schools with similar socio-economic backgrounds.

School Profiles

One of the means of gathering data on schools has been through the introduction of School Profiles, now operated by all the local authorities in England (DfEE, 1996). These school profiles are tables of information on which every school is placed on a point below or above the mean. Those with high costs, or bad results, stand out. Every headteacher knows where his or her school is against the average. It is possible to tell whether certain factors are not being attended to. The most significant point is that headteachers are only supposed to know about their own school. There is no mechanism as yet to use these profiles as means of 'naming and shaming' whole schools. In the light of the research reported here this is significant.

Target Setting

The statistical data that is presented in the profiles include factors such as pupil staff ratios, the percentage of free school meals, attendance rates and financial data like the cost of upkeep of the buildings, as well as the SATs results in English and Mathematics. The schools are banded in clusters according to socio-economic circumstances (SCAA, 1997b). Such information could be useful to schools and could enable head teachers to share with others how they have managed to deal with similar problems. Such information ought to give insights into how individual schools are performing so that there could be more communication and a greater degree of collaboration. Target setting could then become more meaningful. However, the insistence of anonymity and confidentiality of the information to others, other than local authority officials and inspectors, is interesting. This suggests that there could be potential misuse of the information, insofar as certain institutions could be targeted for certain outcomes, like vandalism, over which they have no control.

The Research

> The question school effectiveness research deals with most of the time is what kind of factors within schools and classrooms make a difference between effective and less effective schools. (Creemers, 1997, p.112)

This research explores a different avenue, the reactions of head teachers to the information that is given to them; which parts of the School Profile they found most useful, and what kind of information they would wish to share with others. What emerged from the research revealed something more than reactions to what could be useful. What the headteachers revealed says a great deal about the context in which they operate, the general state of morale in schools and the ambiguous nature of information. All *should* think of knowledge as power; but power is revealed as a double-edge, a sword that is feared for not having just one direction.

The head teachers in this research were from both primary and secondary schools. The schools selected were from a wide range of socio-economic backgrounds. Indeed, in terms of size and location, and number of free school meals, one could hardly wish for a more diverse mix. More than one hundred schools were profiled. Three data collection methods: observation, questionnaires and semi-structured interviews were used to explore head teachers' reactions to information about their schools, as set out in the profiles and in target setting. Both quantitative data - the information within the profile - and qualitative methodology was utilised to enrich the analysis of the findings.

The first data collection tool was the observation of headteachers when they attended meetings on the new School Improvement Initiative set up by the Local Education Authority. At all the introductory sessions, data was collected through analysing and recording their reactions and hearing their reports from meetings with collections of their neighbouring schools. What was learned was both revealing and consistent and established the framework for the more empirical research which was to follow.

The second data collection method of questionnaires elicited information about the size of the school, from under 100 pupils to over 600, the number of free school meals, the headteachers and staff's initial reaction to the initiative, the way in which it was introduced, the meetings they attended, and which parts of the information presented to them were most useful. They were also asked to say with whom they shared the information, an aspect which was explored in far greater depth in the semi-structured interviews. Responses were obtained from 112 schools.

The third data collection method employed was semi-structured interviews with a representative sample of schools, from a range of seven different socio-economic groups as defined by the number of children with free school meals. The interviews followed similar issues to the questionnaires but explored them in greater depth. The questionnaires were used to verify the findings of the interviews, and the interviews to explore in depth the reasoning behind the responses. In each case every means was pursued to make certain that the samples used were representative of the wide range of participants and that any general statement was valid and reliable.

The Questionnaire Survey

Profiles

The initial reaction to the information provided by the School Improvement Initiative was positive. Favourable responses were obtained from 78% of the respondents. Clearly the idea behind the information struck them as useful and helpful and it had been presented to them in a positive light. The positive way in which the initiative was introduced was also indicated by the numbers who actually attended meetings to discuss the profile (74%) and the wish of those who did not do so that they had attended meetings (89%). In addition, and frequently as an alternative, 78% attended group meetings to discuss the initiative. A sense of interest and a feeling that what was being presented was potentially helpful and interesting was widespread. What also emerged from accounts of these meetings is a tension between the sense of overall unity of purpose within the LEA and a sense of solidarity between the heads. This could, and sometimes did, lead to a sense of 'us' against 'them', the 'them' being the Local Authority Officers and Councillors, seen as representatives of the State.

Target Setting

All the heads involved shared the view that all information on their schools and the attendant aspects like targeting and benchmarking were fundamentally useful and helpful tools, but they were also uniformly suspicious about the uses to which the information might be put. In a different educational climate they would have welcomed the information and been prepared to share it, but with the current emphasis on competition, inspection and punishment for failure, they felt unable to do so.

Information Sharing

The information in the School profiles was, therefore, considered by the headteachers to be potentially helpful. But the issue of whether this information could be more widely disseminated proved, again, to be more equivocal. The sense that knowledge could be a weapon, either for the arguments of the headteacher, or *against* the performance of the school, was overwhelming. The governor that tended to be chosen to share the information was the Chair who, it was suggested, could be trusted with selected information on the grounds that he or she would not wish to do harm to the School. Even so, 22% of heads did not share any information whatsoever with the Chair of Governors. When it came to sharing the information with parents, just 1% responded that they had done so. Given the comments in the interviews, this was hardly surprising, but it should also be interpreted as disappointing. Primary headteachers, in particular, constantly affirm the importance of opening up their schools to parents, and to the communication of what is happening. And yet the information contained in the profiles appears to be jealously guarded. This lack of communication could be caused by the suspicions reported above, but could also arise from lack of time. The expression of goodwill towards parents is undermined by the increasing constraints on time - a fact that is strongly felt by parents themselves (Cullingford, 1996).

The Interviews

Profiles

All the headteachers, despite seeing merit in the profile, felt unease about the use to which the information might be put:

> We felt unease, at first it seemed a good idea ... we are united. We approve of benchmarking, are doing it already. It's well used. Unease came from questioning the sort of information. Who might have access. Some heads wouldn't be able to use it without training.

The usefulness of the profile depended on the extent to which it provided 'various factors you can't explain away'. This was the sensitive issue, because heads felt that there were some circumstances, especially in a small school, that could be 'explained away' - but only by those who really understood the unique circumstances.

The information provided by the profiles, then, is seen to be both potentially useful and potentially destructive. 'There is always a danger of comparing unequal'. Small rural schools were felt to be particularly vulnerable to misinformed criticism. 'Sometimes you didn't want to see it'. 'It could be used against us':

> - no-one would own up. Stood out a mile. Percentage differences are huge when it's a matter of one or two children. This might be ammunition. This could be closure stuff.

All head teachers expressed their concern at the potential misuse of the information - by governors, by parents or by their LEA. They articulated the 'atmosphere of current thinking' where 'people will ignore circumstances'.

One pervading response, mitigated by time and the need to do other things, was that the profiles could lead to headteachers trying to find the reasons for the outcomes that made their schools different, like salaries, supply cover or the rates for dinner ladies. What interested them were the comparisons between schools - so that the most 'dangerous' information was also the most useful. For some, the most significant of all were the SATs results, which they knew about, but not in the overall context of other schools, except through League Tables. They all agreed that these were matters on which they would take action, or protested that they were already taking action, before the profile revealed the comparison with similar schools. For others the profiles provided new information of a different kind, like energy costs - 'gave me pause for thought', grounds and maintenance - 'how do they do it? Do the parents do it?' or supplies and services - 'about average; good news to me'.

Target Setting

All the head teachers pointed out that the School Improvement Initiatives, with their detailed information, comparisons against similar schools and the emphasis on target setting, were part of an overall context of eliciting as much data as possible on which to base judgements. They spoke about both the 'atmosphere of current thinking' and the numerous schemes which were being set up to 'raise standards'. Whilst they found this useful, they saw it as part of a pattern of events. A typical response was:

> I'm a bit dubious of cycles ... all this is lots of things that all form part of one system ... you're just running systems ... you're so bogged down in the planning cycle, when do you have time to do anything?

There was constant tension in the heads' reflections, between the need to learn from others and the difficulty of trusting them. They drew a distinction between the possibility of learning new approaches – 'How did you do that?' and the competitive climate. They kept reiterating that 'outsiders don't know the context' as if the 'outsiders' were looking for negative evidence with which to blame the school. They pointed out the tension between people, the fascination with league tables, and the fact that very small differences in measurable data can have a crucial impact.

This has implications especially for the setting of targets. The sense of constant measuring, and therefore interpreting such measurements as a starting point for setting goals and plans against which the head and the school could be measured, was paramount. It suggests that the information presented, like SATs results, is both useful and dangerous. It also suggests that the headteachers were very careful about which piece of information they wished to highlight (or explain away) and which particular target they would choose to set.

Information Sharing

One of the central ideas of the School Improvement Initiative is that like should be compared to like, so that schools will be able to compare notes and, therefore, increase understanding. As one of the headteachers demonstrates, the potential of learning from others – 'how do they manage that?' – is clearly recognised. Despite this, just 40% of the headteachers had had any contact with other similar schools, even considering the context of group meetings which gave them every opportunity to do so. Those who had made contact again reported the ambivalence that shadows the information. Those who made contact with other schools found that this was useful (30% of the whole cohort). Yet just 7% reported that they would take this further and actively co-operate in helping each other. This suggests a suspicion of letting out too much information, as if the creation of league tables inhibits any mutual collaboration, or learning from each other.

The most interesting findings, given that schools have access to SATs results, are those which, to use a word often invoked by the heads, can be used as 'ammunition' either for or against the school, or within the school. Two examples illustrate this well:

> What really hit me is that we are the most financially supported and resourced first school. That gives me ammunition.

> We have the lowest take up of LEA courses by staff. It proved what I've guessed at; the staff passivity.

Plans for Sharing or Disseminating the Information

Given the sense of 'ammunition' and the suspicion of the potential misuse of the information, it is no surprise that the heads were very wary of sharing the profiles, although the number of people they were thinking of involving did vary. What is clear is that they would all be very selective about which parts of the profile they would communicate, and very selective in which governors and which staff they felt would understand the information. No head suggested that he or she would disseminate the profile figures freely to anyone either within or outside the school.

Dissemination to Parents

The constituents of the school who were under the greatest suspicion were the parents. It was felt that some of the information could be misused or misinterpreted, although it was acknowledged that some parents would know some of the material anyway. But the suspicion held against some parents was strong:

> I daren't show it to parents. They are clued up. Have statistical knowledge.

At best parents would see carefully selected parts:

> They would make it an issue to back up their arguments or complaints.

> Parents would use their power in the wrong way.

It is noteworthy that whilst the headteachers all stressed the importance of the collaboration of parents, the information provided in the profiles caused them to revert to suspicion, even fear. Parents were then depicted as being unhelpful to, rather than supportive of, the school.

Dissemination to Governors

If the parents are that vague outside threat, like a Government Inspector, then it could be argued that those ostensibly within the system could be relied upon to understand the meaning of the information and the context in which it is placed. But whilst parents were held in a kind of aspic of suspicion, most governors, supposedly part of the functional operation of the School, were almost equally held back from the information.

The headteachers intended to censor very carefully the graphs held within the profiles. Their reasons varied. Some said that the governors were 'supportive but ill-equipped'. 'They don't have time. They lack knowledge. They wouldn't understand the context; they might misinterpret'. Others felt that governors could become openly hostile.

Some heads did express carefree assumptions about the fact that there would be no particular difficulty in communicating with governors, that they would naturally be involved. But it is a matter of concern, given the role and status of governors, that in the majority of cases they were regarded as if they were outside agents.

There is something structurally fallible about headteachers' suspicion of their own governors. It can be traced to the power that governors wield if they so wish. But it is also due to the pervasive culture of fear that seems to imbue the heads' outlook. Accountability is all very well; but it should not imply that the main function of a school is to protect itself against it. When one reads the headteachers' inner thoughts, it is clear that they regard the setting of targets not just as a way of improving standards but as another threatening measure which could expose the failure of their own school.

Dissemination to Staff

If there appears to be an element of the unpredictability of the use by governors of the information gathered, there is an identical caution towards the teaching staff of the school. There was a tension, once again, between the selection of staff seen as capable of interpreting the material and the selection of material as being capable of interpretation by staff. The comment included that the staff 'would not be ready yet' and 'I wouldn't show it to them in that form'. Even within the school management team there was a conscious decision to use the material selectively.

Conclusion

It seems impossible to separate the School Improvement Initiative from the context in which it takes place, including earlier and more recent initiatives of which the headteachers were aware, whatever their particular circumstances. The sheer amount of new information and new demands were seen as a blight, in which each new idea blotted out all else, to the detriment of almost any original or useful idea.

There is no doubt that the information that the school profiles provide will be useful to the schools, but improvement year by year depends on the confidence of heads to be able to talk to each other and share information. We constantly heard the two refrains:

> I'd love to find someone with a similar intake who is doing better to discover how they've done it, but I daren't!

And:

> These figures are one off and there are exceptional reasons for them but I fear that will not be taken into account.

Information about schools is essential if there are to be judgements made about their performance. In a climate of belief in School Improvement Initiatives the more information that is collected the better; this is not just to make schools accountable but to make sure they have enough data to know what they should do, which problems they should address and how they compare with other schools of a similar intake. No one doubted that the information they received was useful. No one questioned the potential, and yet the information remained undisseminated and unused. This was despite the best intentions of local authority officers to reassure the head teachers.

This indicates a curious anomaly. The educational climate in which schools operate is one of comparisons and competition. They are striving to do better against each other, or against targets. The information on which judgements of comparative success or failure are based is crucial. Teachers generally, and head teachers in particular, welcomed the information but they rejected its use. The question remains whether competition between schools leads to secrecy rather than collaboration, or whether because of a plethora of so much information, schools have little time to deal with it.

Continuing professional development is usually based on the notion that improvement can be seen and measured. Annual reviews are based on information like the success rates of pupils and attendance figures. Whilst there might be questions raised about whether the things that are most worthwhile can be easily measured, a desire for improvement should be based on clear information. Once there is a suspicion of the uses to which it will be put, then all the effort in gathering it will not be worthwhile. Here we have revealed the kinds of tensions which undermine the connection between institutional development and personal needs. The information was potentially helpful, but not shared even with staff, let alone anyone 'outside' the immediate milieu of the school. In terms of the professional development of individual staff therefore, including the headteachers themselves, the usefulness of the information was undermined by suspicions and a lack of communication. In terms of institutional developments, such information was seen more as a threat than a support, more a means of prevention of change than a means of managing it to construct a more productive future.

References

Creemers, B. (1997) *Effective Schools and Effective Teachers: an International Perspective.* Warwick: CREPE.

Cullingford, C. (1996) *Parents Education and the State*. Aldershot: Arena.

DfEE (1996) *GEST Supported LEA School Improvement Projects*. London: Department for Education and Employment.

SCAA (1997a) *Value Added Indicators for Schools*. London: Schools Curriculum and Assessment Authority.

SCAA (1997b) *The Value Added National Project*. London: Schools Curriculum and Assessment Authority.

11 Whole School Development Policies: A Case Study

CHRISTOPHER GREENFIELD AND CEDRIC CULLINGFORD

Introduction

Whatever the cultural differences in the outlook of 'management' and the attitudes of 'academics', the arguments are centred on the needs of the students. Indeed, in the extremes of both positions, pupils can be used as a weapon. The justification of educational institutions lies in their 'outputs', their 'products'. Even if not expressed in this way, the most humanistic of teachers will agree with the focus of attention. This gives a somewhat different slant to the management of professional development.

In the tension between the needs and purposes of the whole institution and the personal development of individuals lies the holy grail of an integrated policy which involves everyone. In schools, a common source of purpose which influences the behaviour and attitudes of staff and pupils alike is constantly sought. It might not be easily measured, but the notion of 'ethos' remains a powerful concept (Rutter et al., 1979; Mortimore et al., 1988). A school has the duty of delivering the National Curriculum and preparing its pupils to do well in examinations. It is also expected to pay attention to the 'hidden curriculum' of discipline, communication skills and belief systems.

The concept of self-management of schools has had a profound effect on the 'ethos' of schools. Freed, to a degree, from Local Education Authority constraints, they are seen as autonomous, certainly in a financial sense (Bush and West-Burnham, 1994). The question remains whether the pupils in a school can be part of a central policy of both professional and institutional development. They are usually seen as the 'outcomes' of a school, the results of other people's actions, despite the numerous statements that remind people that they are the sole raison d'etre of schools. Certainly, from the pupils' point of view, they do not feel central (Cullingford, 1991). What would then happen if a whole school policy was implemented that involved all pupils and teachers and involved behaviour as well as the curriculum?

For many schools the formal mechanisms of management are quite distinct from the everyday complex experience of individuals (Murgatroyd and Morgan, 1993). The aim is to bring the two together.

There are occasions when the formal and informal aspects of school overlap; when the ethos of the school is itself a subject. This is particularly true of the recent developments in citizenship education. The idea that formal schooling can be used to shape attitudes towards social behaviour has long been accepted and indeed, has been argued since Plato (Brennan, 1981). The recent initiatives supported by the British Government have suggested that schools have a duty not only to inform pupils of their position as citizens in a democratic society, but to instil some of the values implicit in that position (Crick, 1998).

Citizenship education is an addition to a curriculum dominated by Maths, English and Science. It relies heavily on the accumulation of knowledge of the constitution, of the functioning of political parties and the rights of individuals enshrined in legislation. To that extent it continues the tradition embedded in the 1904 Code of Regulations for Public Elementary Schools, the report of the Association for Education and Citizenship in 1934 and the 1943 Norwood Report that anticipated the Education Act of the following year. However, in all these reports the concern with knowledge is driven by a concern for attitudes and behaviour. Unlike the core curriculum, there are values attached. It is assumed that more knowledge will reduce rather than increase narrow prejudice. Citizenship education might be a small part of the overall curriculum, but the values it represents are implicit in the purpose of educational institutions.

It seems to be in accordance with the dictates of common sense that attitudes promoted by a school should have *some* effect on the political and social attitude of students. However, there appears to be little published material on the precise extent to which curricular input can affect educational outcomes related to citizenship attitudes. Such work that has been published would indicate that there is some linkage, albeit slight. For example, the study conducted by Osborne and John (1992) concluded that schools with 'traditional' or 'democratic' structures appeared to influence, but only slightly, the attitudes of the students attending the schools. Harber (1991) suggested that schools' organisational structures tended to socialise pupils politically, but again only to a very limited extent.

Clearer evidence of children developing attitudes which accepted the imposition of hierarchies was found by Bowles and Gintis (1979) and Cole (1988). However, pupils are not empty vessels waiting to be filled up with whatever the designers of school curricula wish to put in. Pupils daily arrive at school and daily leave schools, as intelligent individuals who absorb influences from all around them. The influence of parents and then the wider family must have at least as much impact as a school curriculum, no matter how carefully designed. Other influences will arise from 'significant others' in a child's experience and will also have an impact on that child's attitudes. Anxieties about the influences on young people of the 'pop culture', 'video games' and other mass media are almost daily expressed in our tabloid newspapers. All of these influences will have an impact on the development of attitudes towards society. It can be questioned whether many attitudes towards society are actually acquired from school (Cullingford, 1992).

Even within schools, is it simply the curriculum that can influence a child's attitudes? The evidence seems to indicate that the curriculum itself has less of an impact on a child than the cumulative school 'ethos'. The way in which adults act towards pupils, and towards each other, may be at least as effective in influencing the attitudes of pupils as what pupils are told are the correct ways to relate to one another. Even the 1943 Norwood Report recognised that citizenship education was not merely linked to the cognitive domain of education. 'The most valuable influence', the report said, was 'the general spirit and outlook of the school - what is sometimes called the 'tone' of the school' (p.49).

Citizenship education draws attention to one of the underlying purposes of schools. They are small institutions in which many of the norms of society are demonstrated. Disciplined behaviour, attention to and understanding of rules, and the organisation of groups affect all those involved in schools, teachers and ancillary staff as much as pupils. Teachers cannot function, they cannot take their personal interests forward nor develop their subject, unless there is an understanding of shared behaviour in which all comply. From the point of view of staff development therefore, let alone the development of the institution, a code of conduct and a policy of inclusion is always needed.

An Investigative Project

The following research study was undertaken to explore the impact of a management decision to involve the whole school in a development policy. A school which had a clear commitment to education for citizenship, and had policies in place which were designed to influence both the cognitive and affective aspects of development of the pupils, was identified (as school 'C'), and permission obtained from the school's officers to conduct a three-tiered project.

The comprehensive school selected for the project had many features which could class it as 'typical' of its kind. It was suburban with a catchment drawing on large areas of subsidised housing as well as more middle class areas. It was located in a stable area, and almost all of the children had attended only the one comprehensive school and one of its feeder schools for their whole educational career.

An ethnographic study was designed to investigate education for citizenship on three levels. Firstly, there was the educational input of the curriculum created by the official school policies agreed by the School Governors, Head Teacher and other School Management Team members. Secondly, the outcome of this curriculum would be investigated, as far as was possible, by examining the views of pupils on social issues and the school itself. The third level, and one which the present writers believe has been overlooked to a great extent in previous consideration of citizenship education, was the role of the teacher practitioners themselves.

The policies of the school, in the main, are passed to the pupils through the teachers and in this process the policies will be interpreted to pupils in different ways by different teachers. Since the attitudes of pupils can be influenced by the attitudes of teachers (Cullingford, 1991), the views of teachers themselves will be significant. In particular the attitudes of teachers towards official school policies could be relevant to the outcomes of citizenship education at the school. Conforming to all five characteristics of an ethnographic social research study identified by Hammersley (1990), the project aimed at constructing a picture of the inner world of the school with reference to the teaching and learning of citizenship.

The project was to use four of the six sources of evidence for case studies which have been identified by Yin (1984), by using interviews with administrators, teachers and pupils, by making observations of individuals, by analysing available documentation and by using field notes of visits. Yin's two neglected categories (archival records and physical artefacts) were judged to be irrelevant in this project.

The Head and Deputy Heads were interviewed as representatives of the school administration, and twenty four year 9 pupils were interviewed as a cross-section of pupils in the school. The sample was selected on a modified random basis, using every fifth name on the class list and adjusted by the

Head of Year to take account of the overall profile of the school in terms of gender, ethnicity and ability.

To gain the views of the practitioners, six teachers were interviewed. They were asked not only about the official policies of the school, but about their views of pupils and how they approached their task of teaching. For example, they were asked about classroom management and methods of discipline. Each of the interview subjects was met by a researcher using an open-ended question technique which was designed to supply a frame of reference for respondents' answers, but which put a 'minimum restraint' on those answers (Kerlinger, 1969). Pupils, for example, were asked about their sense of identity, their ideas about constructive social activity, their ideas of anti-social behaviour, their experience of the influence of the school, and their sense of personal empowerment and authority. Indirect questions were also included as recommended by some researchers (e.g. Wilson, 1984). These questions were designed to reduce the risk of the respondents giving answers which they anticipated would be pleasing to the researcher, rather than expressing their true opinions.

The Curriculum for Citizenship Education

To establish the nature of the curriculum for citizenship education at school 'C' researchers looked for evidence of the three essential aspects of education for citizenship identified by Porter (1983): status, volition and competence. In all aspects there was clear evidence which suggested that school 'C' had taken education for citizenship seriously in the past, and had planned a suitable curriculum.

For example, the school official policy cast the students as 'partners' in the school. The school prospectus declared that pupils were 'encouraged to be active and to participate both in their learning and the life of the school generally'. The school behaviour policy was clearly stated to have been the product of co-operation between the staff of the school and the students.

The staff handbook reminded staff to respect the dignity of pupils, for example, by delivering rebukes (when required) low key and in private. The opinions of pupils on school matters were encouraged in the Code of Behaviour, and a policy aimed at upholding the personal dignity of pupils (the 'anti-bullying' policy) had also been formulated recently through staff-pupil consultations.

Overall the policies of the school, and their practice, indicated that each child had a significant status in the school, commanding respect and being accorded dignity. Policies encouraged pupils to feel that the school was a place where they are entitled to express their views, which would be taken seriously. The older pupils, at least, learnt about British political structures and were encouraged to think critically about them. The policies fitted well with the expectations of the Qualifications and Curriculum Authority in its document (QCA, 2000) on *Citizenship at Key Stages 3 and 4*. Building on the report of the Crick Committee, the QCA expected that the themes of political literacy (competence), community involvement (volition) and, perhaps significantly, not 'status' but 'social and moral responsibility' should 'run through all education for citizenship'.

Thus, taking evidence from interviews with senior staff, analysis of official school documents and observation of official school occasions, school 'C' appeared to be enlightened in its approach to education for citizenship, even foreshadowing the elements of the programme to be added to the National Curriculum in 2002.

Outcomes

In the light of the significant evidence that school 'C' had taken education for citizenship seriously, and had followed at least some of the procedures identified by academics as being essential to education for citizenship, a good outcome in terms of pupils' attitudes to citizenship might have been anticipated. It was therefore, something of a surprise to the researchers that in the interviews with year 9 pupils, as well as in observation of their activities, that the school's policies and curriculum did not exert any detectable influence on the citizenship attitudes of these pupils.

For example, most of the students interviewed did not feel that they had any significant status within the school. In fact only one of those interviewed named the school as being a 'community' to which he belonged. Most seemed to feel impotent within the school and viewed the teachers as the 'high-status' people, with themselves as 'low-status' people:

> … one thing I don't like is when teachers treat me, I know they are in authority, they are in charge of us, but I don't like being treated like I don't exist, or that I don't have a brain, because that really annoys me, by anybody, but particularly a teacher …

Despite these criticisms and reservations, not one of the students interviewed challenged the authority of the teachers either to punish or to take arbitrary decisions. It is perhaps relevant to students' ideas of their own status that they generally felt that bullying was the most serious misdemeanour that could be committed in a school. However almost all the students interviewed felt that the teachers regarded 'talking in class' as the most serious misdemeanour!

The sense of powerlessness that these views indicate permeated through into the students' views on participation. None of the students interviewed suggested a re-distribution of power within the school. For most of them, the kind of changes that they would like to make in the school were very minor - almost trivial - such as the girls being allowed to wear some items of jewellery, or the class being allowed to eat their packed lunches in the classrooms instead of going to the dining hall - but very few had bothered to express these views in form periods or to any of the teachers. Most claimed it would be 'pointless' to air their views, and could lead to them 'getting into trouble'.

Overall the picture emerged of the school policies being worthy but ineffectual in terms of educational outcomes. Accepting that the year 9 pupils were still rather immature and perhaps still seeing themselves as being 'children' rather than young adults, the results still showed a uniformity in self-image which was significant. The researchers accepted that perhaps after only two-and-a-half years in school 'C', the encouragement offered by the school to more positive citizenship attitudes had not yet had an effect. Would the views of these students remain the same even when they had completed year 11, i.e. after five years at school 'C'?

The researchers had little opportunity to observe the behaviour of the students outside school, and were therefore not able to judge whether the attitudes expressed by students in school were reflected by their behaviour outside of it. Nonetheless the observation of the conduct of students around the school, their interaction and attitude towards day-to-day situations in the school were consistent with the views they had expressed in their interviews with the researchers. It was not possible, of course, for the researchers to make any guesses about what attitudes these students might hold by the time they left school, or by the time they had entered adult society, but one can surmise that their views would not change (White with Brockington, 1983).

The Delivery of the Curriculum

The researchers felt that one clue to the dissonance between the educational objectives and outcomes of the school 'C' might lie in the way in which teachers presented themselves as role models or interpreted the school's rules to the students. Accordingly six members of staff, each teaching a different subject and of different ages and gender were interviewed about the attitudes they would take with them into the classroom, and which they might convey to the pupils.

As well as the formal curriculum of the school, the informal curriculum presented through the 'ethos' and through other influences has an effect on students. 'Teachers influence their pupils' (Cullingford, 1990) because 'schools are relatively small organisations in which personal relationships are very important' (p.178). Research by Getzels and Smilansky (1983) also showed that problems linked with the attitudes and styles of teachers were identified far more frequently by pupils as being 'problems connected with the school' than any other matters.

Professional experience suggests that even when all teachers are teaching the same syllabus there are variables in the processes which mean that results achieved by different teachers will be different. The variables might include the different relationships created by the different personalities of the pupils being taught, the different circumstances of each classroom, and the different personalities of the teachers themselves. Everyday experience also suggests that politicians and lawyers can refer to the same facts, and yet come to totally contradictory conclusions. It is unreasonable to expect that teachers will be able to refrain from deliberately or subconsciously making value judgements about the curriculum they are required to deliver to their pupils. This may be particularly significant for the delivery of a curriculum like citizenship education which itself may be dealing with value judgements.

The researchers attempted to explore the attitudes of the interviewed teachers towards their pupils, towards the policies of the school, and even towards larger society. All of these have some relevance to the curriculum that would be received by the pupils of the individual teachers.

The National Curriculum Council document on Spiritual and Moral Development (NCC, 1993) makes a link between the formal curriculum (*what* is being taught) and the informal curriculum (*how* it is being taught) that is relevant for citizenship education:

> Teachers are, by the nature of their profession 'moral agents' who imply values by the way they address their pupils and each other, the way they dress, the language they use and the effort they put into their work. (NCC, 1993, p.8)

When interviewed, and after observation, it was perhaps not surprising that the teachers at school 'C' proved to be a representative cross-section of all main-stream political views. Whilst two enthusiastically embraced the school's official policy, two implicitly rejected the idea of treating children as 'partners' in their education. All teachers felt that it was perfectly proper for them to pick and choose which aspects of the school's policy and curriculum they delivered, and which they ignored or treated superficially. Ideas of 'model pupils' ranged from the well-behaved child to the well-behaved *and* intelligent child! And by 'well-behaved', it was evident that most teachers meant 'obedient'.

Nonetheless there was considerable variation in classroom practice and in the quality of the relationship teachers had with their pupils. Some teachers wanted a more prescriptive code for discipline, specifying particular punishments that would follow particular offences, while others wished to have greater discretion.

Some of the teachers recognised that pupils were receiving contradictory messages about values and standards from different teachers, such as this observation by a teacher who revealed:

> It's difficult for the kids. They're doing one thing in one lesson that may be breaking school rules, but the teacher isn't picking them up on it, and then the next teacher says, 'You are breaking school rules! Go to the Head of Department!' It must be quite confusing; they need to know where they stand.

Other teachers, however, were less concerned about the possible inconsistency of the messages being received by the pupils. Another teacher, said she often pretended 'not to notice' breaches of some school rules, adding:

> I think I can understand what the school strives for, but from my working in the classroom, I think I am probably not always what the school would ultimately want in terms of getting the system working perfectly, but then I think I often have fewer discipline problems because of my attitude to them [the pupils].

Attitudes towards pupils varied from keeping them tightly disciplined, and allowing them very little flexibility in, for example, where they sat in the classroom, or how they entered or left the classroom, to others who were much more 'laid back'. Whilst this may be teaching pupils a valuable lesson about the inconsistencies of society, for those who designed the school curriculum it will mean that pupils are receiving different messages from those they intended. The possible value of such inconsistency has been recognised. Edwards (1996), for example, said:

> However long it is debated consistency will not be absolute. Guidelines and a broad sense of direction will be valuable in assisting teaching in helping pupils to develop their own personal sense of values. Pupils are very adaptable and perceptive. They learn from a range of adults, making their own judgements and seeing variety as an advantage, not a disadvantage.
>
> (Edwards, 1996, p.177)

Some of the teachers at school 'C' seemed to go further than interpreting guidelines differently. For some it amounted to almost a rejection of the guidelines themselves. For example, one teacher said in his interview:

> We seem to be so wrapped up in policies for this and policies for that, we haven't got the time to deal with one of the fundamental things of how a school can run - and it's having some sort of discipline in the school.

One teacher who felt that she was more 'liberal' was sending a contradictory message to the pupils in her classes when she refused to uphold the school regulations on, for example, the wearing of school uniform, or jewellery. She also turned a 'deaf ear' to bad language which was specifically not allowed according to the school code of behaviour or the staff manual.

Practice More Than Policy

The pupils at school 'C', therefore, received an inconsistent interpretation of the whole-school policies on education for citizenship. Not only was the curriculum conveyed in an inconsistent way, it was sometimes conveyed by teachers in a way which gave contradictory messages to pupils. The problem was compounded by the fact that most teachers felt they had little, if any, responsibility for education for citizenship. Even form tutors had their own priorities as to which of the school rules they felt they should impress on their pupils, and which they felt free to interpret generously or to ignore. The traditional autonomy of British teachers is an important issue for practitioners, and the judgements made by teachers at school 'C' are part of the practical manifestation of this autonomy. Whilst the teachers interviewed varied in their views of most things, including the extent to which they themselves were involved in making the regulations of the school, they would certainly have perceived a clear message about their own status as citizen-teachers if the administration had ruled more firmly on how they should interpret the school policies to their pupils.

It is perhaps significant that the latest government initiative on citizenship education lays more stress than hitherto upon the preparation of teachers to deliver a citizenship curriculum, especially during initial teacher training. There is also more stress upon the effect of the overall impact of the school ethos. For example, the QCA states:

> Citizenship should reflect and be reflected in the values and ethos of a school ... the school ethos embodies the values held by a school's communities and creates the atmosphere for life in and beyond the school itself.
>
> (QCA, 2000, p.1)

To make the teaching of citizenship more effective at school 'C', the school could benefit from developing a more coherent citizenship education policy throughout the school, and in devoting more resources to the preparation of teachers to deliver this curriculum. In particular there should be greater consideration given to the development of skills of participation and responsible action. The QCA document referred to above gives many examples of good practice which could be adapted to local needs. A thorough-going review of the whole of the curriculum offered by school 'C', to ensure that the hidden or informal curriculum is consistent with the official aims of the school, would also be helpful.

In summary the project carried out at school 'C' shows that for effective education for citizenship more than good intentions are needed. School 'C' is probably typical of many schools in England and Wales, which have a positive official attitude toward citizenship, yet which are failing to convey the curriculum effectively to pupils.

The difference between a whole school policy, full of good intention, and its impact on staff and students is clear. Any centralised policy which is aimed at improving the performance and understanding of all members of an institution is laudable. Without the full participation and support of teachers in particular it can also be meaningless. All the literature on continuing professional development, on lifelong learning, on institutional effectiveness, and on the need for coherent policies as well as targets, emphasises the importance of involvement and communication. A concern like citizenship, having an impact on the everyday life of the school, should only be welcomed. It is clearly a 'good thing'. In this case study it was supposed to be central. The results, however, suggest that a note of caution should be sounded. To put good intentions into actual practice is more difficult than we think.

References

Board of Education (1904) *Code of regulations for public elementary schools.* London: HMSO.

Bowles, S. and Gintis, H. (1979) *Schooling in capitalist America.* London: Routledge and Kegan Paul.

Brennan, T. (1981) *Political education and democracy.* Cambridge: Cambridge University Press.

Bush, T. and West-Burnham, J. (1994) *The Principles of Educational Management.* Harlow: Longman.

Cole, M. (ed) (1988) *Bowles and Gintis revisited.* London: Falmer Press.

Crick, C. (1998) *Report of the Advisory Committee on Citizenship Education* (The Crick Report). London: HMSO.

Cullingford, C. (1991) *The nature of learning.* London: Cassell.

Cullingford, C. (1992) *Children and society.* London: Cassell.

Edwards, J. (1996) Planning for values education in the school curriculum. In Halstead, M. and Taylor, R. (Eds.) *Values in Education and Education in Values*, pp.163-179. London: Falmer Press.

Getzels, J. and Smilansky, J. (1983) Individual differences in pupil perception of school problems. *British Journal of Educational Psychology* **53** pp.301-316.

Hammersley, M. (1990) *Reading ethnographic research.* London: Longmans.

Harber, C. (1991) Educational contexts for political education. *Educational review* **43** (3), pp.245-255.

Kerlinger, F.N. (1969) *Foundations of behavioural research.* New York: Holt Rinehart and Winston.

Mortimore, P., Sammons, P., Stoll, L., Lewis, D. and Ecob., R. (1988) *School Matters: The Junior Years*. London: Open Books.

Murgatroyd, S. and Morgan, C. (1993) *Total Quality Management and the School*. Buckingham: Open University Press.

National Curriculum Council (1990) *Curriculum Guidance no. 8: Education for citizenship*. York: NCC.

Norwood Report (1943) *Curriculum and examinations in secondary schools*. London: HMSO.

Osborne, A. and John, P.D. (1992) The influence of school ethos on pupils' citizenship attitudes. *Education Review* **44** (2), pp.153-165.

Porter, A. (1983) *Teaching Political Literacy.* London: Institute of Education papers.

Qualifications and Curriculum Authority (2000) *Citizenship at Key Stages 3 and 4.* London: HMSO.

Rutter, M., Maughan, B., Mortimore, P. and Ouston, J. (1979) *Fifteen thousand hours*. London: Open Books.

White, R. with Brockington, D. (1983) *Tales Out of School: Consumers' Views of British Education.* London: Routledge and Kegan Paul.

Wilson, M.J. (1984) Styles of research. In Bell, J. et al. (Eds.) *Conducting small scale investigations in educational management*. London: Harper Row.

Yin, R.K. (1984) *Case study research: design and methods*. Beverley Hills: Sage Publications.

12 Leadership for Sustainable Development Education

JOHN BLEWITT

Introduction

One factor which has implications for institutions and individuals is the concept of sustainability. The development of a Sustainable Development Education Strategy (SDE) for Yorkshire and Humber is indicative of the growing significance of sustainable development policy and the increasing significance of regionalisation in the planning of education and training. Sustainable development education is only slowly being integrated into the work of formal education institutions and the informal learning process. Taking a theoretical approach derived from ecological and systems thinking, this integration indicates the importance of two things: the need for sustainable development education leadership within organisations and appropriate policies and practices that will enhance, encourage and embed sustainability principles in the consciousness and behaviour of all stakeholders.

> Sustainable development education is about the learning needed to maintain and improve our quality of life and the quality of life for generations to come. It is about equipping individuals, communities, groups, businesses and government to live and act sustainably; as well as giving them an understanding of the environmental, social and economic issues involved.
>
> (DETR, 1998)

Formulating a Regional Sustainable Development Education Policy

As policy making becomes more significant at the regional level, education, training, employability and sustainability are being slowly integrated in the decision making process, according to principles of need and subsidiarity. The Regional Economic Strategies produced by the Regional Development Agencies are informing regions' developmental frameworks for the next ten years. Other regional strategies are also being developed - on spatial planning, tourism, technological innovation, culture and sustainable development. Indeed sustainable development is becoming increasingly important as arguments against exponential economic growth, environmental hazards and the problems associated with social exclusion gain greater currency. Education is not immune from this, although the dominant thinking here still focuses on a narrow dual conception of employability and vocationalism: skill development and updating, information technology, employability, regeneration and renewal. However, in order to be prepared for the risks and uncertainties of the 21st century, individuals need more than a few National Vocational Qualifications. National Education Targets promote a credit-based and quantitative approach to progress, but more qualifications do not in themselves further sustainable development (Reid, 1995; Trorey, Cullingford and Cooper, 1999). Lifelong Learning must improve human well-being as well as serve the economy. As John Prescott and David Blunkett have written in the Foreword to Yorkshire and Humber's SDE Strategy:

> Sustainable development education is about forming and informing people: individually and in communities, at work and at play. It helps people to recognise the impact of their actions on the world around them, and to make choices and decisions that improve the quality of life of others. It offers those on the edge of society a way back into it, it can enhance employability and citizenship, and can make businesses more competitive, all the while ensuring that we protect and enhance the environment.
>
> (Yorkshire and Humber Education for Sustainability Forum, 2000, p.1)

The key concepts of SDE are:

- Interdependence.
- Citizenship and stewardship.
- Needs and rights of future generations.
- Diversity.
- Quality of life, equity and justice.
- Sustainable change.
- Uncertainty and precaution in action.

The future success of the regions will depend on the extent to which sustainability imperatives are successfully addressed. These imperatives include democratic renewal, subsidiarity, social capital, community capacity building, pollution abatement, integrated transport, improved biodiversity, social inclusion and meaningful employment. Yorkshire and

Humber have produced a detailed set of sustainable development objectives and indicators, incorporated within a sustainable development plan, which inform and attempt to set the parameters within which other strategies will evolve. Sustainable development education is a necessary condition for the creation of a healthy, vital and prosperous region.

The concept of Sustainable Development Education is holistic and inclusive, sometimes running counter to popular perceptions of education as that taking place exclusively within the formal institutions of schools, colleges and universities. In acknowledging the significance of informal learning, connectivity and partnership working, the Lifelong Learning agenda sees education as broader than this. Sustainable development education prefigures a paradigm shift in educational policy and practice. It places emphasis on the significance of informal learning networks, the nurturing of social capital and community capacity building, the value of diversity, the limits to growth and the need for precaution, the needs and rights of future generations, equity and environmental justice, the connective role of the communications media, global and corporate citizenship and business efficiency and effectiveness incorporating the whole spectrum of civil society. These issues are not yet central to the perspectives of many decision-makers inside the new regional bodies or in formal education institutions, although the influence of systems thinking and the ecological concept of self-organisation underpins the attempt to construct a holistic, joined-up, approach to policy making and practice.

Following the *Lifelong Learning and Sustainable Development* Conference held in Harrogate in October 1999, funding was secured from the Environment Agency, the Regional Assembly and the Government Office for Yorkshire and Humber to develop a regional SDE strategy. Extensive consultations took place with major stakeholders in the first half of 2000 and, with due recognition of the Regional Economic Strategy, six key objectives were identified in the Strategy report:

- Develop the sustainable development competence of the existing workforce - to facilitate sustainable growth.
- Promote the region's commitment to sustainable development - to foster a positive regional identity.
- Develop the sustainable development competence of the future workforce - to ensure preparedness for the 21st century workplace.

- Develop the sustainable development competence of all the region's citizens - to facilitate social inclusion and active participation in sustainable development.
- Increase opportunities for sustainable development volunteering - to enable all citizens to contribute their time and/or expertise to improving the quality of life in the region.
- Promote the sustainable management and use of the education community's physical, cultural and environmental assets.

(Yorkshire and Humber Education for Sustainability Forum, 2000)

Two of the fourteen accompanying priority actions attracted immediate interest from potential sponsors. These were for the development of teacher training initiatives and secondly, a leadership programme. The latter is particularly important, because SDE challenges the dominance of economic instrumentalism, individualism and the Newtonian conception of linear causality - more qualifications causes a fairer society and a more effective economy. Instead, the world can be understood as a complex, interconnected, unpredictable and non-linear ecosystem. SDE is an approach to learning that cannot be managed but must be led, cannot conform to an unchangeable blueprint but must evolve in a self-organising fashion. In a complex world, institutional strategies are most effective where 'implementers become formulators', where the people on the ground are able, and do, effectively influence the evolution of the organisation.

Theoretical Perspectives: complexity and self organisation

Complexity is usually associated with living beings, manifesting itself at the level of the system itself. A complex system is comprised of many elements which richly interact both physically and in relation to information transfer. These interactions are fairly short range, each element operating in ignorance of the overall nature of the system itself. However, they may have consequences far in excess of their localised existence. The effects are therefore non-linear in scope and not necessarily predictable. Feedback loops may enhance or stimulate development or alternatively may hinder or inhibit it. Most importantly, complex systems are not closed, for they constantly interact with the external environment, adjusting or not adjusting according to their degree of internal flexibility and capacity to accommodate, manage or mediate the variety of flows they experience. In the network society some time-sharing social practices may not be contiguous, so new spatial dynamics will be established. This is as every online learner already knows. Finally, complex systems only achieve equilibrium when the possibility of change is exhausted. There is no such thing as a stable state. Individual 'elements' within formal education institutions experience constant change; therefore what needs to be considered is the nature, organisation and trajectory of that change. Cilliers offers a working definition of self organisation:

> The capacity for self organisation is a property of complex systems which enables them to develop or change internal structure spontaneously and adaptively in order to cope with, or manipulate, their environment.
>
> (Cilliers, 1998, p.90)

The behaviour of a complex system is not determined primarily by the priorities of the individual components or elements of the system, but is the result of complex patterns of interaction. Hence the whole is greater than the sum of a system's constituent parts and its structure is something that is not so much designed and imposed as one that emerges from the various interactions taking place between the system and its relation to the environment. This is not to deny the significance of human agency in human or social organisations, or in human beings themselves, but it is to qualify any notion of purely voluntary action. A self-organising system selects or filters flows of information or influence. What it integrates is not so much a product of conscious decision making, but rather the system's capacity to make sense of, to re-articulate or re-design itself in accordance with what it encounters. A self organising system is not determined by an established series of specific goals or targets. Rather it may be said to have a function shaped by and within the overall context in which the system operates. The function of a college can only be understood within the context of the education system and the political, economic and other processes operating within the wider society. The same may be said for specific nodes, departments or sections within the organisation itself. According to Cilliers:

> the process of self-organisation cannot be driven by the attempt to perform a function; it is rather the result of an evolutive process whereby a system will simply not survive if it cannot adapt to more complex circumstances.
>
> (Cilliers, 1998, p.93)

A self-organising system will attempt a balance between rigid order and chaos. In order to survive and adapt, the organisation needs to learn. In order to learn the organisation needs to understand the flows and influences it encounters, and for its individual elements to take the lead in responding intelligently and creatively to these influences. Consequently, any complex, dynamic system may be seen as continually being transformed by both its environment and itself. Self organisation is a self transforming and reflexive process. Control does not come from a single source, and if for any reason this does happen then the system itself will start to degenerate and die.

Capra (1996) argues that a basic set of principles, derived from our understanding of ecosystems as autopoietic networks and dissipative structures, may serve as guidelines for building sustainable human communities of practice, experience and hope. These principles would include interdependent and networking (Capra's 'web of life'), non-linear relationships involving multiple feedback loops, cyclical processes, flexibility, partnership inferring democracy, enrichment, personal empowerment and systemic limits to growth, particularly in relation to increased economic activity and material consumption (Capra, 1996).

The principles of sustainable development and the concept and direct experience of the risk society have become increasingly pertinent as stories of diseases jumping the species barrier, genetic modification of foodstuffs, global warming and sunbathing and skin cancer penetrate more deeply into the social consciousness. The green slogan *act local, think global,* which accompanies many environmental campaigns and pleas for more sustainable practices, also articulates a moral and relational responsibility. My actions, my university's purchasing decisions, affect others near me as well as others further away, both spatially and temporally. For Cilliers, 'altruistic behaviour' is a necessary characteristic for the flourishing of a system. Systems thinking *does* harbour an ethical implication, contrary to that despaired of by Beck in his seminal *The Risk Society*:

> One can do something and continue doing it without having to take personal responsibility for it. It is as if one were acting while being personally absent. One acts physically, without acting morally or politically. The generalised other - the system acts within and through oneself: this is the slave morality of civilisation, in which people act personally and socially as if they were subject to a natural fate, the law of gravitation of the system. This is the way the "hot potato" is passed in the face of the threatening ecological disaster.
>
> (Beck, 1992, p.33)

Many of these risks and hazards, like the air we breathe, are invisible, universal and unspecific. Victims may not be aware or cognisant of the potential threats unless knowledge and understanding are gained through formal or informal learning - a college course, a media report, observing the disfiguration of a tree, a cyclist wearing a gas mask ... The degree and the extent of endangerment are fundamentally dependent on external knowledge and our reflections-in-action. The problem is to address the incompetence that pervades the decisions that determine our own and others affliction. Without education for sustainability, we will not attain the 'cognitive sovereignty' necessary for health, well being and survival. As Beck writes:

> the harmful, threatening, inimical lies in wait everywhere, but whether it is inimical or friendly is beyond one's own power of judgement, is reserved for the assumptions, methods and controversies of external knowledge producers.
> (Beck, 1992, pp.53-54)

Is this beef safe to eat, this mobile phone safe to use, this product morally right to purchase? How can I distinguish between corporate citizenship and corporate green washing or propaganda? Has Monsanto really changed its spots? Educationalists and educational organisations are inextricably and inevitably involved in the social, economic, political and ecological relationships that constitute and reproduce this risk society. Having interpreted this world in various ways, the point may be to change it before it is too late.

Sustainable Development Education Leadership: towards implementation

In 1990, Senge noted that the prevailing view of learning organisations was that of giving emphasis to increased adaptability but, for him, what was of greater significance was a focus on generative and creative learning, stimulating new ways of looking at the world. Generative learning requires seeing the systems that control events. 'When we fail to grasp the systemic source of problems' he says, we are left to 'push on' symptoms rather than eliminate underlying causes. Adaptive learning is simply about coping but coping is not enough. To create a learning organisation and sustainable human communities, a form of non-hierarchical, lateral and co-operative leadership is needed:

> Leadership in learning organisations centres on subtler and ultimately more important work [than simply energising the troops]. In a learning organisation, leaders' roles differ from that of the charismatic decision maker. Leaders are designers, teachers, and stewards. These roles require new skills: the ability to build shared vision, to bring to the surface and challenge prevailing mental models, and to foster more systemic patterns of thinking. In short, leaders in learning organisations are continually expanding their capabilities to shape their future - that is, leaders are responsible for learning. (Senge, 1990, p.489)

Consequently an SDE leadership programme will require the learning organisation to learn that innovation from below is something to be nurtured and not controlled. Innovation will require the ability of leaders to address challenging situations in such a way as to integrate learning and apply it creatively and reflexively to other situations. Educational improvements must be seen in more contextualised ways than is usually allowed for. Fortunately the seeds of a paradigm shift are already present in the policy references to mentoring, networking, partnership relationships, credit frameworks, learning webs and in the recently published Further Education National Training Organisation (FENTO) standards for FE teachers whose value base stresses collaborative working, collegiality, reflective practice and creativity in continuing professional development.

With clusters of SDE leaders operating horizontally and vertically within a learning/educational organisation, relationships will be established whereby new modes of thought and action are developed locally. Leadership within this context may not only have non-linear systemic effects, but may also create learning experiences, cultures and practices that move beyond the formal curriculum or the specified targets of management-determined strategic action plans, which by their very nature exhibit qualities of rigidity and adaptability. In words borrowed from Lave and Wenger (1991), SDE leaders and the leadership process will help bring about ecological and sustainable *learning* curricula in various parts of the organisation. A learning curriculum consists of situated opportunities for the improvisational (creative) development of new practice, 'a field of learning resources in everyday practice *viewed from the perspective of learners*'. For Lave and Wenger, participation at multiple levels is entailed in membership of a community of practice, of which the SDE leader would be a fully participating member. This community need not necessitate co-presence or a well-defined group with socially visible boundaries. However, 'it does imply participation in an activity system about which participants share understandings concerning what they are doing and what that means in their lives and for their communities'. This is not to deny the significance of power relations, established habits of behaviour or attitude or other pressing influences and conditions that delimit possibilities of evolutionary change. What it does suggest is that SDE leadership encompasses generative learning rooted within emerging communities of practice in an overall context of complexity and self organisation. Consequently learning, and leadership, is not merely situated in practice, for it is an integral part of a generative social practice in the lived-in world of experience and action.

Creativity is a defining characteristic of such leadership encompassing as Seltzer and Bentley (1999) state: 'the ability to formulate new problems; the ability to transfer learning across different contexts; the ability to recognise that learning is incremental and involves making mistakes; and, the capacity to focus attention in particular direction'. With time the complex organisation changes in a relational and interdependent manner, drawing in others from the margins and inferring an overarching ethical imperative that returns, in part maybe, a cognitive sovereignty to all of us at risk in our social and ecological environment:

> A community of practice is a set of relations among persons, activity, and world, over time and in relation with other tangential and overlapping communities of practice. A community of practice is an intrinsic condition for the existence of knowledge, not least because it provides the interpretative support necessary for making sense of its heritage. Thus participation is the cultural practice in which any knowledge exists, is an epistemological principle of learning. The social structure of this practice, its power relations, and its conditions for legitimacy defines possibilities for learning (ie. for legitimate peripheral participation). (Lave and Wenger, 1991, p.98)

SDE is becoming increasingly significant for schools, colleges and universities, and is recognised as a contributing element to regional skills development planning and the production of sustainable development frameworks (DETR, 2000). It features prominently in Yorkshire and Humberside's report *Advancing Together: Towards a Sustainable Region* launched in March 2001. The need for leadership in the implementation and delivery process at micro and macro levels is self-evident, for without it Sustainable Development Education will remain simply words on paper.

Figure 12.1 Developing leaders for sustainable development education

1. Leadership is required to ensure that sustainability principles and practices are introduced, developed and embedded within the culture of organisations and the consciousness of practitioners. In this way SDE leaders may need to adopt an advocacy role and one that communicates a transformative and creative approach to pedagogy.
2. Potential and actual SDE leaders will benefit from professional development opportunities that enhance understanding of both SDE and the methods by which the direction of change within a learning organisation may be influenced. This may be achieved through a critical engagement with the teaching and learning curricula, ranging from new units of formalised or accredited study, widening participation and nurturing informal (generative) learning networks.
3. Generic knowledge, understanding and ability outcomes may be identified according to key questions, issues and conceptual domains pertinent to SDE leadership:
   - What is a leader? What does a leader do? How can he/she make a difference?
   - How do leaders facilitate change? They may seek to initiate change or innovate with view to changing ideas, beliefs, attitudes, interests, practices and procedures.
   - How might leaders develop a strong sense of purpose as well as the ability to communicate a vision of the future in a clear and distinct manner to others?
   - Leaders inspire and motivate people. They are able to creatively engage with a range of issues, problems and challenges. They generate trust, active participation, commitment and community.
   - How might leaders effect change if they do not exercise formal power or authority within their organisation? Leaders align people towards achieving and attaining goals. Leaders are often people-centred, exhibiting high levels of emotional and linguistic intelligence.
   - Leaders have the capacity to learn and elicit the desire to learn in others. They have self-knowledge and the capacity to make choices justifying action on the basis of knowledge or expertise.

This leadership, articulating ecosystem norms and values, could become part of an individual's continuing professional development or an aspect of an organisation's strategic staff development programme. Leadership is already a major issue for senior managers and frequently appears in some form on existing pre-service and in-service teacher training programmes. The task is to fully embed SDE leadership in the culture, consciousness and practice of the compulsory education sector. The interest generated in the Yorkshire and Humber SDE Strategy is an encouraging sign that the 'education renaissance' of *The Learning Age* could facilitate a further shift towards the ecological paradigm in thinking on education quality, school improvement and professional development. Clarke writes:

> Human groupings are self-organising and emergent and the flow of information through an organisation takes its own course and, if people are connected and meet in a conducive organisation environment, the resulting interactions will be beneficial and will reframe their activity in purposeful ways.
>
> (Clarke, 2001, in press)

To effect systemic change within an organisation the whole organisation has to move. It requires all those working within it or in some way associated with its operations and purpose to share and contribute to the process of change. Relatively small actions may in time have quite significant and perhaps unexpected outcomes. Although prescribed outcomes and targets characterise contemporary educational management, from an ecological perspective it would be mistaken to predict the exact nature of those outcomes. In other words, outcomes, like objectives, need to be more expressive as well as sustainable. In practice various tensions may develop. An individual, for example, may wish to effect or influence change but find his or her organisation's plans, targets and criteria are constructed unsympathetically. Suggestions and even small actions for change may meet with the type of disheartening resistance that comes with it being 'not a priority' or being allowed but not financially supported for the very same reasons.

However individuals are by their very nature capable of being change agents because of the relational nature of human agency. Without growth complex organisations, including people, die. For Dewey (1933), growth was the primary goal of education and personal development. Many teachers working to green the curriculum or render an institution's services more sustainable may find themselves with modest development opportunities, a far cry from Giroux's (1992) notion of the teacher as a 'transformative intellectual'. Within schools they may establish green clubs, within colleges they may participate in enrichment programmes or emphasise those elements of sustainability that already exist in units or modules currently being delivered. Non-academic staff may have similar opportunities and although the 'making the best of' approach may benefit staff and students and may, like the proverbial butterfly, lead to major changes, they equally may not. Without leadership, desired and desirable change will remain uncertain, haphazard and random. The political, policy and other priorities of the institution and the wider environment need to inter-relate and evolve towards greater sustainability.

EcoCampus: in practice

The EcoCampus project, derived from work undertaken by the University of Central Lancashire on environmental management systems and Going for Green's commitment to greening educational institutions, offers opportunities for SDE leadership and systemic change. It may serve as a useful example of what might possibly be achieved when the policy and practices of an organisation and its wider environment connect. A principal aim of Going for Green's earlier *Sustainable University* and its *Sustainable Communities Project* was to develop a means to support and reward institutions of further and higher education seeking to improve their sustainable development performance. The interest generated in this work led Going for Green to realise that further and higher education institutions were looking for a sector-specific management system, for which accreditation would be a recognised measure of commitment to their improvement in sustainable development performance. The scheme, currently being piloted by a number of further education colleges and universities in England and Wales, will allow these institutions to be recognised for addressing key issues of environmental sustainability, and eventually gain accreditation for improved sustainability performance. The management system software has been developed by Nottingham Trent University. The key aims of the pilot are to test the EcoCampus model in preparation for a UK launch in 2002. From a management perspective, the benefits of EcoCampus are, according to Going for Green, likely to include the following:

- financial savings through improved resource productivity, reduction in energy consumption and landfill costs

- help with establishing compliance with environmental legislation and a reduction in the risk of penalties for breaches of legislation and policies
- enhanced student recruitment potential by providing evidence of responsible practice
- improved external perceptions of the institution
- addressing the needs and expectations of external stakeholders for environmental, sustainability, social and economic performance
- practical sustainability issues, such as waste, emissions, traffic and transport addressed
- creation of an enhanced learning environment
- staff and students becoming involved in the institution's activities, helping to create a sense of community and ownership
- environmental/sustainability issues established as a key policy/strategy element.

(Going for Green, 2000)

The EcoCampus awards will be made in 11 key areas of environmental sustainability and for overall progress towards sustainable development. The award areas are for:

- Transport.
- Ethical/sustainable procurement.
- Curriculum greening.
- Resource use (including energy and water).
- Waste.
- Community involvement.
- Policy.
- Environmental sustainability reporting.
- Built environment.
- Environmental sustainability training.
- Health and safety.
- Overall progress towards sustainable development.

In this way, the EcoCampus programme can be undertaken in manageable sections, allowing institutions to focus on areas which they identify as being of importance, enabling an institution to be rewarded for initiatives already undertaken. They also represent key elements of Castells's (1996) *Space of flows* and an organisation's *function*. EcoCampus is not based on institutional comparison and is intended to operate along the following lines:

- Establishment of leadership, commitment and resources.
- EcoCampus champions to take the work forward.
- Establishment of an EcoCampus steering group to provide a forum for guiding and implementing the work.
- Undertaking a comprehensive environmental review of activities and procedures, using guidance materials supplied by EcoCampus.
- Preparation of a policy for sustainable development and action to realise it.
- Prioritisation of the significant environmental sustainability impacts and putting measures in place to deliver the requirements of EcoCampus in the short, medium and long terms. Measures should include training for staff and students and a communications programme, ensuring all are aware of their own responsibility to the environment and to the implementation of EcoCampus.
- Identification of documentary methods that will allow for both internal and external verification.
- Monitoring, reviewing, reporting and arranging for external verification with a view to receiving the EcoCampus award.

The identification of champions acknowledges the role of lateral leadership and the need to engage persons interested in pursuing the sustainability agenda. They may operate in their own particular localities, influencing others through their immediate physical and non-physical relationships, and gradually and incrementally acquiring the capacity to effect systemic change assuming the system/organisation is not 'hard wired' against it. This lateral leadership may expand well beyond the formal spatial boundaries of the organisation through its curriculum developments, purchasing policies, energy conservation methods and approaches to green transport practices. Champions/leaders may find themselves affecting the thinking and behaviour of people and organisations in a wider community. The search for ways to promote sustainable transport practices will mean encouraging cycling, walking and the use of public transport, as well as changing attitudes to mobility and access, therefore involving issues relating to social disadvantage, health and fitness, finance and planning. All manner of phenomena may arise which may serve to either help or hinder positive action in this area, and those championing this will need to seek creative strategies to make things happen, to anticipate problems that have not yet arisen and to engage in dialogue with others outside the organisation. Pragmatism is likely to be essential to the SDE leader's approach to issues, as is a sense that what she or he is doing is an end in itself, worth doing for its own sake, to be replicated in numerous other areas. This change may initially have a modest, perhaps a traditionally environmental focus, but may prove a powerful force if integration between the elements and the work of the champions occurs; harmony, complexity and sustainability will be realised. It will also contribute to changes in our own personal and professional selves. If I change myself something may happen as a consequence that may lead to a change in the world.

Figure 12.2 Leeds Metropolitan University's call for EcoCampus champions (2000)

Energy and Environment Champions: Leeds Metropolitan University

LMU seeks volunteers to be the 'eyes and ears' of departments and faculties in a bid to reduce the university's environmental impacts.

We are looking for E&E Champions that **represent all staff** and functions of LMU – academic and non-academic. Energy and Environment Champions will look for ways of reducing avoidable energy/water waste, etc. Some measures will require direct action that will encourage others to do the same. E&E Champions will help identify projects that the University should undertake and help implement new ideas in partnership with the Estates Division.

'Green Teams', made up of Energy and Environment Champions within faculties will be created, with a nominated team leader. The Team Leaders will form a Green Taskforce that will report directly to the Environmental Policy Steering Group and the Energy Working Group.

References

Beck, U. (1992) *The Risk Society*. London: Sage.

Capra, F. (1996) *The Web of Life: A new scientific understanding of living systems*. New York: Doubleday.

Castells, M. (1996) *The Rise of the Network Society*. Vol.1. London: Blackwell.

Cilliers, P. (1998) *Complexity and Postmodernism: understanding complex systems*. London: Routledge.

Clarke, P. (2001) (in press) *Learning Schools, Learning Systems*. London: Cassell.

DETR (1998) *First Report of the Sustainable Development Education Panel.* London: Department of Employment, Transport and the Regions.

DETR (2000) *Guidance on Preparing Regional Sustainability Frameworks*. London: Department of Employment, Transport and the Regions.

Dewey, J. (1933) *How we think*. Chicago: Henry Regnery.

Giroux, H. (1992) *Border Crossings: cultural workers and the politics of Education*. London: Routledge.

Going for Green (2000) *The EcoCampus Award Scheme*. Leeds: Going for Green.

Lave, J. and Wenger, E. (1991) *Situated Learning: Legitimate peripheral Participation*. Cambridge: Cambridge University Press.

Reid, D. (1995) *Sustainable Development: an introductory guide*. London: Earthscan.

Seltzer, K. and Bentley, T. (1999) *The Creative Age: knowledge and skills for a new economy*. London: Demos.

Senge, P. (1990) The leader's new work: building learning organisations. In Pugh, D.S. *Organisation Theory*. Harmondsworth: Penguin.

Trorey, G., Cullingford, C. and Cooper, B. (1999) Lifelong Learning for a Sustainable Future. In Oliver, P. (Ed.) *Lifelong Learning and Continuing Education*. Aldershot: Ashgate.

Yorkshire and Humber Education for Sustainability Forum (2000). *Education Strategy 2000-2010.* Leeds: Yorkshire and Humber Education for Sustainability Forum.

13 Institutional Development and Professional Needs: Some Reflections

CEDRIC CULLINGFORD

The Politics of Accountability

Whatever the context of the studies in this book, from Universities to Primary Schools, some consistent themes emerge which suggest something about the tone and culture of the times in which we live. There are ever increasing external demands placed on institutions and individuals, and systems of accountability. There are not only growing amounts of information but more organisations involved in its dissemination. The pressure placed on individuals to conform to prescribed processes is strong, and made the more astringent by the tension between market forces and centralised control, within as well as outside institutions.

All these lead to consequences which we experience in our professional lives, and which we all recognise, and cope with, in our different ways. The continual additional demands of new initiatives, with deadlines both short and soon to be replaced by others, demonstrates an urgency of political will in entering and controlling what used to be seen as the 'secret garden', not only of the curriculum but of the personal privacy of teaching and learning. This 'policy hysteria' of overlapping and even conflicting policies affects all (Ball, 1994; Stronach and Morris, 1994).

One of the pervasive, if unintentional, themes of our time is that of mistrust. There is an unspoken assumption, beneath the system of accountability, of inspection and judgement. The exposure of those who must be 'named and blamed' and the scrutiny of professional practice would not be necessary if it were assumed that people were doing as good a job as possible, developing their own professional practice and continually improving.

Being brought to account forces a defensive position. There is a symbiotic relationship between accountability and self-justification. This is an age of triumph for those who are able to market themselves. It is not enough to do a good job. The evidence for what is done is as important as the quality of the job itself. Those who believe in the role of inspection will argue that demonstration will itself lead to higher standards. The old fashioned notion that *Possunt quia posse videntus*: 'They can because they think they can' (Virgil) has been replaced by the idea that people do what they need to in order to justify themselves. Every inspection requires not only a visitation but extensive paper work. The quality audits, the offices of inspection and the research assessments all depend on how well the work of institutions is presented. Some cynics might suggest that we live in the age of 'spin', of marketing, of presentation, as if we were all party politicians. All would agree that the response to external inspection is the development of strategies to justify every action carried out.

The Consequences for Professional Development

These strategies have significant consequences for personal and professional development. Those days when staff development was a matter of individuals identifying their own needs without considering the institution are long past. Personal concerns are supposed to focus specifically on organisational goals and be justified on those grounds. Intelligent individuals can, of course, gear their requirements to the strategic plan, and many would see this as a positive step, but it is also a new style of thinking. The outcomes of institutional success are measured in technological terms, in competencies and skills. The requirements of governments are perhaps necessarily mechanistic. The creation of wealth, the demands of competition and the development of advanced labour forces are all seen as the prerequisite of national and institutional health. Even concerns like lifelong learning often actually mean utilitarian outcomes, those skills required by society as a whole, and those skills which reward the individual financially. There are also some ironies in the setting up of many more official bureaucracies designed to improve institutions through staff development.

One question that arises from continuing professional development is whether people learn what they want to. There can be a gap between personal interests and the requirements of the institution. The skills shortages, even in a time of high unemployment, suggests that demand does not so easily create supply, that such a mechanistic view of learning is not altogether accurate. There are many studies, often in Scandinavian countries, which demonstrate that, when they are given a choice, individuals will wish to learn subjects that appeal to them rather than those which are deemed to be useful, and those subjects which 'appeal' are philosophy rather than engineering, and astronomy rather than computing, (Marklund, 1986). If personal development and personal interests were all bound up in the necessary skills of wealth creation, the policy makers would be content.

The desire for control is natural in governments. Policy makers are concerned with broad outcomes rather than the personal well-being of individuals, with measurable economies rather than the feelings of workers except, perhaps, on the day they vote. Inspection, therefore, is to do with institutions. Inspectors are meant to assess overall standards of performance, and to compare one institution, whether University, School or College with others. The question is the extent of control that inspectors have over the daily habits, even the thoughts of the individuals who make up the institutions. Personal motivations and dedication are essential, but the moment they become a central part of accountability, all kinds of questions are raised.

The Individual and the Institution

In the wealth of management literature, especially in the business world, the sense of the person fitting into the corporate whole is a pervasive theme. Whilst there are many models from command structures to collegiality, dedication to a particular product, belief in mission statements, and the pursuing of the same goal are all the essentials of management. Like the term 'ethos', the corporate whole is a concept which is difficult to measure or analyse, despite all the performance indicators which are supposed to be precise about its outputs (Rutter et al., 1979; Mortimore et al., 1988). There is a corporate institutional whole, a welding of a body of people into one that is the holy grail of management. The desire for shared 'visions' and collective understandings run deep, for this is where institutional success is supposed to lie.

If institutions consist of the people in them, the obvious response will be, in the light of the policy makers' own experience of themselves, the focus on 'leadership'. The role of the Vice-Chancellor or Principal or Head Teacher has been the subject of a great deal of analysis (if less research) for many years. The argument is simple. Appoint the right person to head an institution and the rest will fall into place. The new 'leadership' colleges, and the 'Headlamp' training, as well as other management courses, demonstrate this belief. The changes in the approach to headship over the last twenty years or so have been interesting. The earlier analysis tended to be about personal styles, from those who were over-authoritarian to those who were less assertive and more facilitative. More recently the tendency is to assert the specific skills needed in a head teacher, and the demonstration of certain practices. The assumption of the importance of the 'leader' remains. It is the primary focus of OFSTED inspections.

The personal needs of the head teacher are rarely mentioned. The head is often depicted as a powerful functionary who galvanizes an institution with clear and well thought out policies and actions. The managerial 'vision' is to create an institution whose success is measured in terms of clear outcomes, both personal and financial. The head's success is accounted for in terms of systems in which individuals are subsumed. In this approach a successful institution has clear policies and systems which can overcome any messy problem that might confront it. 'Events', in the way that politicians dread, no longer affect the smooth running of the operation. This, at least, is the dream of policy makers. Human resources are managed. All in the institutions share the same beliefs and carry out similar actions. All obey the requirements of its centre.

The Idea of the Manager

Management literature is consistent about the ways in which systems operate and the influence and functions of managers. As a concomitant to the regimes of inspection and accountability, the heads of institutions not only bear a heavy responsibility, but are assumed to be capable of certain kinds of functioning. They are deemed to put the needs of the institution before their own, just as they are required to make sure that their staff do the same. Operations and systems predominate. Whether concerned with 'improvement' or 'effectiveness', the functions of 'chief executives' are the subject of a literature that demonstrates its belief in the efficacy of efficient systems over individuals, promoted by individuals in power over others.

The power and status of effective leaders is demonstrated not only in the management appointments of the City and big business but in the development of the powers of Vice-Chancellors even at Oxford and Cambridge (the Masters of Colleges used to take a role in turn) and the emphasis on the accountability of heads. The irony is that, in parallel with this prevalent belief in the power of command, we detect a growing emphasis on the individual as a member of a corporate body having his or her own particular role to play. Schoen's notion of the 'reflective practitioner' even if it is almost unrecognisable from his first publications, is a powerful influence. The way in which the notion is interpreted is telling. It implies not only thinking about the job but remaining 'on task'. It means that thoughts must be directed towards every aspect of the role. Individual interests are subsumed in those of the professional. It is no wonder that the notion that all individuals share the functionary thoughts of leadership, of dedication to the task in hand, has led to institutions like the Institute of Learning and Teaching (ILT) in Higher Education. External bodies, such as the ILT and *Investors in People* have been given the responsibility for promoting individual development. These bureaucracies (not used here as a term of disparagement) naturally rely on the paperwork which attempts to describe what actually goes on.

Questions of structure and agency, the ways in which individuals are formed by institutions, will always be of prime importance. Yet we have never lived in a time when public institutions are so subject to outside interference. The autonomy of schools, colleges and universities are under threat. They are governed and inspected. Their funding is continually questioned and liable to measures of performance. They are no longer 'free' as they once were. This has, in turn, effects on leadership and on all staff. It also reminds us of the tensions underlying prevailing notions of lifelong learning, reflective practice, action research and professional development by which individuals use systems to nurture quality.

The Effects of Managerialism

One of the effects of the prevalence of regimes of inspection is on the personal lives of individual teachers and lecturers. The rise in accountability is marked by raised levels of stress. One reason for this is the different approaches, even the different languages used by inspectors and the professionals they are inspecting. The technical approach used by OFSTED (Cullingford, 1999) contrasts with the holistic and humanistic values espoused by teachers. There is a sense in which the personal selves of teachers in their professionalism is assaulted and abused. The tensions between the different values can be traumatic, and the way in which teachers feel they can best cope is to have weakened commitment to their ideals, to give up values and become technicians in their turn (Jeffrey and Woods, 1990).

Notions of Human Resource Management are based on the significance of the market and the power of central directives. Menter et al., (1997) attack the 'Post Fordist' management approaches which they feel are destroying relationships and destabilising professional identities through the clash between internal and external pressures. They also relate stress to the ambivalence caused by clinging to professional values when they are no longer required or admired.

One example of the spread of institutional rather than individual values into general policy is the Literacy Hour in schools. This is a policy much lauded by politicians. It makes clear exactly what teachers are supposed to do and how and when they are supposed to do it. It turns teachers and pupils into passive recipients on an 'outsiders' curriculum (Hancock and Mansfield, 2001). The teacher is driven by the need to go through prescribed material 'briskly' in four timed mini-lessons. The teachers are technicians, made to carry out tasks it is assumed they would not do were the tools, objectives and orders not available.

Some have argued that the whole of the National Curriculum has a deleterious effect on the professionalism of teachers (e.g. Butroyd, 2001). It is prescribed and imposed. Those who accept it without question survive best. Pupils also see it as a monument to what the State requires, since even teachers are perceived as fulfilling other peoples' criteria, making the pupils' submission even more impersonal (Elliott, 1998). Universities are also invaded by external demands on the curriculum, notably in the requirements of the Teacher Training Agency. Those involved either adapt or experience difficulties (Woods et al., 1997). There are tensions or there are constraints in adapting to the demands of managerialism, since individuality and collegiality tends to be replaced by micropolitical action. Teachers and lecturers are faced with the choice between restricted roles or greater stress:

> one of the ways for teachers to avoid much negative trauma is by shifting identity and status from professional to technician. (Woods et al., 1997, p.xii)

Such external constraints have changed the nature of institutions and make earlier analyses of school effectiveness or improvement somewhat dated. In the research on the characteristics of good schools it used to be agreed that one could recognise them easily (e.g. Joyce and McKibbin, 1982). The 'self-actualising school' – the ideal type – was one in which staff development was central in terms of a free interchange of ideas, and warm and informal interchange in which individuals were supported by the systems. The 'comfort' school might be supportive but not 'synergetic', and the 'survival' school (or college or university) would have a phobia about change in which individuals would remain covert about their own efforts. These possible differences no longer apply in the same way. The interchanges and the ideas are overt and measured. Any 'actualising' cannot be done autonomously.

The idea behind the notions of school effectiveness imposed from outside is that the shared agreement about what is effective can be systematically transposed from one institution to another. As if what 'works', like the meaning of 'ethos' is agreed (Ruddock et al., 1994). Shared vision and goals, professional identity, a supportive environment with high expectations and a focus on teaching and learning are all part of checklists of effectiveness that are often repeated, since Rutter's work. What happens to them when they are imposed? Are they so good and original that they need to be insisted upon? Again we see a tension between the managerial systems: 'this is how you must be', and the goals that are difficult to impose. It is like saying 'you *must* think for yourself without questioning'. No wonder 'critical thinking' is a term and concept which is becoming sidelined in schools (Quinn, 1997).

The Management of Professional Development

Since staff are so important, staff development has become a significant movement in itself. There have always been different types of staff development activities, from those led by 'thinkers' and 'doers' (Fleming, 1995) to 'brokers' and 'strategists', those brought in from outside to control the operations. There are many more staff development officers and agencies than ever before because, as never before, staff development is increasingly policy led (Beaty, 1995). It is directed towards the management of change (changes being imposed from outside) and towards the instrumental concerns of the development of up-to-date specific skills, or towards new (and more efficient) means of curricular delivery like distance learning. Staff development is increasingly tied to institutional development and therefore to accountability.

In larger institutions, like universities and colleges in particular, there are tensions that surround the question of whether staff development should be managed as an academic entity, like an additional department, or carried out within its existing academic framework, or both. Just as there are new bureaucracies devoted to national initiatives of personal development so, partly because of the needs for measurement and accountability, there are increasing numbers of personnel devoted to more formal processes of staff development, delivery, recording and evaluation. Again, it appears that personal reflection is imposed from outside. This could be, like action learning sets, a positive move but it does mark a shift in emphasis. The individual uses the system, but there is no opting out, at least formally. The increased formalisation of individual development is also a result of the increasing abstraction of human activities from their traditional sites in the family, or neighbourhood or workplace. Even learning is being globalised, especially through information technology. The tensions in 'lifelong learning' between 'growth' (of the economy) and human wellbeing are the more marked (Strain, 1998).

The prevailing view surrounding institutions is that they are formal systems with clear and simple processes. Their performance can be measured the more easily if they depend simply on the quality of the inputs and other quantifiable matters. This, in turn, is supposed to depend on good management on which judgements can then be made. The hierarchies are essential. Managers use rational means and pursue clear goals. Whilst it is the manager's responsibility for achieving these goals, they spend their time pursuing the delivery of these goals through others. The systems and structures are clear: people are told what to do. This is a model both simple and assumed by governments. You place the right person 'at the top' and your instructions will be carried out. Staff development in this model is a matter of coercion and instrumental outcomes.

Professional Development *as* Institutions

This institutional model is a far cry from the collegial one of the past in which institutions were assumed to be organic wholes. There the power was shared among all the members of the organisation who would agree policy through both consensus and an agreed, collective vision of what they were supposed to be doing and how they were going about it. Personal and professional development was the starting point for all actions and not an addendum. The ideas of the individuals were assumed to be important so that any support to develop them – staff development as a profession in itself – was encouraged. Even in dysfunctional institutions where chaotic 'office politics' reigns, the same distinction between the collegial versus the managerial approaches can be made.

From the point of view of external agencies this 'old-fashioned' view of educational institutions as complex, humane, organic and personal is regarded with suspicion. It is not measurable. It might not instantly respond to external demands. More significantly, it suggests freedom of decision making, ownership and autonomy.

The ways in which institutions as a whole behave can also be explained in other ways. Some are highly political. Conflict is regarded as endemic, as each decision is a result of a bargaining process that reflects the compromises of negotiations. Far from being collegiate, such a place would assume that all members are only concerned with their own self-interests. Staff development there is a sign of individual power.

Descriptions of the way in which institutions operate reveal some of the difficulties of effecting change from outside. To a great extent these descriptions are subjective, given that institutions are the creations of the people within them. They are also uncertain and unpredictable, since decision making processes depend on different people at different times. Institutions are also bound by their cultural traditions. They are the result of long held values and ideologies; not according to the whims of individuals but according to the 'hidden curriculum' of shared encounters, arguments and assumptions. In such places staff development is almost an alien concept, even where it takes place.

It is interesting that at a time when 'scientific realism', those chances of personal whim and chaos theory, are accepted as being a realistic description of the world, and held up, indeed, as the proper mainstream of action and the main basis of decisions, educational institutions are assumed to be controllable and accountable in a different way. The theories of human action, based on research, seem to head in a different direction from that of policy. The obsession with measurement is such that there is a desire to include that difficult ground of personal development. Policies are easy to formulate. Actual change is not.

The notion of market forces, that continuing mantra of modern policy makers, is an ambiguous one. It assumes both clear outcomes and measures of accounting, like success or failure, and deep uncertainties and subjectivities. What holds it together is the essence of competition, of an hierarchy of successes, measured in financial or other terms. League tables dominate, and every action is presumably taken to present the institutions in the best possible light. Personal development in this context could be seen as a strength, or as a self indulgence.

The Tensions in, and Solutions to the Problem

The prevailing spirit of the time is of mistrust of people and systems, leading to inspection, and yet belief in the way in which the same people and systems market themselves; that which is inspected. It is therefore, convenient to picture institutions as so simple that they can be held accountable. Systems are all. The question remains whether institutions really are so formal and unambiguous.

Cohen and Marsh's seminal book views the personal development of individuals and institutional needs as in implicit and perpetual conflict. They cast doubt upon the prevailing notions of leadership, and the power of management. In reality we treat goals as hypotheses, institutions as if they were real, and treat experience as a theory. As they point out:

> Human action is frequently corrupted by an exaggeration of its consequences.
> (Cohen and Marsh, 1974, p.204)

Managers occupy a minor part in the lives of many people. Many issues have a low salience for many people. The total educational system will always have high inertia. Such relative observations would gall the bureaucrats. They wish to see change, and to see it as a result of their will. This means the power of delivery, and this in the hands of its 'leader'.

There are many complexities in the tensions between the professional development of individuals and institutional needs. The individual personality will always be a factor – whatever the system. The needs of institutions are provoked and changed by external factors. As this book demonstrates, there are all kinds of repercussions of policy, all more subtle than the theories that motivate those who wish to control. The balance between individuals and the organisation to which they belong, and between organisations and policy, has shifted dramatically over the years. The question remains whether it is possible for anyone to have at least a sense of autonomy. Are there still professionals or are there only functionaries who carry out the orders of others? And who are the people who drive the system? Any empirical study of education must reveal the eternal questions between the individual and the system, and must question why simplistic policy notions persist despite all the evidence to the contrary. Nowhere is this conflict more apparent than in this book.

The other prevailing impression that the research in this book makes clear is the continuing strengths and power of individuals, whether despite the system or because of it. On the whole the 'system', like formal professional development reviews, means well, even if policies have the opposite effect to that intended. Even when they do not, the individuals, despite the stresses, still prevail. Nowhere are the ambiguities of individual will and collective policies clearer than in the uses and misuses of Schoen's notion of the 'reflective practitioner'. Whilst no one would argue with either reflection or good practice, the term has tended to be applied in an instrumental, measurable way. Those skills and competences that can be readily observed prevail; and are invoked at every moment. Does one learn a new 'skill' every time one attends a conference? That seems to be what is being demanded during the reviews of ones own development – its learning (on reflection) is both conscious and deliberate.

What 'reflective practice' in its current use misses out is that supremely complex human ability to employ intuition, to deal with many different things (and people) at once. James (1890) made much about the centrality of human instinct. Intuition is very informed and very refined. There will again be a time when the inner complexity of individual development will be recognised. It persists but it persists despite, not because of, the institutional policies to promote learning.

The chapters, the case studies and the analysis presented here all draw out the tension between the forces of central control and the creative freedom of the individual. This theme is always at the forefront of arguments about culture and organisations, and the examples given represent something deeper than particular institutional decisions. There is, throughout, a deep suspicion of managerialism, of de-professionalisation through performance-related competencies. Strategic goals appear to run counter to their delivery through professional development.

But do they? These chapters also celebrate not only the power of individuals to survive, not just through 'retreating', but their ultimate abilities to influence the communities in which they live through their individual actions. Concepts like complexity or meta-abilities draw attention to the ultimate goal, which is to create reflecting institutions, or learning organisations where the culture and cultivation of individuals are the prime force. Professional development might exist despite central control but clearly needs to inform it. In place of the battle between institutional needs and professional development must come the creative tension of their symbiosis. We hope this book demonstrates both the possibility of answers, and their necessity.

References

Ball, S. (1994) *Education Reform: A Critical and Post-structural approach.* Buckingham: Open University Press.

Beaty, L. (1995) Working Across the Hierarchy. In Brew, A. (Ed.) *Directions in Staff Development*, pp.146-157. Buckingham: Open University Press.

Butroyd, B. (2001) National Curriculum Subjects are Repositories of Values that are Under-Explored. In Cullingford, C. and Oliver, P. (Eds.) *The National Curriculum and Its Effects*, pp.173-192. Aldershot: Ashgate.

Cohen, M. and Marsh, J. (1974) *Headship and Ambiguity.* New York: McGraw Hill.

Cullingford, C. (Ed.) (1999) *An Inspector Calls: Ofsted and its effects on school standards.* London: Kogan Page.

Elliot, J. (1998) *The Curriculum Experiment: Meeting the Challenge of Social Change.* Buckingham: Open University Press.

Fleming, N. (1995) Academic Staff Development: A Comparative Perspective. *Higher Education and Development in Australia* **14** (1), pp.3-15.

Hancock, R. and Mansfield, M. (2001) The Literacy Hour: A Case for Listening to Children. In Collins, J., Insley, K. and Soler, J. (Eds.) *Developing Pedagogy: Researching Practice*, pp.96-108. London: Paul Chapman.

James, W. (1890) *The Principles of Psychology.* New York: Holt.

Jeffrey, B. and Woods, P. (1990) Feeling Deprofessionalised: The Social Construction of Emotions during an Ofsted Inspection. *Cambridge Journal of Education* **26** (3), pp.325-343.

Joyce, B. and McKibben, M. (1982) Teacher Growth, Status and School Environments. *Educational Leadership* **40** (2), pp.36-41.

Marklund, S. (1986) *Integration of School and the World of Work.* London: Dept. of International and Comparative Education.

Menter, I., Muschamp, Y., Nicholls, P. and Ozga, J. (1997) *Work and Identity in the Primary School: A Post-Fordian Analysis.* Buckingham: Open University Press.

Mortimore, P., Sammons, P., Stoll, L., Lewis, D. and Ecob, R. (1988) *School Matters: The Junior Years*. London: Open Books.

Quinn, V. (1997) *Critical Thinking in Young Minds.* London: Fulton.

Rudduck, J., Harris, S. and Wallace, G. (1994) Coherence and Students' Experience of Learning in the Secondary School. *Cambridge Journal of Education* **24** (2), pp.197-211.

Rutter, M., Maughan, B., Mortimore, P. and Ouston, J. (1979) *Fifteen thousand hours – Secondary Schools and their Effects on Children.* London: Open Books.

Strain, M. (1998) Towards an Economy of Lifelong Learning: Reconceptualizing Relations between Learning and Life. *British Journal of Educational Studies* **46** (3), pp.264-277.

Stronach, I. and Morris, R. (1994) Polemical Notes on Educational Evaluation in the Age of Policy Hysteria. *Evaluation and Research in Education* **8** (1), pp.5-19.

Woods, P., Jeffrey, B., Troman, G. and Boyle, M. (1997) *Restructuring Schools, Reconstructing Teachers: Responding to Change in the Primary School.* Buckingham: Open University Press.

Index